CHILDHOODS REAL AND IMAGINED

Volume 1: An introduction to critical realism and childhood studies

This book explores and charts the relation of dialectical critical realist concepts to many of the aspects of childhood. By demonstrating their relevance and value to each other, Alderson presents an introductory guide to applied critical realism for researchers, lecturers and students involved in the study of childhood.

Each chapter summarises key themes from several academic disciplines and policy areas, combining adults' and children's reported views and experiences and filtering them through a critical realist analysis. The first volume deals with the more theoretical as well as practical aspects of childhood, while the second volume will widen the scope to concentrate more on politics and childhood. Each chapter demonstrates how children are an integral part of the whole of society and are often especially affected by policies and events.

Through developing the dialectical critical realist analysis of childhood and youth this book will be of great interest to critical realists, childhood researchers and policy advisers.

Priscilla Alderson is Professor Emerita of Childhood Studies at the Social Science Research Unit, Institute of Education, London. She teaches on an international MA in the Sociology of Childhood and Children's Rights and her work on children's competence, wisdom and rights has been widely published.

Ontological Explorations

Titles in this series include:

CHILDHOODS REAL AND IMAGINED

Volume 1:
An introduction to critical realism and childhood studies

Priscilla Alderson

Routledge
Taylor & Francis Group

LONDON AND NEW YORK

First published 2013
by Routledge
2 Park Square, Milton Park, Abingdon, Oxon, OX14 4RN

Simultaneously published in the USA and Canada
by Routledge
711 Third Avenue, New York, NY 10017

Routledge is an imprint of the Taylor & Francis Group, an informa business

British Library Cataloguing in Publication

British Library Cataloguing in Publication Data
A catalogue record for this book is available from the British Library

Library of Congress Cataloging-in-Publication Data
Alderson, Priscilla.
  Childhoods Real and Imagined / Priscilla Alderson.
  v. cm.—(Ontological explorations)
  Includes bibliographical references and index.
  Contents: v. 1. An introduction to critical realism and childhood
  studies—
  1. Children. 2. Child development. 3. Child welfare. I. Title.
  HQ767.9.A426 2013
  305.23—dc23   2012042922

ISBN: 978–0–415–68097–4 (hbk)
ISBN: 978–0–415–68098–1 (pbk)
ISBN: 978–0–203–80535–0 (ebk)

Typeset in Times New Roman
by RefineCatch Limited, Bungay, Suffolk

Printed and bound in Great Britain by
TJ International Ltd, Padstow, Cornwall

CONTENTS

ACKNOWLEDGEMENTS

This book draws on my 30 years of social research with children and adults. I would like to thank all the hundreds of people who have helped me, by giving interviews, by allowing me to observe and write about them, by advising on the research projects and by providing funds and much other support.

I am grateful to many colleagues and co-researchers, and to everyone whose publications have informed and challenged my own work. Thank you to my doctoral students, and to the students from around the world who have taken part in our childhood and children's rights MA course.

Thanks are due to Roy Bhaskar for commissioning and advising on the book, and for holding the fortnightly postgraduate seminars on critical realism at the Institute of Education, as well as to all who have attended the seminars including Tamaki Yoshida, Alan Norrie and Mervyn Hartwig. For generously reading and commenting on draft chapters I thank Berry Mayall, Ginny Morrow, Christopher Goodey and Pat Gordon-Smith – although I am responsible for any shortcomings in the book.

For help with editing thanks to Damian Mitchell at Routledge, Heather Cushing of RefineCatch and Jon Ingoldby of Jon Ingoldby Publishing Services.

And thank you my dear expert advisers on realism, my grandchildren: Hari, Amy and Robbie; Chloe and Toby; Claris and Sian.

PART I
Background

1

INTRODUCTION

Absent children

The obstetrician, Ignaz Semmelweis (1818–1865), worked in a Viennese hospital where women knew that they were more likely to die in the maternity ward staffed by doctors (around 16 percent), than in the one staffed by midwives (around two percent). The two wards opened for admission on alternate days, and many women gave birth in the street to avoid being admitted to the first ward. Semmelweis researched why the second ward was safer, even for women who stayed there after a birth in the street. For years he kept detailed records and tested every possible variable; his methods included a small controlled clinical trial. He concluded that puerperal fever, a septicaemia/blood infection, was somehow spread by doctors' unwashed hands, often stained with putrid matter from the autopsy rooms. When he introduced the routine washing of hands and equipment in chlorinated lime, maternal mortality rates fell almost to zero. Semmelweis's work was rejected, opposed or ignored by obstetricians internationally and, despairing, he died in a mental asylum of septicaemia.

(De Costa 2002)

Semmelweis's story is one of countless examples that illustrate key themes in this book. Before considering the themes in this example, I will briefly outline this chapter.

Absence is a central concept in dialectical critical realism (DCR), and this book is concerned with the absence of children and childhood from almost any report, book or film on politics, economics, trade, armed conflict, housing, transport, climate change or any other major topic of public concern. Yet children and their interests are actually central to all these 'adult' matters. That is why, to illustrate this point, this first section will consider three examples of absent, though crucially involved, children. I will then describe the groups of readers for whom this book is written, and define some terms, before reviewing a few statistics about numbers of children and young people in the world, one-third of all human beings.

'Childhood' variously refers to the *status* of being a minor, the early-life *state* of immaturity whether actual or ascribed, and the *process* of growing towards adulthood. Traditionally, research about children has concentrated on examining the state and process of childhood as if these are taken-for-granted facts. Childhood studies recognise that childhood largely consists of a conferred status; many attributes are imposed on or ascribed to children, such as ignorance, dependence and volatile emotion, when they are not necessarily integral to childhood and when many children and young people demonstrate their knowledge, generous interdependence and reliable wisdom. Researchers examine how children and adults reproduce or resist stereotypes of childhood and youth, instead of assuming they are factual or inevitable.

Childhood studies have been developing for around 25 years, and their vital contributions, besides their differences from the older discipline of child psychology, will be recorded in this introduction. There are, however, problems, disagreements and limitations in childhood studies, some shared generally among the social sciences, and these will be noted. Chapter 2 will further analyse splits between, for example, qualitative and quantitative, empirical and interpretive childhood research, to prepare for the subsequent chapters on the main topics of this book. These will be about how DCR contributes to childhood studies and works to understand and resolve the present problems, gaps and splits.

DCR is not a version of sociology. It is a philosophy of the natural and social sciences. The aim in DCR is not to dominate research or dictate how it should be done, but to serve it, by clarifying underlying assumptions and contradictions, and by showing the necessary conditions for the existence of the objects and subjects we research, and for the knowledge we produce. Before introducing DCR, first I review, in this chapter, debates about the relationship between sociology and philosophy. The Introduction ends with an outline of the contents of this two-volume book.

To return to the above Semmelweis example, my first theme is the absent, unmentioned children in the historical records of maternal deaths, which seldom mention the perinatal death of babies, the time when a child is most likely to die. Even today, well over one-third of births in the world still go unrecorded and unregistered, which means that states do not formally acknowledge these children, or their rights, which exist in the states' responsibilities towards them enshrined in the *Convention on the Rights of the Child* (UN 1989).[1] The adult-centred accounts of Semmelweis's work with other doctors and with women rarely refer to the babies whose births were the primary reason for the adults to meet and for the maternity services to be provided. The unheard and unseen children accounted for the opening of maternity clinics around Europe, partly in an effort to reduce the scandal of frequent infanticide. Disadvantaged women including prostitutes were offered free maternity services and the opportunity for their babies to be taken into care. In return, the women's bodies were used for clinical training and research in the wards and post-mortem rooms. Daily teaching rounds between both these areas multiplied cross-infection, while they were also revolutionising medical science. Children are further hidden and implicitly blamed in the term 'puerperal fever' (*puer* – boy/child) although, ironically, the main cause lay in adults' hands.

The second theme concerns the power of theory and the limits of research methods. Semmelweis applied respected research methods with impressive results and his colleagues were avowed positivists, but they refused to accept his conclusions. They could not recognise an underlying mechanism, logic or theory that might explain and validate his findings. Still influenced by Galen (circa 131–217 CE) with his medical theories of the internal rebalancing of the four humours in each unique patient, and vague notions of bad air that are echoed in 'malaria', they had no theory or methodology of germs or of living micro-organisms that could transfer, invade and multiply. Joseph Lister (1827–1912) succeeded with his antisepsis regime so soon after Semmelweis had failed because theories of germs and cleanliness had become respectable, albeit before they were fully understood.

Semmelweis and Lister illustrate how new paradigms, patterns or frameworks of thinking have to be recognised and accepted, and theories have to change, before new knowledge can be recognised. The mass care of poor patients in clinics gradually moved the medical gaze away from Galen's individual, unique cases and towards the science of generic causes and conditions (Foucault 1993). Economics played a part when doctors, who had mainly attended individual wealthier patients at home, were employed to tend hordes of anonymous workers and paupers in charity hospitals.[2] Semmelweis's meticulous research evidence and methods were necessary but not sufficient to change understanding, and they showed the essential power of theory to validate and make sense of research and its connection to practice. Whereas scientific theories explain the underlying mechanisms of the findings, theories are also often moral and political. Semmelweis's colleagues could not accept that, as respectable, professional, healing men, they were sources of disease, particularly when they saw themselves as diametrically different from the bodies and corpses of poor, dirty, 'fallen' women and their babies. This book will examine changing scientific and moral theories about childhood, and their primary importance in research and policy.

The third theme is the well-being of children and how, often from well-meant intentions, adults' interventions in children's lives can bring great benefit and sometimes great harm. Just as mothers' and babies' mortality rates soared and later fell, because of obstetricians' changing practices, so science and technology have brought benefits and also dangers to children. Later chapters will examine how adults can further children's, and adults', interests when they are influenced by varying kinds of childhood research theories and methods, values and aims.

From Vienna in the 1840s to Pakistan in May 2011, a second example illustrates continuity in these themes about childhood. Almost a decade after the 9/11

(2001) attack on the twin towers in New York, the Americans ended their search for Osama Bin Laden in a house in Pakistan. Extensive news reports debated whether the soldiers should have arrested Bin Laden instead of assassinating him, and what right they had to do so in Pakistan. The debates covered further topics relevant to this book – relationships and politics and justice between nations in the wealthy minority world and the poorer majority world – but the overriding theme is the invisible children at the heart of each event and society.

Some weeks later the world was told that Bin Laden's identity was checked, while the raid was being planned, by a DNA test of blood taken from a child in his household. This was obtained by a health visitor during a 'fake' hepatitis B local vaccination programme. The international charity Médecins Sans Frontières (2011) was concerned that the deceptive use of the programme by US forces would bring healthcare staff and international aid agency workers into greater danger and mistrust from the people they aimed to help, who were already fairly sceptical if not hostile towards western health programmes. The US deception might jeopardise the polio vaccination plans to complete the worldwide elimination of polio.

Pakistan had the highest rate of polio infection in the world, with 84 reported cases in 2011. In Khyber Agency, 2009–2011, over 200,000 children missed being immunised (Saleem 2011), partly because some Muslim clerics feared that immunisations cause impotence and infertility, although other clerics worked hard to dispel that myth. This is an example of debates about morality, politics and health, which centre on, and take urgent meaning from, disputed concepts of children's welfare on which societies' future depends. Providing treatment solely for the military aim of catching Bin Laden violated the medical ethics of doing no harm, and of always treating patients, including children, as ends in themselves, never as means to other people's ends (Beauchamp and Childress 2001). The deception further exploited an exceptionally vulnerable community where Bin Laden was living and there were serious unmet healthcare needs. Hepatitis B prevention requires three injections over three months, but only one was administered.

Typically, reports about Bin Laden's death cover relations between the adult groups, their politics and reputations, but gloss over the pawns in the politics – the children. What happened to the children in the household and what did they observe? One year later, the 11 children who were living in the house were reported to be still in prison. And how many children in the town received only one vaccination? What are the likely effects for them, to receive only one-third of the full dose? Were there plans to complete their immunisations?

A year later, the World Health Organisation (WHO 2012) reported that the quest to eradicate polio from the world was faltering. The $2.2 billion being spent on the programme needed to be nearer to $3 billion if every child at risk was to be vaccinated. The Taliban had banned polio vaccination programmes in north-west Pakistan, they said until the US ceased the drone strikes there, and they also blamed the vaccination ploy used to capture Bin Laden for local hostility to the programmes. So 560,000 children in three areas of Pakistan received no vaccinations in 2012,[3] and this illustrates a little of the vast unrecorded, unrecognised effects of armed conflict on children.

Occasionally children play a central, though generally passive part in reported public affairs. For example, problems of journalists hacking into celebrities' mobile phones and then publishing their secrets in tabloid newspapers have been publically reported for years (Davies 2008; Rusbridger 2011). There had been little public interest until, in 2011, in London, the scandal suddenly erupted into the headlines and the heart of public and political concern. The catalyst again concerned a young girl, in this case Millie Dowler, a 13-year-old who had been murdered. Public tolerance of phone hacking suddenly seemed to snap at the idea that a journalist might have hacked into the dead girl's phone. In order to hear more messages from her desperate parents, the journalist might have deleted some of Millie's messages to make space for her inbox to receive new messages, giving her parents the false hope that she was still alive. It was as if an event involving a child (Millie's youth and status as a daughter were emphasised) served as a litmus test of the turning point between public acceptance and outraged protest. This private trouble opened public scrutiny, including the Levison Inquiry, into years of concealed domination by the Murdoch News International empire over politicians, the police, the mass media and democratic processes.

These examples, from countless possible ones, have been given to illustrate how children and young people are ignored in many adult-centred concerns. If children are mentioned in the mass media or policy debates they are usually portrayed negatively as 'villains or victims', or as needy dependents,[4] and their wide-ranging views and activities are seldom reported in the way adults appear in the media (Franklin 2002). However, children and young people are so large and central a part of humanity that information and policy become skewed by their seeming absence, which this book will address.

To the readers

Childhoods Real and Imagined is written for people who care for and research, work and make policy for and with children and young people, and also for those who are interested in adults, since it is neither useful nor possible to understand the generations separately. I am specifically writing for researchers who cope with tight budgets and deadlines, as I had to do for many years. This book is also for teachers and students of university and professional courses about childhood, society and research, and for the interested general public.

'Social research' includes the social sciences, psychology, education, the arts and humanities, law, economics, business, journalism and much healthcare research: everything that relates to the social and is not exclusively in the natural sciences.

DCR was developed over decades, beginning as critical realism. I have chiefly relied on Roy Bhaskar's series of books, on Alan Norrie's overview of this work in *Dialectic and Difference* (2010), on Mervyn Hartwig's edited *Dictionary of Critical Realism* (2007) and on the contributions that all three of them, and many other people, have made to the fortnightly seminars on critical realism held at our Institute since 2008. I have not attempted to trace the detailed development of DCR and, for brevity, have referred to insights from critical realism and DCR all under the heading DCR. The tenets of DCR have been developed and justified in immense detail, and rather than repeat these many analyses I have concentrated on explaining basic details and showing how they can illuminate and be applied to social research. Readers who want to know more about the underlying analyses are referred to the extensive DCR literature.

I also hope to interest readers, who are already familiar with critical realism, in childhood studies if they do not yet know much about them. As this book is written for a wide readership of both experts and novices with different interests, I trust that readers will accept sections that might seem to them too elementary or too challenging. This book is about applying DCR when researching and understanding childhood and children's and young people's – and therefore adults' – places in the world today. I aim to show how childhood studies and DCR can mutually inform one another, and gain from the interchange.

The book is illustrated with practical examples from research including my own projects (see Appendix 1). The challenge of rethinking my past research in relation to DCR, and of writing this book, has helped me, and I hope will help readers, to see how DCR enlarges research theory and analysis. Since learning about DCR, I have revised some of my former ideas and discarded others, on the continuing journey of learning and change.

Children and young people in the world

'Childhood' is defined here as beginning at birth, and ending gradually and uncertainly. Babies will often appear through the book, to show how they are human beings too, and to explore how they expand concepts of childhood, human nature, human rights and human society. Older children and childhood generally are often infantilised into misleading, belittling stereotypes, which I hope to avoid. In their body size, experiences and abilities, beliefs and behaviours, status and responsibilities, many children are 'like adults'. In majority world countries, 8-year-olds may head a household, run a small street business, or work in an army. They raise profound questions about what the concepts 'child' and 'adult' mean. 'Younger generations' will sometimes mean people aged under 25, when they all share common interests and experiences, challenges and opportunities, or are discriminated against and disadvantaged because of their youth.

It is often claimed that 'women are half the world'.[5] However, Socialnomics (2010) estimated that 1.8 billion or 26 per cent of people on the planet were aged 0–14 years in 2010, and 52 per cent were aged 0–30 years (see Table 1.1). Since a third of births and many deaths go unrecorded, population numbers can only be estimated and are continually revised. Complications include the missing birth

TABLE 1.1 Mid-2010 estimates of the world population

Total population	6,852,472,823
0–4-year-olds	621,484,971
5–9-year-olds	600,725,107
10–14-year-olds	595,369,490
15–19-year-olds	597,734,190
Total 0–19 years	2,415,313,758

Source: adapted from Census.Gov 2010

records of innumerable babies of illegal migrants. Millions of Chinese children suddenly appear on school rolls although under the one child policy their births were not reported.

These groups aged up to 19 years include young men and women, many paid workers, and many who have children of their own and other 'adult' responsibilities. The terms 'children' and 'childhood' will usually loosely refer to the first two or three groups, and 'youth' and 'young people' to the third and fourth groups. The UNCRC (UN 1989) includes everyone from birth up to 18 years.

During 2011, in the two largest nations, an estimated one-third of Indians and 17 per cent of Chinese were aged under 15. The richer, whiter minority world tends to have lower percentage rates of children aged 0–14 years: in 62 nation states 12–20 per cent of the population were children (UK 17 per cent); in 70 states children were 21–33 per cent; in 50 states they were 34–43 per cent; and the poorest states tended to be among the 23 to have the highest proportion of children at 44–49 per cent. These states include areas that endure serious unrest and violence: Iraq and the Palestinian Territories (43 per cent); Zimbabwe, Ethiopia and Afghanistan (44 per cent); Yemen and Somalia (45 per cent); Congo (46 per cent); and Niger (49 per cent) (see www.socialnomics.net).

Child psychology

Although both the psychological and sociological approaches to childhood are complex, wide-ranging and overlapping, they broadly differ in their theories, methods, aims and links to policy and practice.

Child psychology tends to emphasise the empirical and behavioural study and measurement of children's development towards the end-stage of adulthood. Psychologists assess development as normal or abnormal, and test how types of problems and assistance affect psychological growth. Following a broadly medical model, clinical and educational psychologists specialise in identifying, assessing and arranging treatment for problems in individuals and groups. Psychology has great public appeal in its claims to be scientific, to deal with precise evidence objectively, and to offer remedies for psychological ills. (Sociology in contrast is often more cautious about its empirical claims; it deals with partly abstract complex topics such as 'race'; it risks seeming subjectively political; and it offers no directly useful, clinical service.)

For over a century, child psychology has informed research, policy, services, professional training and expertise, public and mass media understanding and the 'common-sense' of adult–child relationships generally in children's daily life and care. Psychology offers scientific support for everyday concepts of children's dependence and very gradual development through universal, genetically deter-mined though socially varied stages (Harris and Butterworth 2002; Harris 2008, among countless examples). Over the twentieth century, child psychology has encouraged more practical understanding, and perhaps more patience and toler-ance generally, towards children's early immaturity. Growing 'child-centred' and 'youth-centred' approaches have been expressed over the past century in the wealth of new toys, games, books, clothes, entertainment, food and educational aids designed to appeal directly to children and young people. The many advan-tages that 'child-centredness' brings also incur the potential disadvantages of overly positioning children and young people into separate 'worlds', over-emphasising and even imposing a perceived vulnerability and needy dependence on them, while underestimating their competencies and freedom rights. Paradoxically, moves to over-protect children – and women – can increase their vulnerability and social exclusion and reduce their means to resist oppressive power (Holt 1975; Rose 1999). Psychology examines the individual rather than agency–structure interactions in social and political contexts.

So to summarise very broadly, while recognising that important child psychology research verges into social psychology (for example, Hart 1997; Penn 2005; and see Burman 2007; Morss 1990; Woodhead 2011 for critical reviews by psychologists), psychological *theories* of childhood are influenced by concepts of normative childhood and universal developmental stages; *methods* of research tend to be based on natural scientific observations and assessments; the *aims* of child psychology and their links to *policy and practice* are predominantly to help children to develop into adults while enjoying a 'good childhood'.

Childhood studies up to 1990

In contrast to child psychology, childhood studies, established around 1990, are multidisciplinary, ranging across sociology, geography, anthropology, history, social psychology, social policy, law, education, economics, religion, nursing, cultural and youth and international and development studies. The studies cover practical social policy research (although offering information and analysis rather than the direct intervention psychology provides) and also more theoretical socio-cultural research. A key difference from psychology is that childhood studies see matters such as competence not as fixed and measureable facts but as shifting, contingent, social experiences, co-constructed between children and adults. So with children's competence, much depends on the information, respect and support that adults give, and on adults' competence in helping and understanding children, as well as on the child's abilities.

Researchers work with a range of *theories and methods*, and defy easy generalisations. However, they tend to consider that childhood and child–adult relations vary greatly across time and place; there are few biological or universal features that are not varied and socially contingent; and a major theme for reflexive analysis is childhood itself, especially in how adults and children perceive and constantly reconstruct childhoods through their local beliefs and behaviours, including interactions during research projects.

Feminists, particularly from the 1960s, challenged bio-psychological concepts of women as essentially and inevitably emotional, irrational, dependent and inferior to men. Instead, feminists showed how these are often self-fulfilling concepts and ideologies that conform to powerful, ancient, sexist traditions. These social behaviours rather than biological facts involve the hermeneutic dyad. This occurs, for example, not only when dominant men interact with subordinate women, but when they repeatedly reconstruct and reinforce one another's roles and the differences between them. Similarly, childhood studies critically analyse how children and young people are constantly reconstructed as if they are emotional, irrational, dependent and inferior, in relation to rational, dependable adults. Childhood studies, however, see childhood and youth as important fulfilling times of life, worthy of respect and study in their own right; childhood is taken to be a conferred social status rather than an inevitable biological state; children and young people are social actors who can form and express valid, important views. These tenets began to be set out in international edited collections (James and Prout [1990] 1997; Qvortrup *et al.* 1994).

Before 1990, the historian Philippe Ariès (1962: 128) was among the first to analyse the very varied beliefs and behaviours associated with different childhoods. He asserted that the modern concept of childhood did not exist in medieval times although 'this is not to suggest that children were neglected, forsaken or despised'. Modern ideas of childhood evolved or were invented during the growing prosperity of seventeenth-century Europe as a life stage between dependent infancy and independent adulthood. Other scholars contended that there have always been childhoods, a space between infancy and adulthood, although they continued to develop Ariès's interpretive approach when exploring the great variety of childhoods through history and across the world. A few examples include Michel Foucault (1977), Jacques Donzelot (1977) and Nikolas Rose (1999) who analysed how childhood was controlled and reconstructed through power relations.

It is claimed that childhood, if it existed, was of little interest until about 300 years ago, but who was not interested? Pieter Bruegel's painting of over 80 children's games records lively interest in childhood play in 1560. Even if literate men, on whom historians chiefly rely, did not think of children as a topic to write about, that does not mean that all the unknown, unrecorded children, women and men were uninterested in such aspects of childhood as birth, infancy, games and play, childhood illnesses, starting to laugh, walk, talk and dance. If there was no attachment, pleasure or interest between poor parents and children, given the arduous labour of feeding, clothing and teaching them to survive and to work, what might parents' motives have been for not abandoning their children? Were they simply seen as free future labour? Jo Boyden (1997: 192) believed that 'innocence and nobility were first associated with children' during the eighteenth century, and yet the medieval rooms in western art galleries are filled with reverent paintings of 'holy' childhood and motherhood.

Harry Hendrick (1997: 35) considers that historical records can hardly convey either the immensely complicated and contradictory variety of childhoods and parenthoods existing at any one time, or the reality of working-class childhoods. He notes that the middle classes who organised the evacuation of British city children during World War II, away from the enemy air-raids and into the country, were shocked and surprised by two things: the dreadful living conditions for families in the slums; and the very close ties between the parents and children. In contrast, middle-class parents expected to have distant relationships with their children, consigning them largely to the care of servants and then to boarding schools. And so they assumed that working-class families would not mind being separated. In fact, many children returned to the cities, as like their parents they dreaded separation from their family more than the deadly dangers of the bombing raids. By chance, the war effort gave the middle classes a glimpse into the realities of working-class life, and their surprise suggests that their previous histories of the working classes had hardly been reliable. Christina Hardyment's (1984) review of fashionable advice in childcare manuals over three centuries revealed wild swings between harsh or indulgent parenting, demonstrating that normative beliefs about child–adult relationships are far from fixed or inevitable and that much of the literature on childcare was propaganda rather than description.

Children were seriously respected by notable individuals over the twentieth century. Appalled to see starving children around Europe after World War I, Eglantine Jebb founded Save the Children in 1919 and she persuaded the League of Nations to adopt her International Charter of Children's Rights in 1924. Janusz Korczak (Eichsteller 2009) democratically shared the daily management of their orphanage with children in Warsaw during the 1930s and 1940s. They had a children's newspaper and parliament. He chose to share their suffering in the Jewish ghetto and death in the gas chambers. The third and most emancipated version of Jebb's Charter, inspired by Korczak, was the UNCRC (UN 1989). John Holt (1975) advocated respect for children's rights as soon as they can understand and exercise them, including rights to vote. Margaret Macmillan in the earlier part of the twentieth century, and Susan Isaacs around the mid-century, were among numerous educators and psychologists who carefully observed and listened to children and created child-friendly nurseries and schools informed by their findings. Bertrand Russell continued the tradition of philosophers who were deeply interested in early education and who established schools. Although it is sometimes claimed that childhood studies create new ways of respecting, observing and talking with children, they often follow long-held traditions.

Other precursors to childhood studies included Margaret Donaldson (1978), an innovative psychologist who used a 'naughty teddy' to reveal how interviewers' methods, humour and rapport with children greatly alter how competently children perform during tests. Scottish children from 3 years of age laughed at the teddy for being 'silly' when he asked repeated questions and firmly repeated their initial replies. However, when Piaget had asked the same insistently repeated questions of Swiss children aged up to 6 years, they had seemed to want to please him by providing differing answers. He attributed their inconsistencies to their intellectual immaturity, rather than to their subtle, polite responses to his odd behaviour. Ironically, Piaget projected his own psychological and relational failings onto the children by labelling younger children as egoists, unable to understand another's viewpoint.

Alice Miller (1983) and Virginia Axline ([1964] 1990) demonstrated the importance of detailed psychoanalytic study of troubled children. Jean Liedloff's ([1975] 2004) study of indigenous children in the Amazonian rain forest vividly illustrated contrasts between childhoods in different times and places, and the impressive competence of babies aged from 9 months. The anthropologist Myra Bluebond-Langner (1978) observed and talked with severely ill and dying young children about their own profound views, experiences and understanding of their cancer treatment. Colin Ward (1978, 1988) examined the city and the country from the viewpoint of childhood. Ben Bradley (1989) related how child psychologists such as Skinner and Piaget used babies as empty pages on which to write their own 'visions of infancy' drawn from their autobiographies and their earlier research with animals. Further great sources of insight into differing childhoods, child–adult relations and adults' perceptions of children are found in biographies and novels since the eighteenth century, many informed by the authors' own childhoods including Tom Jones, Jane Eyre, Maggie Tulliver, David Copperfield and Huckleberry Finn onwards.

Progress in childhood studies since 1990

Around 1989/1990, childhood studies as the formal social science study of childhood itself as well as of children's lives, could be said to have been established, and university childhood centres began to open around Europe, Australia and New Zealand. Since 1989, there have been numerous multidisciplinary reports, international conferences, degree and other courses, and funded research projects about childhood in a range of social sciences. Jens Qvortrup and colleagues (1994: x) noted that 'sociology has no tradition for studying childhood', and they aimed to 'contribute to knowledge in terms of theories and methods' (1994: xiii) on the socioeconomic forces affecting children in 16 European countries. They found falling numbers of children, rising numbers living in poverty and a neglect of children in national statistics and economic policies. There was growing concern about child physical and sexual abuse but less about the general risk to childhood itself of social exclusion. Qvortrup and colleagues agreed that there are many different kinds of childhood, but that it is still vital to establish childhood generally as a social phenomenon, which should be central to public attention, policy and records (Saporiti 1994). When children are recorded independently in national statistics, and no longer concealed inside adult-led groups such as the family, new findings emerge, such as that young British children are most likely to share rooms and to be in households with less than one room per person, whereas old people are likely to have several rooms each.

Edited collections of research reports critiqued the many former omissions and misunderstandings about childhood, and mapped out new areas and methods through which to collect new evidence about children's lives and well-being, with more respect for their diverse interests around the world. However, children's own voices were seldom heard in these books (James and Prout [1990] 1997;[6] Qvortrup et al. 1994;[7] Stephens 1995b), although there were compelling exceptions. Njabulo Ndebele (1995: 330) asserts, during and after apartheid in South Africa:

> that children are at the centre of these events – sometimes as victims, sometimes as perpetrators – is at the root of the problem, for our goal is nation building. What can we expect of children who have witnessed [and been victims and] sometimes participated in these gruesome events?

Sharon Stephens's (1995b) book includes Ndebele's chapter, and Stephens reports Norwegian children's views and drawings about the effects of the Chernobyl power station nuclear explosion on their lives. Chapters explain political contexts of children in Indonesia, and of schooling in Japan and South Korea where exam results are seen as the products, children, teachers and mothers are the labourers, and politicians control the inhumane means of production. Research is expanding, for example, about child workers (Fassa et al. 2010; Morrow and Pells 2012) and child soldiers (Honwana 2006; Rosen 2005; Drumbl 2012).

Interest rapidly grew in interpretive social *theories* of childhood as a crucial time of life, with children able to form and express valid views in empirical studies (see Alanen and Mayall 2001; Alderson 1993; Barry 2005; Brett and Specht 2004; Dunn 2004; Field 2007; Hill and Tisdall 1997; Honwana and De Boeck 2005; Hörschelmann and Colls 2010; Invernizzi and Williams 2008; John 2003; Katz 2004; Mayall 1994, 2002; Morrow 1998; Murray and Andrews 2000; Penn 2005; Qvortrup et al. 1994, 2011; Scheper-Hughes and Sargent 1998; Serpell 1993; Siegal 1997, 2010; Stern 1977; Tisdall et al. 2006; Winter 2011; Yoshida 2011, from many more examples). There are also reflections on meanings of childhood and children's part in society (Hill and Tisdall 1997; Holt 1975; Jenks 2005; Lee 2001, 2005; Morss 1996; Nadesan 2010; Percy-Smith and Thomas 2010; Prout 2005; Stainton-Rogers and Stainton-Rogers 1992; Wall 2010; Wyness 2006). Many of these sources will be considered throughout the book. The theories have encouraged ethical, respectful *methods* of research with children (Alderson and Morrow 2011), which include discussions, interviews, children's focus groups and essays, art and drama, mapmaking, photographs, games and online chat-rooms, as well as ethnographies and action research conducted for, and with, and sometimes by, children (Christensen and James 2008). Connections to *policy and practice* in childhood studies put less emphasis on how to fit children into adult society, than on how to adapt society towards meeting children's needs and interests. NGOs (non-governmental organisations) around the world have encouraged children's research, practical projects and protest movements to campaign for justice and better conditions for children at school, at work and in their healthcare.[8]

Governments that have ratified the UNCRC (UN 1989) undertake to report regularly to the Committee on the Rights of the Child in Geneva on their progress in implementing the Convention in law, policy and practice. Although government reports are somewhat evasive and complacent, regular parallel reports by NGOs working for children, and reports from children themselves, tend to be more accurate and critical.[9] The UNCRC has encouraged researchers in academia and in NGOs to work with children and young people to promote their rights, through their research aims and topics, stages and methods, conclusions and recommendations (Percy-Smith and Thomas, 2010; Qvortrup *et al.* 2011, from many examples). The Economic and Social Research Council (ESRC) (the main funder of academic social research in Britain) sponsored the programme 'Children 5–16' during the late 1990s. The 22 research projects varied widely in their scope, topics and methods, and the programme included international conferences, a series of edited books, and many other published papers (see Appendix 1.3). The hope was to strengthen and establish childhood studies as a recognised subsection of sociology and related disciplines.

I have been very fortunate to work in childhood studies since 1989, and to share with many colleagues in the rewards of mapping new areas of research. For example, a paediatrician told me (after my book of the project was published in 1993 – see Appendix 1.2) that in 1989 he had advised that my funding application should be rejected. He thought that my plan, to interview young patients aged 8–15 years, was unrealistic, and it was impossible to interview anyone aged under 12 years. Notions of competent children have changed so much since 1989 that profound interviews with 4-year-olds are now published (Alderson *et al.* 2006a, 2006b; Gordon-Smith 2009; Solberg 1996; Winter 2011). Researchers interact with babies to discover how they 'form and express their views' (UN 1989, Article 12) (Als 1999; Murray and Andrews 2000; Alderson *et al.* 2005a). New findings in the theories, methods and processes of childhood research from around the world are published in numerous books and international journals.[10]

Problems in childhood studies

However, there are problems in childhood studies, and some are shared with social science generally (Holmwood 2011),[11] including disappointment that research reports seldom directly influence policy. The first disadvantage concerns *funding*. In Britain, charitable trusts, such as Nuffield, Rowntree and Wellcome, which have funded imaginative, innovative childhood projects, do not grant the overheads university managers now require, so that many researchers may no longer apply to them. Researchers increasingly rely on fewer sources, mainly government funded research councils and government departments, which do grant overheads. However, to limit the permitted funders increases the numbers of applications to them and therefore the failure rates of the very time-consuming work of writing applications. Funders now tend to set their own (government influenced) detailed research agendas on which they invite researchers to bid and compete. Commissioned research about childhood favours large, 'a-theoretical', quantitative, longitudinal birth cohort studies, assessments, evaluations and systematic reviews instead of small qualitative studies in which researchers engage with child participants. Funders also increasingly prefer large research centres, and teams led by economists, statisticians and business experts, over theory-based social research. The former are seen as more reliable bases for policy-making and for the impact universities are expected to make. Their hopes for future funding can discourage researchers from conducting and publishing reports of research that is critical of potential funders such as government departments.

A second set of disadvantages links to *repetition*. So many studies have been published about different ages and types of children and young people, engaged in different activities in different countries, that new reports are interesting but seldom really original or informative. The required format of empirical papers in childhood journals and chapters in edited books comprises background, topics and questions, sampling and methods of collecting and analysing data, findings, brief discussion and conclusion and many references. This is repetitive and allows little space to develop new thinking, to critique published work, and to develop and explain alternatives. Overwhelmed by hundreds of printed and online reports, researchers have to sub-specialise when trying to keep up to date, which can lead to ever more narrowly confined research on smaller areas of childhood.

A third problem is *time*. Five years can easily pass between early plans for a funding application and eventual publication of the research, half a childhood away, or after an elected government's whole term of office. The lengthy process cannot examine urgent questions, and is further held back by peer review journals that lack a forum for rapid response and debate, unlike newspapers with their letters columns, online blogs and email debates. The academic format of empirical reports often expects critical debate about a published paper to be voiced in a similar research-based paper, eventually produced years later.

Time is also a problem for contract researchers who are so pressured to raise funds, conduct research rapidly and attend to administration, that they have little time to spare for studying theory. I have only been able to come to terms with critical realism during semi-retirement. DCR cannot solve these three problems. However, the aim of this book is to present DCR in terms that I hope even very pressured researchers will have time to digest and then apply in order to address the following concerns.

The fourth problem is when *reputation and alliances* are compromised by scientific and moral uncertainties. Childhood studies have not become part of mainstream sociology[12] and, like Semmelweis, researchers encounter scientific and moral opposition. Serious social scientific disagreements between positivists and interpretivists (see Chapter 2) feed doubts about whether the social sciences are scientific, reliable or reputable. These uncertainties are compounded by ideological criticisms, such as by critics of children's rights (their views are critically reviewed in Freeman 2007). Theoretical disagreements between social researchers can compromise ideals of their fair, objective peer review of journal articles and funding applications written by those with whom they disagree. Childhood researchers have a higher chance of publishing in childhood journals than in mainstream ones, but this further excludes childhood research from the mainstream, and leaves non-childhood readers and reviewers puzzled by themes which childhood researchers take for granted. These uncertainties link to the dwindling part social science generally plays in informing and influencing public policy and debate.

The related fifth and underlying problem is the *unresolved disagreement* among social scientists about their theories and methods, the nature and reality of the objects of their research, their relationships to these objects and to their knowledge, and how they can explain or justify or validate their findings convincingly. Ways to analyse and resolve the disagreements will be main themes throughout this book.

A sixth problem is that, although founders such as Qvortrup and colleagues aimed to free childhood away from developmental psychology and into membership of mainstream society, and in the Nordic countries they may have been successful, other researchers emphasise *separation* into the sub-specialty of childhood studies. For example, Allison James (2011: 215–16) states that childhood studies research 'begins, and to some extent ends, with the study of children and childhood', examines 'the ontological status of both children and childhood', and involves three agreements: to regard children as social actors; 'to access children's views at first hand'; and to see that 'childhood as a biological moment in the life course, should nonetheless be understood as a social construction'. The summary raises vital questions about where and when childhood begins and ends. Can it be separated from 'adult' societies, markets, states, economies and policies? Do these separations, if they exist, help or harm children? How far is childhood biological or social, natural or cultural? And how do positivist and interpretivist traditions further the study of the ontology and the social construction of childhood?

Partly concerned with the problems listed above, some researchers call for new directions in the sociology of childhood. Hugh Matthews (2005: 272) queries whether well intentioned childhood research may become 'adultist, exclusionary and oppressive'. Horton and Kraftl (2006: 139) list colleagues who share their uncertainties and their concern that children's geographies could be 'more useful, more engaged in policy and weighty contemporary issues', more relevant, purposeful and applied, and less 'self-referential, endlessly re-citing an all too familiar body of work . . . a rationale for itself . . . a comfort zone . . . cosy and unchallenging'.

The idea that childhood is socially constructed could help to release children from ascribed and imposed dependencies. It might free them from claims that children are inevitably immature and therefore need such controls. It might recognise that many of the restrictions serve adults' power and convenience rather than children's interests, just as feminism recognised the power of sexism and worked to emancipate women. Yet instead, childhood studies have tended to become a refuge from mainstream social science and society, where children are appreciated but nevertheless contained and excluded from 'policy and weighty' matters. DCR offers ways to strengthen the validity of critical social research with children and young people. This could help to increase its credibility, and its potential influence on public thinking, policy and practice.

Sociology and philosophy

Theories are the living centre of research. This section reviews different kinds of theories and how they involve philosophical questions. Childhood studies examine how theories and values are at the heart of the understanding of childhood and youth, just as they were central to Semmelweis's research. His colleagues were asked to accept the scientific and moral reality that their hands could transmit disease. They had to transcend their presumed dichotomies between disease-free male doctors and impure women and babies. They also had to see that seemingly dead matter could be actively infectious, before they knew about the living microbes it contains. Their unexamined theories and assumptions about morality and biology confused and obscured new ways of thinking.

Childhood studies create conceptual space for understanding similar abstract, invisible, and deeply assumed notions. This involves seeing how childhood, youth and child–adult relations are not simply universal, biological and inevitable; they are also partly varied, changeable constructs worthy of critical scrutiny.

'Theory' means 'to look', and researchers' choice of theory shapes how they look at evidence, and how they question, collect and interpret it. Theories range from explicit hypotheses and research questions, to working models and frameworks of thinking about reality. Theories include *epistemology*, thinking and basic beliefs about what counts as knowledge, how it is produced and how we can know anything, and *ontology* or being in the existence, purpose, nature and function of things. Each discipline from history to biology has its own theories in terms of ways of seeing things and technically describing them. Provisional working theories are accepted until they are superseded by more powerful explanations. Theories may explain personal values, aims and motives, priorities and preferences. Theoretical frameworks include *empiricism* that sees the world in terms of facts, and *interpretivism* that attends to constructs. Moral beliefs about society, policy and relationships may be *functionalist* or *critical*. In extreme terms, functionalism sees society as an organism that functions for the general good of all, so that protestors should be silenced, punished or excluded. Childhood involves being socialised into rules and roles; dissatisfaction or *anomie* is treated by restoring people to their normal personal roles in society. Critical theory, however, sees society as basically unjust, when rival groups compete for control and resources. Dissatisfaction involves people being oppressed by injustice and *alienated* from their true selves. The remedy is to transform society towards greater political justice.

Sociologists have long been concerned about serious inconsistencies and limitations in their work. Among a range of colleagues, Norman Denzin and Yvonna Lincoln (2000: 575) warned that qualitative social research had reached a 'crisis of legitimation'. Clive Seale (1999: 26) admitted to 'fateful moments' of doubt, which he aimed to tackle through a pragmatic middle way, 'between the extremes of objectivism and relativism, realism and idealism and the deduction/induction dispute'. Seale wanted to use 'political and philosophical debates as resources for achieving certain mental attitudes' but not as 'principles from which all else must flow, creating unnecessary obstacles to flexible and creative inquiry . . . we bracket out deeper existential or ontological questions in order to get on with life', only occasionally 'requiring episodes of philosophical thought'. Seale aimed to avoid 'dominance' by philosophy over sociology, which, he thought, risked 'laying foundations for truth', wholesale constructivism and 'a descent into nihilism'. He believed all these influences would lead to 'profound uncertainty and distrust'. Instead, he wanted

> qualitative researchers to establish a new consensus around exploring shared meanings for positive purposes, drawing on the strengths of a constructed, imagined research community [to provide and] agree standards of judgement for the plausibility, credibility and relevance of research reports.
>
> *(1999: 29)*

Seale has been quoted in some detail because he summarises so well the doubts that many social researchers share, along with efforts to examine and resolve them. However, he raises several problems. First, he seems to wish to smooth over differences with renewed professional consensus. Second, the 'plausibility, credibility and relevance' of any professional work cannot wholly be judged by a group selected from within that profession. Social research involves groups across society with varied views, including research subjects who agree to give their time and data, research funders, those who read, and learn from, and perhaps apply research findings, and very many groups who are affected when research reports influence public opinion and policy relating to them. Criteria for assessing research, which all these groups could all find convincing, will have to extend beyond sociologists' interests. Third, the selected academic 'community' is likely to involve conservative leaders, reluctant to probe too deeply into the foundations on which they have built their reputations.

Fourth, Seale is mainly concerned with research methods, the craft of research, whereas the deeper problems concern theories and philosophy. Fifth, Seale in his first quotation above, with Hammersley (1995) and others, tends to assume that if philosophy is invited in, it will only dominate sociology. They overlook how philosophy is integral to everyday and research thinking, and that a main task of philosophy is to be an under-labourer, clearing away rubbish and laying foundations, and not always the master builder. The philosopher Mary Midgley (1996) compares philosophy with plumbing. These can both be ignored and taken for granted until they are not working well, when the problems of blocked drains, floods and empty taps (and their equivalent in clear logical thinking) become obvious and have to be fixed.

As mentioned earlier, DCR is not a version of social science. It is a philosophy of the natural and social sciences that does not dominate or determine methods, theories, topics or findings. Instead, it clarifies the necessary conditions for scientific and social activities and structures to exist, and for social science knowledge to be produced (Bhaskar 1998a: Chapter 1). DCR aims to analyse, explain and validate social research, to draw on the strengths of empiricism and of interpretivism and to overcome their limitations. DCR shows the importance of moving beyond describing and documenting, to include analysing, making connections, explaining and working to resolve contradictions.

Philosophy is not artificially introduced into social science. It already exists in innumerable theories and questions, such as whether agency is free, or determined, or some combination of these. The above examples of social researchers' unease indicate the need for the kind of under-labouring that DCR can offer, and which this book shows can be applied to childhood studies – though it is relevant to all kinds of social science.

Childhoods real and imagined

DCR is about critically recognising that real existence (ontology) is separate from thought and imagining (epistemology). Real children, for example, exist independently beyond researchers' concepts and analysis and data. Researchers, however, as mentioned, tend to reduce being into thinking, ontology into epistemology, things into thoughts, to mistake their perceptions and reports for reality, or to deny that there is an independent, essential reality. This reduction and loss of reality into ideas, termed the *epistemic fallacy* (Bhaskar 1998a), is at the heart of social science and childhood studies. From countless examples, here is a summary of research on infants' 'theory of mind':

> Towards the end of the first year, it [*sic* meaning 'the infant'] is able to participate with others in shared activities . . . Yet infants . . . are still not

aware of distinctions between their own mental attitudes towards objects and the attitudes of others with whom they interact. They merely enter into and share such attitudes with significant others. Not until the second year do they become aware of themselves and others as having distinct attitudes towards the same objects or events.

(Martin and Barresi 2006: 272)

These views are based on rigorous laboratory tests, but they ignore reality. It is impossible to feed a newborn baby unless this is a shared interaction between the carer and the baby, who is the main agent. And babies quickly become aware of differences between their own 'mental attitudes' and those of other people. This is shown when they frequently and vociferously protest if others stop them from doing or having something they want. Yet the misleading theories are often believed. The psychologist Michael Siegal (2010) called for better research methods, to discover young children's deep knowledge that is well beyond the levels discovered so far by psychological tests. Also vital are new theories that explore how and why misleading views have been so widely believed.

Another way to learn about babies is to be with them, and I will say a little here about my being and doing as well as thinking. I helped to care for my five younger siblings, and the two youngest were born when I was 10 and 18. My mother shared with me her radically changing views about childcare, mainly learned from being with her children. Between us, my mother (for 25 years), one of my sisters (22), one of my daughters (19) and I (14) have spent 80 years mainly caring for our children before moving on to combine this with paid work. Three of these 15 children died of different incurable conditions, and three others have long-term illness/disability, which has led us to reflect on the value of brief and restricted young lives. In our extended family, I have almost always lived with children aged under 5 or been in close touch with them, when each new baby has reminded us about children's 'marvellous minds' (Siegal 2010). While I was working on this book, my three youngest grandchildren were born, each reawakening the questions: What does it mean to be human? And how far is humanity innate and universal, or learned and local?

One of my grandchildren lives among chickens, goats, dogs and horses, each species with its closely organised group and power hierarchies and rituals. When I was trying to work out how, as a baby, she differed from other social species, I found Mary Midgley's (1979, 2010) Darwin-inspired philosophy about social animals helped me to appreciate the ontology of newborn human babies as highly social, interacting beings. This leads to the questions to be considered later: When does morality begin and what are its origins? Is it taught and acquired, a synthetic epistemology, or is it partly innate in authentic human ontology? 'Innate' is not necessarily blind instinct or biological determinism, and can involve dispositions, potential and emerging capacities. Babies help to highlight relations and tensions between childhoods real and imagined, which DCR helps to analyse.

Outline of the book

I would like to summarise here the ways in which DCR uniquely contributes to childhood research, so that readers may know what to expect. Yet I cannot describe its usefulness effectively without first explaining what DCR consists of, a task that takes up most of this volume. So instead, this Introduction concentrates on a few of the main concerns that DCR addresses.

Chapter 2 will review the problems of present research methods in detail. Chapter 3 will present 12 tenets of DCR. Present splits between disciplines, such as between economics, psychology, moral philosophy, ecology, politics and education, result in limited, fragmented views of human life. The DCR concept of four levels or planes of social being provides a framework for connecting disparate parts of complex humanity and society. Chapter 3 explains the first plane of social being – real bodies in material relations with nature. Chapter 4 addresses the second plane – interpersonal relations and agency. The third plane is social relations and structures (Chapter 5), and the fourth plane, in Chapter 6, concerns human nature and the ethics of inner being, alienation and flourishing. This involves questioning assumptions that social science should be value-free. Volume 2 returns to the planes with greater emphasis on politics and practical change: in Chapter 9 relations between childhood and the ecology and the natural world; in Chapter 10 interpersonal and international relations within the economics of scarce resources; and in Chapter 11 inter-generational relations and structures through evolution and history. Chapter 12 will consider ethics, emancipation and flourishing as the good life in the good society, how good societies might respect and include children and young people more, and how DCR and childhood studies together can open new practical approaches to research theories, methods and social influences. Dynamic change is central to childhood and humanity and society, and DCR offers ways to analyse change, emergence and transformation through a four-stage dialectic, explained in Chapters 3–6 and 9–12.

Childhoods Real and Imagined breaks unwritten conventions in sociology: that childhood is different and separate from the 'adult world'; and that each academic should stay within a narrow sub-speciality (although multi-disciplinary work can be a cautious meeting of different experts). Other assumed rules are that each author should thoroughly survey the great wall of related preceding work, attribute almost every point to previous authors, and then attempt to add only a small block of new thought. Anxieties behind these sociological rules are analysed in Chapter 2. This book, however, is about the serious problems that arise from splitting apart childhood and adulthood, and splitting academic disciplines into sealed compartments. I have not kept to the sub-speciality of childhood, and instead will consider many interrelated topics and disciplines. Far from claiming to be an expert in all these subject areas, I agree that an edited collection by a range of specialists would cover each topic with far deeper knowledge. Yet that could perpetuate the partitions. Instead, I aim to be a sufficiently informed general reader to attempt to analyse related areas from the perspectives of the sociology of childhood and dialectical critical realism. Besides peer-reviewed academic work, I have drawn on reports and commentary from the mass media and NGOs. All these sources take particular slants on childhood and youth. NGOs, for instance, often exaggerate children's problems in order to encourage the public to give them more support and donations. The sources will therefore be used for their information and analyses, and also as examples of varying attitudes towards childhood.

So far, DCR has mainly been 'pure' (debated among philosophers and theoretical sociologists) rather than 'applied' to practical social research, although there is a growing range of applied critical realism work. I have related DCR to practical research, partly by reviewing social studies that have applied DCR, but mainly by showing serious, general, current problems in research and how DCR seeks to resolve them.

This is not easy. For almost 40 years, DCR has aroused strong criticism, although it has gradually convinced leading former critics (Norrie 2010). A main problem is that the DCR literature tends to be dense, hard reading; another is that there are many complicated terms and concepts. There are several things that make for hard reading. One is an obscure writing style, which I have tried to avoid. A second factor in hard reading is when complicated ideas are, at first, hard to grasp and take some effort. I've tried to explain these ideas as clearly as possible, sometimes gradually by returning to them thoughout the book. A third factor is when the ideas challenge the reader's assumptions in ways that feel hard, inconvenient and even painful. Yet surely the point of writing or reading a book is to consider challenging ideas that offer a new way of looking at the world, and to think about them critically but fairly. On jargon – every discipline and trade has what seems to outsiders to be jargon and to insiders to be necessary, unique terms. DCR has plenty of complicated terms. I have aimed to avoid unnecessary jargon, and I have selected DCR terms that seem most useful to researchers. Learning a new discipline or sub-discipline, from physics, to mechanics, to DCR, is partly like learning a new language, and gradually realising the range of subtle meanings and associations that each word and phrase holds.

Although I concentrate on children and young people, I do not wish to imply that they are more important, valued or worthy of respect than men and women, simply that they are of equal human value.

To conclude, here are some of the major questions to be addressed throughout the book:

- How can methods in natural science possibly apply to social science?
- How can we understand change and becoming as well as being in childhood?
- How can philosophy serve social science without dominating it?
- How can we understand reality, and validate our understanding?
- And what are the differences between reality and our understanding of it?
- Do universal truths exist, or is everything contingent and provisional?
- How do human agents and social structures interact?

- Why are absence, non-identity and dialectic so important?
- Is social science ever value-free, and should it be?
- How can we reunite many aspects of society, usually separated in research, but which can only be understood in relation to one another?

2
TRENDS IN RESEARCH ABOUT CHILDREN, CHILDHOOD AND YOUTH

A mother was bottle-feeding her 15 week old baby. She turned to gaze at his face. He turned his head to gaze back at her. He stopped sucking and smiled faintly. Her expression changed, her eyes widened with a look of anticipation. His eyes locked on to hers and she suddenly said 'Hey!' opening her eyes wider 'and throwing her head up and towards the infant. Almost simultaneously, the baby's eyes widened. His head tilted up and his smile broadened . . .' His mother began saying, 'Well, hello! . . . heell'o . . . heeello'ooo!' each time was longer, more stressed and at a higher pitch. 'With each phrase the baby expressed more pleasure, and his body resonated almost like a balloon being pumped up, filling a little more with each breath.' They paused and 'the shared excitement between them ebbed, but before it faded completely, the baby suddenly took the initiative and intervened to rescue it. His head lurched forward, his hands jerked up, and a fuller smile blossomed. His mother was jolted into motion' and they repeated and extended the game.

(Adapted from Stern 1977: 11–12)

We have long known about babies' early social interactions, their awareness and responsiveness to other people, and their initiatives in sustaining intensely close emotional relationships. Such examples raise questions, to be considered throughout this book, about how social research can increase our understanding of babyhood, childhood and youth, and of human nature and relationships, in order to inform policy, practice and public opinion. Parts of this book concentrate on babies because they are such complicated and often underrated human beings and sources of knowledge. Living at the edges and beginnings of human thinking and being, they have much to show about whether, and if so how, they are primarily social or natural beings, or whether such a distinction is helpful.

This chapter reviews social research about children in the contrasting empirical-naturalist, interpretivist-cultural approaches. It considers some current influences from these two approaches on knowledge and policy about childhood. Most research with children involves market research (Beder 2009; Buckingham 2011; Klein 2000; Savage and Burrows 2007), and also traditional psychological and epidemiological research that takes little account of childhood studies. The first example is from positivist birth cohort studies and the public policy they have informed. The second example is a childhood studies interpretivist view of babies' needs. Limitations and problems for childhood studies in the two approaches will be reviewed, and later chapters will show how DCR seeks to resolve the problems.

Natural science traditions

The traditions include empirical (sensed, observed) research, positivism (testing theories against empirical data), and naturalism (that unites methods in natural and social research). When August Comte (1798–1857) coined the term 'sociology', he adopted natural science models of organising empirical data into patterns of predictive laws and rules. He saw positivism as the new religion (Benton 1977). Common-sense empiricism, which takes transferable facts and objects for granted, dominates our daily life. I assume that the words I am typing will appear before your eyes, and convey my approximate meaning. Positivist 'common-sense' concepts of age-stage child development, influenced by the biological sciences, still dominate most matters affecting children in academic research and everyday life.

Charles Darwin joined a tradition of parents who recorded their close observations of their children, and psychological research still follows their methods of animal observation, behaviourism and ethology (applying evolutionary theory to early animal and childhood behaviour), besides developing standardised tests and laboratory experiments. John Bowlby's influential work on babies who were deprived of maternal care was based on research with monkeys (Bradley 1989). For centuries, doctors have guided childcare and psychology, such as the philosopher and paediatrician John Locke (1632–1704) (Hardyment 1984; Stables 2008). Medical influences on social research about children 'biologise' them (Morss 1990). They also tend to pathologise them, in the therapeutic intention to search for problems to be identified and treated, in deeply held notions, that children are largely irrational, pre-social beings through to their hormonal, volatile youth. Child psychologists continue to observe, test, classify and measure children's development within grids of assumedly genetic and universal stages of cognitive growth and moral development.

Many psychologists are cautious and flexible and take account of how subtle interactions between children and researchers can alter their responses (Donaldson 1978; Harris 2008; Harris and Butterworth 2002; Siegal 1997, 2010). However, positivist research is still dominated by perceptions of the science of measureable, 'normal' development. The norm as the statistical average can merge into normative, that is moral, assessments, when the norm becomes the desirable mean, with variations verging away towards 'deviance' or 'dysfunction'. Judgements are still made quite rigidly by researchers, politicians and journalists, as reviewed later. One of the largest, most generously funded areas of research today is the birth cohort study. Such studies purport to examine how different childhoods connect to later adult outcomes. They do so by collecting demographic, social, epidemiological and economic data over decades. The British cohort involving 90,000 babies born in 2012 had initial funding of £33 million. The cohorts illustrate how traditions of the interviewers' objective impersonal detachment from children are reinforced by today's technology. Teams of data collectors electronically record each child's and parent's responses under prescribed headings in order to feed vast data banks ready for statistical multivariate analysis. The digital recording overlooks how human experiences and responses are often complicated and ambiguous.

The aim to be objective still deters some researchers from consciously relating and talking to children. They fear evoking subjective, individual interactions that would stymie their supposedly detached, standardised methods. Ironically, a detached manner tends to intimidate interviewees, who perform less well. Research-based norms therefore tend to underestimate children's and parents' capacities whereas, as mentioned earlier, informal, humorous and empathic rapport can elicit more accomplished responses (Donaldson 1978; Oakley 1981). Empirical social science methods include: abstracting children from their social context and everyday life, like cells under a microscope; observing them in laboratories;[1] and relying on standardised questionnaires.

Genetic and neurological research involve still more direct quests for hard scientific evidence about children's social development and pathologies. Psychiatrists and psychologists aim to find biological proof, such as in the brain anatomy, genes or hormones, to validate their disciplines, and their claims about physical causes of behavioural disorder. Geneticists have, however, moved on from the so far unrewarding search for single gene causes associated with behavioural conditions or intelligence levels. They now search for possible multi-gene associations and predispositions, while epigenetic research on interactions between genes and the environment raises even further complications (Pembrey *et al.* 2006; Plomin and Spinath 2004).

Neuro-researchers claim that their scans reveal brain structures and activities uniquely associated with behavioural traits such as autism and attention deficit hyperactivity disorder (Greenfield 2003; Baron-Cohen 2011). But others challenge these claims as inconclusive, arguing that the brain activities examined are too complicated and are already too much influenced by other factors to be able to provide uncontaminated natural evidence. The factors include social experience (Rose and Rose 2005; C. Fine 2006, 2010) and medication (Baughman and Covey 2006). In effect, the critics question how the biological child can be unravelled from the social child. Yet the popularity of positivist bio-psychological research is shown in bestselling books. For instance, psychotherapist Sue Gerhardt (2004) cites neuroscience to review 'why love matters' and how types of parenting can alter the chemistry and structure of babies' 'social brains'. Educationalist Sue

Palmer (2007) draws on biochemistry for evidence of a 'toxic cocktail of factors' that adversely affect children's learning and development.

Next I will examine an example of positivist research into children's daily lives and its influence on policy, selected from many similar examples. Positivism seems to promise strong, reliable, scientific evidence to validate beliefs and policies about children and young people.

Positivist social research

Normative age-stage theories inform the birth cohort studies. The large databases hold records from questionnaires, interviews and tests conducted regularly with selected cohorts of people born, for example, in 1958, 1970 and 2000. During the early years, parents are the main interviewees. A typical report, by the economists Shirley Dex and Heather Joshi (2005), is about the first nine months in the lives of 18,819 babies born in Britain in 2000. The data are meticulously presented in many tables and figures. The questions to parents cover: pregnancy, birth and early development; family and friends; childcare; babies' temperament and behaviour; parents' health (weight, smoking, drinking), attitudes and relationships, employment and education; housing and income.

The researchers consider that society is willing to invest in cohort studies for these reasons. Society contributes to family budgets. Children are an investment for the future, the labour force that will produce tomorrow's wealth and pensions. And children should not have to suffer the full extent of their parents' low incomes. The 'large cost' of cohort studies is justified, say Dex and Joshi (2005: 237–8), for four reasons. The studies try to identify causal mechanisms in individuals' behaviour. They record comparison groups that might show associations between life events and social problems. They chart social changes and aim to disentangle reasons for them within and between different cohorts. And finally they show how histories of health, wealth, education, family and employment vary and affect later achievements. Dex and Joshi seem to admit that the cohorts can only show possible associations not proven causes, when they loosely conflate 'causal mechanisms', 'causes', 'quasi-causes' and 'associations'. For reasons to be explored later, the cohorts provide stronger evidence and predictions about the physical health/ disease effects of lifestyles and behaviours than about all their other social effects.

Dex and Joshi repeat government policies when they state that their research supports the following aims intended to reduce child poverty: to increase parental employment; to raise standards and results in schools; to promote cost–benefit state frameworks for childcare and health; and to prevent and reduce costly ill health and obesity.

The 2000 birth cohort study uses questions from the 1958 and 1970 cohorts in order to make comparisons across the generations. The concepts and analysis therefore may be dated and underestimate great changes in understandings, experiences and contexts of childhood since 1958, and possibly very different causes for similar results. A report of the 1970 cohort, which connected adult performance back to the babyhood data, was much publicised during 2003. It connects with current international concern about investing in children's 'first 1,000 days' (Black *et al.* 2008). Socially disadvantaged babies were shown to tend to achieve less well in cognitive tests than their peers, when they were aged 22 months and also during the subsequent 30 years. The 2000 cohort yielded similar early results. Comparing the 1970 and 2000 studies, the economist Leon Feinstein (2003a: 24) warned:

> These differences are not set in stone, far from it, but may be hard to break later. This means that policies to reduce inequality and increase average levels of performance that come into play after children have reached primary school age may struggle to achieve the success that one may wish for them.

Feinstein recommended increased state provision of preschool childcare and education, improved pay and conditions for the staff, and increased recruitment and retention of staff to ensure continuity of care and security for the children. Although politicians expressed great anxiety about the data, almost as if behaviour at 22 months is 'set in stone' and determines the whole life course, they did not raise preschool staff salaries. However, also in 2003, the government published *Every Child Matters* (HM Treasury *et al.* 2003), the plan for great investment in childcare and education, which cites developmental research evidence. The next section shows continuing close connections between positivist social research and policy.

Policy influenced by positivist research

This example is given in some detail because it represents many similar research-policy links. It also interweaves key themes for this book: childhood and childcare, biology (including brain anatomy), economics and society, research and policy. The example illustrates how policy-makers select and simplify research findings. They also tend to conflate correlations with causes, and turn possibilities into probabilities and then into facts and certainties. Responsible researchers urge caution, but they continue to publish reports and press releases that play into a desire for simple certainties (Minton 2009; Allen 2011).[2]

By late 2010, the British coalition government was closing down early years services in England, while reinforcing their moral claims about parents' personal responsibilities. The government commissioned an 'independent report' by Labour MP Frank Field (2010) about how 'to prevent poor children from becoming poor adults'; how to end child poverty through increased parental employment and improved state education; how 'a child's home environment affects their chances of being ready to take full advantage of their schooling'; and how to 'enhance life chances for the least advantaged, consistent with the government's fiscal strategy'. Field concluded:

> [There is] overwhelming evidence that children's life chances are most heavily predicated on their development in the first five years of life. It is

family background, parental education, good parenting and the opportunities for learning and development in those crucial years that together matter more to children than money, in determining whether their potential is realised in adult life. The things that matter most are a healthy pregnancy; good maternal mental health; secure bonding with the child; love and responsiveness of parents along with clear boundaries, as well as opportunities for a child's cognitive, language and social and emotional development. Good services matter too: health services, Children's Centres and high quality childcare. [Prevention in the early months is better than attempts at cure later on.]

By the age of three, a baby's brain is 80 per cent formed and his or her experiences before then shape the way the brain has grown and developed. That is not to say, of course, it is all over by then, but ability profiles at that age are highly predictive . . . and the evidence is clear that children from poorer backgrounds do worse cognitively and behaviourally than those from more affluent homes. Schools do not effectively close that gap; children who arrive in the bottom range of ability tend to stay there.

(Field 2010: 5)

Field (2010: 8) noted that despite the expanding, cost-effective, childcare programmes over the past decade, 'current services are also very variable and there is generally both a lack of clear evidence of what works for poorer children and insufficient attention to developing the evidence base'. Targets towards 'abolishing child poverty' in England by 2020 have not been met and, Field concludes, the policy is too expensive.

Well known for his decades of dedicated work on poverty, Field (2010: 16) added a 'personal note'. Since 1969, he has 'witnessed a growing indifference from some parents to meeting the most basic needs of children . . . The most disturbing pieces of research that I have read for this Review is a handful of studies' (Feinstein 2003a, 2003b) on cognition at 22 months. Field asked:

So how do I square these findings – that directly relate the level of income of parents to the success of their children – with my belief that money does not produce the transforming effect we need to counter child poverty at this time?

Field (2010: 16) repeated his earlier list about healthy families that

can transform children's life chances, and trump class background and parental income . . . A child growing up in a family with these attributes, even if the family is poor, has every chance of succeeding in life . . . The simple fact of a mother or father being interested in their children's education alone increases a child's chances of moving out of poverty as an adult by 25 percentage points.

(Blanden 2006)

Moving from incomes to outcomes, Field's view that 'income is not the only factor that matters and that it is not even the main one' led him to recommend granting funds to services and not directly to families, 'as we build the evidence base of effective programmes'. 'All disadvantaged children should have access to affordable, full-time, graduate-led childcare from age two. This is essential to support parents returning to work as well as child development.' Commercially run Children's Centres were given contradictory duties: to cater for all inclusively, yet to 'target' the most disadvantaged. International evidence from schools shows that advantaged families avoid inclusive schools, and disadvantaged children are increasingly segregated into low-standard schools and Children's Centres. Field ignored this evidence when he required that the Centres should be 'welcoming, inclusive, socially mixed and non-stigmatising, but aim to target services towards those who can benefit from them most'. He added that success will be measured when future adults 'secure better paid higher skilled jobs' (Field 2010: 16).

Positivist data also impress journalists, who are concerned about babies' brains and who favour expert care over mothers' care. Polly Toynbee (2010), for example, was worried that the government

> downgraded the qualifications needed by nursery teachers, when all the evidence shows that intensive – and expensive – professional nursery teaching is what works . . . the importance of children being talked and listened to, growing their vocabulary, empathy and understanding. Brains harden by the age of three . . . Every year that passes in children's lives, the chance of changing destinies diminishes.

Toynbee criticised Field's view that 'poverty is not the main reason why people are poor', and disagreed with his policy of 'taking from the poor to pay for the poor'. But neither Toynbee nor Field referred to the leading psychopathologist Michael Rutter's findings (2007) that the most disadvantaged children gain least benefit from Children's Centres. Rutter (2011) also repudiated doom-laden developmental predictions based on brain scans. Field acknowledged, in his phrase 'as we build the evidence base', that no one yet knows how, why or whether the care is effective for disadvantaged children, although it supports his aim to 'support parents returning to work'. He did not mention that this was at a time of rapidly rising unemployment and of low-paid part-time work. Parental employment was not reducing child poverty, and most poor children had parents in paid work but on low wages.[3]

Seven tenets of positivism

Positivists tend to assume that data, such as babies' brain scans and different measures of poverty, can be: (1) objective self-evident facts separated from values; (2) understood apart from their social context and as separate variables; and (3) independent and pristine (whoever observes, records, reports or reads about them sees the same fact). (4) Their essential inherent qualities and (5) stable lasting reality 'out there' in the world can remain unchanged when transferred across time and space. (6) Positivist social research, modelled on the natural sciences, can therefore discover general laws, replicable findings and reliable predictions. (7) This confidence encourages assumptions that 'evidence based' findings can support self-evident conclusions about causes and effects in social life, and provide effective solutions to public and private problems.

Problems with positivism in social research and policy

Positivism raises at least six practical problems. First, there are long-standing disagreements among positivist researchers about methods of defining, collecting, measuring and analysing data. When social research does not produce regular or definitive comparative results (inevitably it does not, see *Closed systems* in Chapter 3), positivists may blame their methods. Belsky *et al.* (2007) argued that they could only have conducted their £multi-million evaluation of the Sure Start early childhood programme thoroughly if the English government had allowed them to conduct a rigorous randomised controlled trial. Yet this would have had to involve turning Sure Start itself in a more centrally, rigidly controlled experiment, without the wide range of local, flexible variations. Second, research statistics show patterns but not definitive causes or explanations. It is unclear precisely which policies promote children's education and development and how they do so. Third, despite or perhaps because of these doubts, there are tenuous links between research findings and the 'evidence-based policy' they are claimed to support. Fourth, this allows politicians to adapt supposedly scientific findings to support and justify their preferred policies. Frank Field continues the long tradition of 'policy-based evidence' by citing malleable data to make government decisions about children look scientific rather than ideological.

Fifth, despite positivist claims to separate facts from values, Dex and Joshi (2005) reinforce current dominant values of cost-effective, future-oriented approaches to childhood. They present babies as cost units rather than as persons, and follow the medical model of checking for problems. Questions about maternal feelings, for example, include: 'annoyance; extent of impatience with baby; resent giving up things because of baby' (2005: 201). Housework, and by implication the work-object babies, are analysed mainly in cost terms, of time, fair division between partners, something to be fitted efficiently around paid work. The questions allow little scope for parents to say what they enjoy or find rewarding and fulfilling. There are implicit values that adults may not enjoy home or family life, and would prefer to be doing paid work and to pay others to care for their child. If this is so, the point of the hard working and earning is unclear, particularly if the work is low-paid and unfulfilling. There is an implied bleak meaninglessness to life: 'Communication [is] for language development' (2005: 250) not for pleasure as in the example that opened this chapter. The survey looks at cost, but not at value, or at parents sharing happiness and the good life with their babies.

'Babyhood' remains an untheorised and implicitly negative prelude rather than a valued life-stage.

Sixth, when positivist researchers and policy-makers predict, for example, that educational disadvantage is fixed possibly for life from the early months, they overlook how their prophecies can contribute to powerful self-fulfilling pessimism. This can lay the blame on disadvantaged families instead of on poor schools and services, which can keep reinforcing early disadvantages. The pessimism may close opportunities and lower the crucially influential expectations of the children's potential, held by the children themselves, and by their peers, parents, teachers, future employers and other adults. The 'objective' detachment of positivism pervades reports and policies, when the authors inevitably select and re-present their data, and when they ignore their own part in the long history of official mistrust of the 'feckless' poor, which still drives public policy (Hendrick 1994; Nadesan 2010; Wacquant 2008, 2009).

Interpretivism

Interpretivism has also been termed 'anti-naturalism', 'hermeneutics' (Bhaskar 1998b) and 'anti-foundationalism' (Turner 2008).

The social construction of childhood

Partly in reaction to positivist social research based on natural science methods, a major influence in childhood studies is interpretive, and concerned with culture instead of biology. Interpretivism broadly includes social constructionism, phenomenology, structuralism, poststructuralism, postmodernism, symbolic interactionism and ethnomethodology. Researchers in this complex range of approaches would reject a common general summary. Yet they tend to share scepticism about the above tenets of positivism, about scientific objective truth, shared taken-for-granted meanings, and universal realities. They emphasise the local and contingent and how meanings emerge through social interactions. These approaches involve seeing things and events as socially produced through forms of consciousness or narrative, discourse or text. Subjects as implacably biological as death are treated as social constructions – for example, in the historical 'invention of infant mortality', meaning the quite recent medical recognition and discourse about the problem (Armstrong 1983). Whereas empiricists rely on sensed experience, social constructionists examine how culture shapes our experiences and perceptions, identities and relationships.

Since the 1960s, feminism and gender studies have challenged supposedly objective, positivist but sexist research, which took 'Man' to represent all adults. Feminists showed how concepts of men and women, and power relations between them, vary in time and place. They are not natural or immutable. Similarly, studies of childhood and generation question the supposedly inclusive objectivity of adult-centric positivism, and show how children and young people are so often excluded. They emphasise that researchers do not simply observe, collect and measure data. They are also selecting, perceiving, constructing and interpreting. Concepts of adulthood and childhood, and power relations between them, therefore vary in time and place and are not static, independent or impersonal (James and Prout [1990] 1997).

To understand childhoods as diverse social constructs, and sets of beliefs and behaviours, can open up freedom to explore alternatives. There is release from assumptions that certain models of childhood, including oppressive and disparaging ones, are inexorable, given or non-negotiable. Childhoods are ideologies about the actual and desirable nature of children and of child–adult relations. In a double hermeneutic, children and adults co-construct childhoods, such as in the interactive dyads of victim child and rescuing adult, needy child and providing adult, or capable contributing child and respectful adult. Beyond genetic or economic determinism, children are recognised as social agents who share in shaping their own lives and influencing the world around them. No longer dismissed as pre-social and pre-moral entities, or as the mainly passive objects of adult education and socialisation, children are respected as reliable research participants and sometimes co-researchers with their own valuable views and experiences (Christensen and James 2008; Percy-Smith and Thomas 2010; Tisdall *et al.* 2006). Childhood studies have involved hundreds of investigations into children's lives, and provided a wealth of new insights into their perspectives and competencies, needs, preferences and contributions to society.

An example of interpretivism: deconstructing needs

I have selected an example about 'need', because need is a central concept in childhood and well-being, and in DCR and natural necessity (see Chapter 3). This much cited example is by Martin Woodhead, a leading proponent of childhood studies and social psychology, an international researcher and policy adviser. Woodhead challenges post-colonial legacies that endure in the export and imposition of potentially oppressive, inappropriate 'western' notions of childhood around the majority world. After summarising Woodhead's analysis of babies' needs, I add some comments.

Woodhead (1997: 63) treats 'needs' as claims, which 'tell us as much about the cultural location and personal values of the user as about the nature of childhood'. He quotes experts who, during the 1970s, claimed that each baby 'needs':

> a 'special' and continuous person or people; daily lives based on somewhere they know as 'home'; [sensitive, patient, personal care] love and security . . . from birth onwards a stable, continuous, loving and mutually enjoyable relationship with his mother or mother-figure . . . new experiences [as] essential for the mind as for the body . . . stimulation . . . praise and recognition . . . and responsibility.

(Woodhead 1997: 63–5)

Additionally, a policy report from 1988 is quoted as asserting that young children 'need' 'to be with adults who are interested and interesting', to relate to other children, 'to have natural objects and artefacts to handle and explore, and opportunity to communicate through music and imaginative play'.

The term 'needs', comments Woodhead (1997: 66), could be seen 'merely as shorthand' and a powerful and 'very credible veil for uncertainty and even disagreement' about children's 'best interests', 'wants', demands or desserts. Woodhead questions the presumption of implicitly timeless, universal qualities of childhood identified in 'children's needs', presented as if they are static, empirical facts identified by astute adults. The claims have emotive force, inducing guilt if they are not heeded, because of the inferred helplessness and passivity of the needy child, and 'the implication that dire consequences will follow if the need is not met', though the consequences are seldom explained. Professional judgments are projected onto children. They are claims made by adults but 'not by the children themselves!' (Woodhead 1997: 68). To present 'needs' as natural and inevitable facts conceals 'a complicated array of personal and cultural values alongside empirical claims about childhood' (1997: 75). The claims require to be differentiated, especially in culturally diverse societies, in order to sort out how far they could be open to personal choice and political discussion.

Woodhead identifies four kinds of needs. (1) Needs can be seen as part of *children's nature* in so far as babies have an intrinsic drive to seek milk/food and they have 'a pre-disposition to seek out enduring human relationships'. But Woodhead is less sure to what degree this predisposition is linked to specific features of early nurturing relationships, commonly prescribed as needs by childcare experts (1997: 69–70). 'Needs' for continuous loving care, and the significance of specific attachment relationships imply a different sense of 'need'. (2) Needs based on '*psychological health outcomes*' are a major area of scientific research, notably the consequences of various kinds of emotional deprivation. Yet Woodhead (1997: 71) draws attention to the challenges of inferring universal 'need' from context-specific research, embedded in particular cultural practices and 'definitions of mental health'. (3) *Social adjustment* criteria for defining need are more normative, and clearly linked to cultural practices, according to Woodhead, who points out that the claims that babies have specific requirements to be mothered by one person (known as 'monotropism') are 'adaptive' to specific family and childcare arrangements common in western societies, but which are far from universal, as evidenced by cross-cultural research. Woodhead also questions whether the 'need to be responsible' is an *ethnocentric*, western concern with independent self-reliance, and he says that parents in Asia, where 'children's economic contribution is highly valued', look for deference and obedience, not responsibility. (4) 'Needs' for music, imaginative play and objects to explore are largely *cultural prescriptions*.

Woodhead concluded that weaker 'needs' (2–4) are too often falsely conflated with the stronger natural need (1), and the term should be avoided, in local and in United Nations global contexts. This would prevent the danger of perversely promoting western values in the 'guise of science', and of pathologising deviance if families do not conform to prescribed childcare practices. Woodhead wanted to defuse western experts' power, and open up debate about the complex scientific, cultural and value basis implied in judgements about 'need'.[4]

My comments draw on DCR approaches to the highly contested views about what human beings need. Kathryn Dean (2007: 323) cites Bhaskar's definition of need as 'anything (contingently or absolutely) necessary to the survival or well-being of an agent, whether the agent currently possesses it or not'. Dean notes the problems of how we can satisfy true needs that advance human flourishing, yet avoid false needs that impede it, with the difficulties of sorting unneeded wants from unwanted needs, and of trying to be free from both of these. That involves balancing subjectivism and relativism in attempts to meet needs that are histori-cally and culturally mediated, yet have real causal urgency.

Interpretive childhood studies risk overemphasising the social and cultural, and underestimating the powerful needs of embodied, emotional relationships. Woodhead seems to qualify all needs as culturally conditioned if not constructed, except food (although choices and rituals around food are of course cultural) and possibly relationships. Yet this overlooks the reality of babies' complex lives, which integrate the physical, psychological and social, as the opening example in this chapter illustrates. Woodhead's criticism of 'monotropism' refers to an old debate (Bowlby 1964). Families have always known, and by the 1970s some experts (Rutter 1972) were asserting, that babies enjoy relationships with a range of adults and children, although they benefit from consistent, affectionate care and become distressed and anxious if left with indifferent strangers. Like adults who do not speak the local language, babies rely on people who know them well enough to understand and respond to their cues and preferences (Als 1999). And 'somewhere they know as "home" . . . continuous, loving and mutually enjoyable relationship[s]' matter to people of every age, for present happiness and not simply for some distant future well-being. Woodhead does not say whether the mental health research he mentions is about babies' well-being or their future adult outcomes. However, Shiner et al. (2009) connect the frequency of violent and broken relationships, and the fairly high numbers of suicides among British men, to their difficulties with attachment in early life.

Woodhead does not say whether the 'cross-cultural research' has found socie-ties where babies routinely have no close relationships. This seems unlikely. Continuing care is not simply 'western', and it occurs in majority world commu-nities and extended families, where babies tend to be breast-fed, to be carried around in a sling for much of the day, and to sleep with their parents at night. Some kind of rewarding emotional relationships would seem to be vital, espe-cially among the billion poorest people in the world, to encourage families who struggle to meet babies' basic needs when resources are very limited. International news reports suggest that parents everywhere grieve if their child is injured, kidnapped or killed, although they vary in how they express grief, and that close relationships count as a basic need for most human beings. 'Need' (unlike interests, wants, desires or desserts) here can mean serious physical and mental suffering if the need is unmet.

Woodhead identifies 'responsibility' with western independent self-reliance in contrast to eastern children's deference and obedience. However, he alludes to 'highly valued' wage-earning children – who have to carry out work responsibly. Like 'needs', 'responsibility' remains undefined by Woodhead. In reality, 'responsibility' can combine independent, reliable initiative and confidence, with deference and obedience to rules and standards set by adults, in ways that confirm and enrich close relationships and mutual respectful appreciation between children and adults. While writing this section, I was observing a child aged 14 months who, like children across the world, insisted on sharing in responsible 'adult' work: in her case, feeding dogs and chickens, sweeping stables and determinedly shutting every farm gate. Robert Serpell (1993: 24–74) analysed complicated, subtle meanings of children's 'intelligence' in several African languages. He showed how *nzelu* involved three dimensions, of wisdom, cleverness and responsibility, all vital for the well-being of rural Zambian communities. Sadly, the local schools were not organised to respect or nurture these capacities, and they left 80–95 per cent of children feeling that they were brainless failures. Richard Sennett's (2008) analysis of adults' anger and despair, when their skills and responsible capacities are denied and devalued, applies to every age group.

This links to 'needs' for music, natural objects to explore, and imaginative play. Woodhead implies these are a lack for children, which adults can choose to remedy. Yet, these are inner compulsions: young children *have* to sing, move to music, touch and explore objects, treat a piece of wood as if it is a dog, a doll or a phone. These are positive needs to be and to do, not negative deficits, and adults can neither construct nor stop such impulses. When talking with colleagues, if I said, 'Babies like music', some would reply, 'How do you know? Where are the research results and references? Do you mean babies in Africa too? Have you asked X [a researcher in Africa]?' These comments suggest that knowledge is preferably derived from formally researched, published sources, and that liking music is culturally contingent and learned, acquired thinking, rather than inherent being and doing.

This cautious, respectful, post-colonial view intends to avoid imposing western concepts and values on to the poorer majority world. Yet it can inadvertently appropriate many vital and universal matters away from the majority world, and imply that these belong only to the western world unless proved otherwise. For lack of contact with the millions of majority world babies, as well as with the rarely seen British babies hidden away in their homes or nurseries, cars or buggies, and still dominated by the theories of Piaget (1928, 1932) and Maslow (1943), the public imagining of babies easily slips into terms of emptiness and absence. Vacant babies may seem to be waiting for adults to meet all their needs while they slowly become human and social. Babies are still mainly missing from childhood studies, whereas they crucially illuminate meanings and origins of later childhood.

The DCR concept of *natural necessity*, what we are compelled to do by our nature, helps with analysis of babies' strong reactions to music from the start: excited by dance rhythms, cheered and comforted by songs, soothed by lullabies and, in their second year, intrigued by the rhymes and tunes they avidly remember and repeat. Music resonates authentically with human being, not simply synthetically with human thinking, in rhythm and melody expressed and enjoyed by mind-bodies. The micro-rhythms that newborn babies engage with in time to human speech (Stern 1977), with its meaningful undulations and inflections, pitch and tone that merge into music, illustrate how babies need to or have to *do* music, rather than passively need to have music provided for them.

Psychological research reveals how music is integral to babies' natural necessity. Trevarthen (2006) cites Bjørkvold (1992: 13, 22) who writes of the 'musicality' of the body: 'Mother and child "swing" together in a common rhythm, and in so doing strengthen each other's identity'. They refine skills of body language and spoken language, humour and songs, the 'fellowship of child culture' and the flow of emotions. Newborn babies know human rhythms, such as the mother's heartbeat, they sense them in others and soon become 'enthralled' by rhythmical play and songs (Trevarthen and Malloch 2002). Chapter 3 will look further at 'need' in the DCR concepts of natural necessity and real human nature.

Seven bases of interpretive research

Despite the variety among interpretive childhood researchers' theories and, as noted earlier, their rejection of generalisations, they are more or less likely to fit into the following summary. The seven points tend to contradict the seven earlier ones on positivism. Interpretivism cautiously treats phenomena as if they are (1) constructed by subjective human perceptions and values and negotiated interactions, (2) within specific social contexts and cultures. (3) Phenomena are contingent, and depend on our individual social selves and perceptions, (4) as if phenomena have few or no essential, inherent qualities and (5) no independent, lasting truth or reality of their own that could transfer intact across time and space. They do not exist 'out there' in the world, but only through the social institutions and cultures that give them meaning. (6) Interpretivism recognises unpredictable human agency, which can be intellectually, morally and pragmatically liberating when it deconstructs ideas of fixed realities, seemingly determined by biology, history, economics or religion. (7) Connections between research data, conclusions, recommendations and later policy-making are questioned as tenuous constructions, instead of being assumed to be self-evident conclusions.

Complications in childhood studies

Positivism and interpretivism have critical strengths but also practical limitations and inconsistencies. Their opposing positions pose problems in childhood studies and social science generally. Positivists' faith in a pristine, stable, factual reality, and their inattention to how researchers' questions, methods and perceptions alter and shape their data and conclusions, are seen by interpretivists as naive and unrealistic. Research methods that can work well with particles in physics cannot simply be applied to social agents who have subjective consciousness, make choices, change the world, are unpredictable, and are driven by many diverse and often unknown influences. Positivist social research therefore cannot produce replicable findings about definitive causes and effects, or predictions or general laws, although these are supposed to be the essential tasks of positivism.

Interpretivists attend carefully to these problems, but they too work with implausible double standards. They reasonably criticise social positivists' certainties, but interpretivists' own caution about reality and their reluctance to generalise weaken their research reports and their potential to influence policies and practices that might benefit children. Latent contradictions emerge when some sections in a social constructionist report are presented as if they have essential, valid, transferable meaning, and others have not. There are double standards when researchers treat children's reported accounts as socially contingent, but rely on the international transfer of their own texts and precise meaning by page or screen. For example, authors who aimed to raise international (therefore transferable) ethical standards in childhood research ended their paper with the qualifying clause: 'The researcher is not the knower of truth but rather the recorder and interpreter of multiple "other" social subjectivities' (Beazley *et al.* 2009: 369). If applied to their whole paper, the sentence would invalidate their aim and this illustrates how untenable social constructionism can be if followed to its logical conclusions.

Another example is when ethnomethodologists contend that language is continuously created and recreated, words are too contingent to have any agreed, clear, extensive definition, and meaning in daily social life only exists when we create and maintain it through talk. Ethnomethodologists therefore analyse the structure and the interpretive rules people use to establish a sense of order, rather than examining the supposedly ephemeral, unreliable content of what they say, and they 'bracket off' large areas of society that cannot hold a constant meaning (Garfinkel 1967; Silverman 2009). Yet ethnomethodologists assume that their own texts retain intrinsic, transferable meaning. Regarding everything as a social construction, Latour and Woolgar (1979: 180–2) assert: 'We do not wish to say that facts [studied by natural science] do not exist nor that there is no such thing as reality . . . Our point is that "out thereness" is a consequence of scientific work rather than its cause', and that 'real' and 'unreal' are socially agreed constructs. This raises vital questions about whether children and adults are the authors or the products of society.

Interpretive researchers consider that it was only when childhood was recognised as socially constructed, not natural or given, that children could be rescued from the natural and behavioural sciences and become visible to the sociological gaze. While this move has greatly increased the understanding of children's daily lives and relationships, views and experiences, and of related power and structures, seven key problems remain. One is when some adults, who research children as 'the other', find it harder to avoid distancing, objectifying and relativising childhood and children than it would be when they research other adults. For example, Nick Lee (2001: 108) notes that a lack of 'self-presence' is sometimes assumed in children. Owen Jones (2008) claims that children are 'other' from, and unknowable to, adults. Yet if children are unknowable, how can we be certain that they are so 'other' from adults? Given that everyone is partly mysterious and unknown, even to ourselves, is age the great barrier or is it simply being human?

Second, publications on any topic are almost always by adults, who take an adult standpoint and voice. Uniquely, children's voices are almost entirely missing from the content and the commentary. A third problem is that however value-free researchers may try to be, and however deeply buried their adult-aligned values and interests, these inevitably shape their research reports to some degree. Fourth, by definition feminist research has the practical and moral goal of equality between women and men, but childhood researchers have no such agreed goal of child–adult equality. There are great unresolved disagreements between adults who wish primarily to protect, or provide for, and partly or alternatively to emancipate children and young people (Alderson 2011). All these problems do not complicate adult-centred research to the same extent.[5]

The fifth difficulty is that childhood researchers are disappointed about the continuing relative neglect of children and their exclusion from mainstream sociology and from society. The more biological age-stage based theories of child development still dominate political, professional and public understanding of childhood. Recommendations from participative research with children have few practical effects (although when adults are consulted there are also seldom direct, practical outcomes).

The sixth problem is relativism, raised by various forms of interpretivism. Unless some stable realities, such as human bodies and universal needs, are recognised, can researchers make sense of other people's experiences and accounts? Can they report these in terms that have shared meaning and relevance for readers and, potentially for policy-makers? If everything is contingent, what is the possibility or purpose of doing research, apart from to explore local differences? Without a sense of real human nature, can suffering exist, or matter? Critics point out that child abuse is more than discursive processes (Hacking 1999). But if there are no universal values, if the history, politics and economics that invest our lives with meaning are deleted or 'bracketed off' from people's accounts, then human values and rights, and the solidarity on which they rely, are empty claims, lost in cultural relativism.

Seventh are the deep conflicts in social science generally between different research methodologies, which erode public trust in their credibility. Whereas positivism is over-reliant on supposedly definite, independent facts separate from researchers' methods, perceptions, values and culture, in contrast, interpretivism, which crucially acknowledges these influences, can be too vague. In reacting against the unduly hard rock of positivism, interpretivists risk falling into a whirlpool of uncertainties. Although many researchers pragmatically try to combine positivism and interpretivism and avoid their extreme forms, this is difficult when the methodologies are largely defined by their opposition to one another, listed in the above sets of seven pairs.

Serious practical and ethical questions remain about the nature, purpose, validity and logic of social research approaches, and how their strengths might be combined and their weakness overcome. Meanwhile, 'a-theoretical' quantitative research by economists and statisticians increasingly dominates social research and public policy about children, and absorbs research funds.

Chapter 3 will consider how DCR addresses these questions, beginning with analysis of a basic error that positivism and interpretivism share.

PART II
Experiencing and imagining childhoods

3

REAL BODIES

Material relations with nature

A British-Nigerian mother described being shocked and sad on first seeing her baby Oludayo, born 15 weeks early and in an incubator, until the nurse told her to speak to her daughter. 'She was looking so helpless and tiny, but then I say something to her and then it was so, she was moving her hands and legs so quickly and right, like trying to recognise you . . . "Yes go on", [the nurse] was saying . . . "this is the one voice she known for a long time, now she can have a sense that she has not been abandoned that you are still here." '

(Alderson et al. 2004: 27–8)

The example of Oludayo works at several levels. There are the premature baby's little known feelings and her possible rudimentary memories and responses. There are the nurse's understanding of these, the mother's feelings and relationship with her baby, her memories and her account of the event. Further layers are my record as the interviewer and the readers' interpretations. There are the social and economic contexts of premature birth and neonatal intensive care, besides the ethos and the training and support for staff in each neonatal unit, which can powerfully affect their attitudes towards babies and parents. Views about babies' early feelings partly depend on empirical and positivist theories, and also on hermeneutic and emergent theories.

This chapter will outline main concepts in dialectical critical realism (DCR). Later chapters will show in more detail how they contribute to social science theories and methods when researching real and possibly imagined childhoods. First, I will say a little more about the background to the neonatal example and the themes that it raises.

'Unthinkable but knowable'

We observed four neonatal intensive care units for months where the staff held vividly contrasting attitudes (see Appendix 1.8). One unit had a mechanistic ethos. Babies were seen almost as faulty machines to be repaired. Parents tended to be treated as extra burdens on the staff, to be managed and excluded as much as possible. At the other extreme, besides maintaining high scientific and clinical standards, staff in Oludayo's unit saw babies as sensitive persons and members of families. Parents were treated as partners with the staff and resources in the babies' healing. Recognising the added emotional stress in family-centred neonatal care, this unit was unusual in employing a counsellor to support the staff, another for the parents, and staff specifically to organise and teach about the emotional, personal responses and needs of each baby. A nurse in Oludayo's unit, informed by Heidelisa Als's (1999) research, commented:

> Yes I definitely think they [babies] have emotions and memories [and] know the difference between the touch of a parent and the touch of a nurse or a doctor, and . . . that [parents have] a loving touch and caring touch. The business-like touch of a doctor is going to be very different. One can almost see the child cringe or tense . . . You see the difference in the reaction when the parent arrives there is an excitement it's incredible, but it may sound mad, but I do think having been looking at the babies for so many years, when their parent arrives the number of times I've said to the parents, 'They know you are here, they are excited to see you, they are pleased.' You can actually tell these things from a 23 weeker [born 17 weeks early], which is amazing. And of course they have a memory. I think they understand whether they are going to have an [intervention]. I think the memory . . . is unthinkable but it's knowable.
>
> *(Alderson et al. 2005a: 41)*

Pads on the babies' skin constantly measured oxygen levels in their blood. They were connected to monitors that enabled the staff to keep checking the level of extra oxygen supplied through the ventilators. To avoid the dangers of too much or too little oxygen, the supply was constantly turned down as low as possible to wean the babies off dependence on the extra oxygen. Alarms rang when the oxygen level was too low, or when breathing or heart rates faltered. In the 'mechanistic' unit, alarms merged with the general noise of radios jangling, bin lids clanging, and staff calling across the large echoing area. In Oludayo's unit, where lighting and sound were deliberately kept low, the alarms rang out sharply and were interpreted by many to denote the babies' rising stress. A nurse described a new doctor who walked briskly past the incubators with noisy footsteps and set alarms ringing in turn along the row. The staff and parents tended to regard the battery of monitors partly as windows into the babies' minds and hearts.

Chapter 2 reviewed how childhood studies have tended to ignore bodies and human nature in order to emphasise children's social and cultural lives. Childhood studies aimed to redress traditional psychological and educational concentration on children's minds, when 'child-centred' too often means 'mind-centred'. This is shown in the inattention of teachers and school design to children's bodily needs (Mayall 1994). Oludayo's unit illustrated how attention to children's expressive bodies can increase awareness of their social and personal life.

In contrast, in the noisy, mechanistic unit, the staff conveyed little sense of the babies being sentient, social persons within human relationships. Among many observed examples, doctors would simply take a blood sample and walk away, leaving the baby to scream. In Oludayo's unit, a nurse would prepare and hold the baby, talk reassuringly, and help the baby to recover. There was noticeably less distress in this unit, showing how attention to children's mind-body feelings and responses can encourage more informed and humane care.

Until around 1990, newborn babies having surgery tended not to be given pain relief, because it was assumed to suppress heart and lung function. The belief persisted that babies could feel no pain because they had no memory (Hatch 1987). Eventually some doctors experimented by giving the routine paralysing medication and anaesthetic to 16 babies having surgery to close a duct near the heart. In addition, they gave analgesia (pain relief) to only 8 of the babies (Anand *et al.* 1987). Against medical expectations, the babies who suffered less shock and adverse effects were those who had the analgesia.[1] However, like Semmelweis's discovery (see Chapter 1), the research results were only slowly accepted and implemented, perhaps partly because they involved doctors having to adopt new moral concepts of newborn babies' capacity to suffer. Our neonatal study raised complex questions about real and imagined childhoods, and how the differing social-emotional beliefs held by the neonatal staff affected their contrasting thoughts, activities and relationships. Almost 10 years later, I can now see how DCR would have advanced our analysis of the neonatal units, and will comment on that at the end of this chapter.

The following brief overview will cover 12 main concepts in DCR. I needed time to understand these ideas and their relevance to practical research, and I still have much to learn. So I hope that it will help readers new to DCR when some points are slightly repeated. Instead of cross-references, the index is intended to help readers to connect different sections through the book on these key concepts. The concepts reviewed here are: *being and knowing*; *transitive and intransitive*; *the semiotic triangle*; *the possibility of naturalism*; *closed and open systems*; *natural necessity* in *natural* and in *social* science (with *induction, deduction and retroduction*); *power$_1$ and power$_2$*; *four planar social being*; *absence and change*; *emergence*; and dialectic through four stages of the acronym *MELD*.

Children's bodies are a main theme in this chapter for several reasons. DCR is about material-physical realism and bodies vividly illustrate this, as well as the different approaches in natural and interpretive research that will be further discussed. The first of the four planes of social being is about material relations with nature, experienced in and through bodies. MELD begins by attending to real difference that exists in the world in, for example, real bodies. DCR began with the philosophy of the natural sciences (Bhaskar [1975] 2008a), and childhood research has similar origins in the biological and medical study of children's bodies, which offer a helpful starting point.

Twelve main concepts in DCR

Being and knowing

(Bhaskar 1998a, 2008a; Hartwig 2007: 173–5)

Chapter 2 summarised contradictions between empiricism/positivism and inter-pretivism but ended by saying that they make the same error. This is the *epistemic fallacy*, which reduces *being (ontology)* into *knowing (epistemology)*, and things (objects, people, events, structures) into thoughts.

As mentioned earlier, *empirical* research emphasises the physical and psychological *being* of children, strongly grounded in sensed/observed biological patterns of age and growth. However, empiricism does not simply observe being-existence. It also involves epistemology in interpreting and making sense of the data. So empirical observation of Oludayo would be absorbed and processed into the researchers' partly personal subjective knowing-epistemology, their values and concepts, and whether they see meaning in babies' movements or not.

In *positivism*, Auguste Comte aimed to reject metaphysical speculation in favour of 'positive' knowledge based on observation and experiment. He wanted to discover natural and social law-like regularities. He thought it was impossible to penetrate to the inner essence or nature of things, and that it was essential to separate fact from value. The problems of attempting to detach children from their essential nature and moral identity and relationships have been reviewed in Chapter 2, when research such as the birth cohort studies misleadingly implies that real mother–child relationships can be adequately conveyed through the epistemology of statistical analysis.

Bhaskar (1998a) contends that researchers displace their search for validation onto their own analyses. Empiricists and positivists concentrate on their *methods*, on rigour, design and avoiding bias in projects such as meticulously controlled clinical trials, 'validated' questionnaires, carefully 'cleaned' and coded databases, and intricate statistical analysis.

Partly in reaction to positivism, *interpretivists* are deeply and explicitly concerned with epistemology. They search for validation in their *theoretical analyses*, and in the complications of how we perceive, interpret, imagine, reconstruct and report childhood. Chapter 2 reviewed how some interpretivists question the gaps between reality and their later representations; some set aside or deny an original reality and instead they see it being 'constructed and reconstructed', or 'performed and presented' through ephemeral beliefs and behaviours.

In these ways, social researchers rely on their *knowing* to provide guarantees and criteria of truth, instead of relying on the *being* of the objects and events originally researched. In an international group of psychologists urgently searching to resolve confusions in their work, one stated: 'That is reality – the *meanings* that we give to the events, experiences, people and things in our lives – it is communally constructed and inherently susceptible to transformation' (Anderson 2000: 202, original emphasis). The statement compounds the original problem: confusion between reality and meaning.

Bryan Turner (2008) distinguishes between three sociological approaches to the body. Foundationalists, who are nearest to critical realism, see the body as a real material entity, constant and functioning although changing. The body is connected to, but differs from, the meanings through which it is represented, experienced and understood in many different contexts. It powerfully structures our lives, societies and social inequalities, and these are all topics for sociological analysis. Among anti-foundationalists or interpretivists, the second approach acknowledges that we each have a body, but that it is only accessed through our perceptions, constructions and discourses, and it depends on these. The third approach, also interpretive, dismisses the separate existence of the physical body, and reduces it entirely into our perceptions and constructions, as the product of our discourses.

Turner considers that sociologists are generally anti-foundationalist. They concentrate on representations of the body, the social processes that produce the representations and, in turn, the effects they produce. Despite his important work on the body linked to human beings' animal vulnerability, Turner tends to split the social and *thinking* about bodies, from the natural and humans *existing* in and as bodies. He states that sociologists are mainly concerned with the former, 'cultural decoding of the body as a system of meaning' and meaning-making (Turner 2008: 15), and he warns us 'not to reify "the body" ' (p. 245). To reify is to treat an abstraction, such as a social relation, as if it is a material thing – which the body already is – so that the original ontology is then lost in the researchers' epistemology.

Turner comments: 'Without a more robust research methodology, sociological interpretations of social texts have the same force or lack of it as literary interpretations' (p. 12). Social science, however, generally lacks the literary force found in fiction, which can intensify vivid physical details with personal imagining. Aravind Adiga (2010: 121–2), for instance, conveys the anger and suffering of extremely disadvantaged people who endure everyday injustice and oppression. Two young boys have just arrived in an Indian city and at night they are led

> to an alley behind the market. Men, women and children were sleeping in a long line all the way down the alley [which] ended in a wall that leaked continuously; the drainage pipes had been badly fitted. A large rubbish bin . . . emitted a horrible stench . . . Keshava could not believe he was expected to sleep here – and on an empty stomach. However bad things had been at home [in the village] at least there had always been something to eat. Now all the frustration of the evening, the fatigue, and confusion combined, and he kicked the shrouded figure [lying next to him] hard. His brother, as if he

had been waiting for just such a provocation, tore the blanket off; caught Keshava's head in his hands and slammed it hard against the ground.

Keshava lay imagining his hunger as a long tunnel with food at the end. He looked hard up at the stars trying 'to block the stench of garbage'. Some ethnographies convey this kind of immediate, tangible realism. They include Cindy Katz's (2004) study of childhood in the Sudan, when village children walk to a distant wood to feast on the luscious berries and light bonfires to make ash to carry back home in buckets. And there is Filip De Boeck's (2005) study of child witches that intensely combines reality and imagining.

Turner, however, considers that foundational and anti-foundational approaches are incompatible. They are defined in opposition to one another, and they fall into either biological or cultural reductionism. Turner attempted an eclectic synthesis, but this has been criticised as incoherent, for example, by Chris Shilling (2012). Shilling advocates research on the relationships between the body in nature and the body in society through his concept of the unfinished body, which is subject to biological and social change. 'Growing numbers of people are increasingly aware of the body as an unfinished entity which is shaped and "completed" partly as a result of lifestyle choices' (Shilling 2012: 174). This adult-centric view regards the mid-life adult body as somehow 'finished', although it is already deteriorating. The young child's unblemished, vigorous body is perceived as somehow lacking. Instead, a baby's body could be seen as 'finished' for babyhood, a young child's 'finished' for early childhood, with features such as large eyes and flawless skin that many older adults spend fortunes trying to replicate.

Bhaskar argues that valid research has to be based not only in reliable theories and methods, but also in the original *subjects/objects* of research – humans and other species, things, events, structures, processes, values), and in how accurately they are understood. The first step in DCR is to distinguish between being and knowing and to recognise their vital differences. To separate the objects' independent, sheer, irreducible being (ontology) from researchers' very different knowing (epistemology) is to avoid the epistemic fallacy. DCR begins by seeing the world existing independently of our knowledge of it (see MELD later on). Sociologists who avoid the epistemic fallacy can combine empirical certainty about the existence of the intransitive objects and causal relationships being researched, with interpretivist awareness of observers' subjectivities. The combination respects parts of both traditions, and the next two sections explain ways of doing so.

Transitive and intransitive

(Bhaskar 1998a: 9–13, [1993] 2008b: 399–400)

Having distinguished knowing from being, DCR also separates them into transitive and intransitive entities. Independent, *intransitive* (though changing) ontology in the objects of knowledge (natural objects, persons, bodies, social structures) lasts over certain periods of time. In contrast, our *transitive* knowledge of them is partial, provisional and changeable.

Knowledge of genetics has gradually developed through theories of plant and animal breeding, evolution, the double helix, genomics and epigenetics. But all these changing, revised forms of partial knowledge have not altered the structure and mechanisms of genetic inheritance that have lasted for millennia. To acknowledge the ontology of genetics presupposes in turn that there is an objective world order, independent of our identification of it, although we can fallibly come to know about it. Transitive knowledge involves how we observe or experience, perceive or understand intransitive objects, differently in the eye and mind of each person involved, through contingent views that change over time.

DCR combines the strengths of positivism's concepts of the essential, intransitive being of objects of study, and interpretivists' attention to limitations and shifts in transitive knowing. Later sections explore how this can apply to the social as well as the natural sciences.

The semiotic triangle: signifier, signified and referent

(Bhaskar [1993] 2008b: 22–3, [1994] 2010a: 52–3)

The ontology, such as of the body, tends to be transformed, evaded or denied through the research process. Researchers then have the problem that they cannot ground or guarantee their work in an intransitive external reality. As reviewed earlier, they search instead for validations in the transitive epistemology of their theories and methods.

An extreme version of this is semiotics when, for example, Saussure ([1916] 1983) refers only to the *signified* (the concept), and the *signifier* (words as sounds or written marks). An example is the concept of dog, and words such as 'dog', 'hound', '*chien*', and so on. By concentrating on this pair of concepts and words, semiotics fall into the epistemic fallacy.

Bhaskar proposes instead the *semiotic triangle*. At the third angle is the *referent*, the independent, real, intransitive dog or dogs being referred to. In childhood studies, the semiotic triangle is a reminder that however abstract and variable concepts and terms about childhood may be, they still refer to actual children, or to the existence of childhood as a social state and status, or to the real personal and political relations between adults and children.

Bhaskar (1998a) criticises hermeneutic research on several grounds. First it is too concept dependent, but it is not concept exhaustive. That is, it reduces physical-material being into concepts, as if the limits of language are the limits of the world. Yet these concepts cannot exhaust or fully comprehend, for example, homelessness, or war, or material social life, which are much more than simply a concept, a *signified*. Second, it does not criticise people's conceptions when they are inadequate, false or superficial, but instead it simply accepts the *signifier*. And third, it leaves out the *referent*.

The possibility of naturalism

(Bhaskar 1998a; Hartwig 2007: 322–3)

How real, though, are social entities in comparison with material-physical ones? And can the same research methods work with both of them? *Scientism* assumes that methods in the natural and social sciences are identical. *Reductionism* assumes that the subjects-objects of social and natural science research are identical. And *naturalism* assumes that there is, or can be, an essential unity of methods in natural and social sciences. DCR analyses how naturalism is possible because the social and natural sciences are more alike than is usually believed.

Interpretive researchers tend to consider that naturalism, the use of empirical, positivist natural science methods in social science, is inappropriate and naive. They argue that social science differs too much from natural science: in its subject matter of social relations, unpredictable agents and contingent, transient social events; in its largely invisible social structures, beliefs and values; in its reflexive, hermeneutic interactions between observed agents and also between researchers and researched; and therefore in the need for appropriate methods beyond those of natural science.

Bhaskar contends that this division follows misunderstandings about both natural and social science. It is as if natural science is supposed only to work with direct experience, the *empiricism* proposed by David Hume (1711–1776). And social science, following Max Weber, should only adopt the *transcendental idealism* of Immanuel Kant (1724–1804) – a reliance on theoretical knowledge that transcends experience. In extreme terms, rejection of naturalism is based on the view that natural science deals with things and social science with ideas. DCR shows how this fallacy ignores common features between the natural and social sciences.

Hume sceptically believed that we should rely on directly sensed evidence. Scientific discoveries therefore should trace 'constant conjunctions' or patterns of observed events. If the conjunctions seem to have a repeated, predictable cause, this should be self-evident. Any contamination from metaphysical speculation should be unnecessary. However, if Hume's empiricism were strictly observed, it would be as if we simply observed numerous falling stones and searched for the cause of falling within the stones, or within repeated patterns or conjunctions between the falling objects. This would fit with Aristotle's belief, held for over 2,000 years, that it was in the nature of stones, their *gravitas*, to fall. Isaac Newton (1642–1727) transformed science by proposing that gravity was the hidden force and cause behind the falling objects and the circling planets. Newton's immensely important advance was that science must recognise that real causes, like gravity, may be invisible and unprovable but crucial.

As noted earlier, Bhaskar explains that empiricism is broader than Hume assumed. Empirical researchers work on theoretical interpretations and on making sense of felt experience. The discovery of general laws can only work when it moves beyond observation towards theories and imaginative hypotheses about invisible causes. Although the theory of gravity cannot be directly sensed or proved, and can only be known in its effects, even so over time and space it still gives reliable, consistent explanations. Evolution too can never be observed or proved directly; it can only be known in its hugely diverse and often unpredictable and random effects. But the abstract cause is generally accepted.

When this combined observing-analysing process of the scientific discovery of visible effects and hidden causes is recognised in natural science, it can also be respected in social science. Variable analysis of many separate factors in children's lives, such as types of parenting, or income, or early learning, follows Hume's empiricism. It is like looking for causes within falling objects and patterns between them. Instead, social science needs to look at deeper unseen causes and powerful structures equivalent to gravity, such as social inequality, class, gender and ethnicity.

Bhaskar (1998a: 123) adds that social activities are very irregular and unpredictable. Natural science method may therefore seem irrelevant to them, if it is thought to be only about making general, predictable laws. But Bhaskar argues that this definition of natural science is too narrow. It assumes that science is solely about simple regularities, whereas science is much broader. It also mistakenly assumes that social activity is always irregular with no discernible patterns. This is asserted 'at the price of rendering social activity quite *unlike* science' (original emphasis). Conversely, interpretivists' ideas about social science are too narrow when they identify ontology as our beliefs and perceptions about the objects of social research (reducing things into thoughts, the epistemic fallacy). Interpretivists then manage 'partially to reconstitute the experience of subjects in society' (the world is more than the identically observed objects that positivism assumes) 'but at the price of rendering social activity *insusceptible* to science' (original emphasis). Each side deletes vital elements from science and from society. 'For the positivist, science is outside society; for the hermeneuticist, society is outside science.' In the confrontation between these misleadingly narrow models of positivism and hermeneutics,

> the weaknesses of the one position find their antithesis in the strengths of the other. Positivism sustains embryonically adequate concepts of the law (generality), ideology and society; hermeneutics embryonically adequate concepts of subjectivity, meaning and culture.
>
> *(Bhaskar 1998a: 123)*

However, each side is necessary in an adequate social science; *transcendental realism* opens ways to resolve this confrontation. It can do justice both to Kant's transcendental (beyond the physical) ideas and to Hume's realism. 'The production of meaning is seen as law-governed but not determined' (1998a: 123). We rely on general social laws, of language, communication and relationship, but we are not completely controlled by them. Social agents' concept-making is seen as 'both necessary for, and necessitated by, social structures, and [is] subject to critique both for what is presents and what it obscures'.

In their seeming concentration on visible and present data, empirical and positivist social researchers resort to superficial behaviourism (Bhaskar 1998a: 134). There is a long history of children being observed like animals (Bradley 1989; Morss 1990). Although children's views were heard in the past, in the 1842 Factory Inspectors' Reports on Women and Children in Factories and Coal Mines,[2] in Henry Mayhew's ([1861–1862] 2010) studies of working children, and in trials at the Old Bailey,[3] London's criminal courts, most research still attends to adults' views about children than directly to children's views and experiences. On the personal level, many adults rely on their own observations and deductions instead of investigating children's inner motives and reasons for their behaviour. On the political level, adults tend to exclude larger, unseen contexts, structures and influences. For example, children's motives and reasons for 'truanting' from school, or 'absconding' from children's homes, are reduced into irrational misbehaviours. Adults then deal with the behaviours, which are effects of deeper problems, by returning and punishing the children, rather than by examining possible causes within the schools and homes. Behaviourism misses the tensions between structure and agency. Human agency can then appear to be unrealistically free from structures. It can then seem arbitrary, when it is unrelated to deeper structural causes. It can also seem overly responsible and potentially blame-worthy when it lacks structural constraints.

Social scientists are acknowledged to tend to be 'critical, self-reflexive and totalising' (drawing together many different aspects and levels of analysis) (Bhaskar 1998a: 134). And they see the objects of their research as 'existentially, but not causally, intransitive'. That is, social objects have independent lasting existence but they do not have inevitable causes and effects of the kind positivism would attribute to them. The objects of social science research – people, relationships, events – are 'concept-dependent, but not conceptual'. That is, they involve concepts but cannot be reduced into them. They are all partly composed of, infiltrated and affected by hermeneutic interactions but, again, they cannot wholly be reduced into these. And the objects are 'transfactually efficacious, but irreducibly historical (that is, bound in space and restricted in time)' (Bhaskar 1998a: 123–4). *Transfactual* means that social objects have partly general, predictable features and effects. The objects (such as children and childhood and intergenerational relations) are transient and vary greatly in how they are expressed in space and time. Yet the tendency still obtains. For example, matches tend to light up when they are struck. That matches often fail to light does not deny the tendency. Children tend to be subordinate to adults, and although many are not always subordinate, that does not disprove the tendency. To recognise underlying transfactual, transferable conditions assists in making comparisons between different objects (see the closing section of this chapter).

To illustrate the contradiction between positivism and interpretivism: on the one hand, child development psychologists map the seemingly inexorable, universal, inherent unfolding of children's new competencies month by month, according to laws of biological determinism. On the other hand, childhood studies researchers emphasise immense differences in young children's skills and behaviours in different settings. They attribute these differences to hermeneutics, in everyone's interacting expectations and histories, beliefs and behaviours. They therefore question general laws.

To summarise: natural scientists rely on speculation and theory as well as on observation, on (Kantian) transcendental idealism as well as (Humean) realism, when they propose unseen structures and causes such as gravity or evolution. Social scientists also rely on both empirical and conceptual work. Although hermeneutics and positivism can seem to be mutually exclusive, they each have essential and partly complementary strengths. The divisions marked out and disputed by theorists do not fully work in practice. Many practical childhood researchers try to resolve divisions between the biological and the social, empirical and interpretive, the structural and the individual.

DCR is useful here in critically examining common assumptions about the natural and social sciences, and in showing how alike they are. They both involve empiricism and idealism. They both explore seen and unseen, natural and social causes, the transitive and the intransitive. All scientists work with things and with ideas. Although this may seem obvious, it is denied when social researchers dismiss reality, or when critics of sociology insist it should observe and report but not attempt deeper causal, structural theories. Two common examples of the criticisms occur in mass media reports about young people who break the law. One is the view that it is soft, misleading and unscientific to attribute causes of (visible) agents' actions partly to their (mainly invisible) social contexts and disadvantages. The second view is that because some young people can overcome disadvantage, therefore they are all free to do so. Social researchers find it hard to counter these powerful views, linked to Humean empiricism and regularities, and to reductionist scientism.

Bhaskar considers that, at best from Weber to Habermas, there have been attempts to patch over the differences between 'the partial insights of the principal disputants' instead of working to combine their strengths. One advantage DCR brings is that, in emphasising the general respect for natural scientists' discovery of invisible causes, DCR endorses research into deeper, invisible social causes. DCR also helps to rescue reality from being submerged under interpretivism, and to rescue interpretivism from being divorced from reality. Some parts of this section on naturalism may seem too obvious, other parts too obscure. However, I hope that the debate on resolving contradictions and uncertainties in social research will become clearer through later chapters.

Closed and open systems

(Bhaskar 1998a, 2008a, 2008b: 401)

This is another useful way to help to resolve assumed differences between the natural and social sciences. Natural science is generally thought to involve *closed systems*: conditions that involve a single causal force and effect, and always produce an identical, inevitable reaction. Molecules behave in consistent, predictable patterns, in a 'constant conjunction of events'. For example, given usual conditions, water boils at 100° centigrade.

In reality, closed systems are rare. They are so unusual that scientists have to construct them in order to produce effects, ranging from randomised, controlled, clinical trials, to the physics experiments in the CERN tunnels under the Alps to search for 'the God particle'.

Usually there are *open systems*, in both the natural and social sciences, when two or more forces are present. Real structures and forces obtain and work consistently in closed and open systems but they can have varied effects in open systems. For example, gravity applies in all physical activities and contexts, whether in road traffic or moon rockets. Yet in open systems, despite gravity, birds and aircraft fly, and falling leaves spiral upwards in strong air currents.

These exceptions seldom raise doubts about deeper, natural, causal systems such as gravity, even though the systems are unseen and unproven except in their effects. It is less often accepted that open social systems can have consistent powers despite the usually varied effects. There is growing evidence and agreement about the harms of social inequality. Yet since inequality interacts with countless other social structures and agents it has partly inconsistent effects or *trends*.

Social positivists treat the social world as if it is a closed system and as if, therefore, social research should produce replicable, generalisable, inevitable results and predictions, with a search for uniform or at least strongly majority findings. Chapter 2 quotes Field's (2010: 16) conclusion that treated parenting as if it is a one-way closed system, not an infinitely open series of interactions and relationships:

> A healthy pregnancy, positive but authoritative parenting, high quality childcare, a positive approach to learning at home and an improvement in parents' qualifications, together can transform children's life chances, and trump class background and parental income . . . A child growing up in a family with these attributes, even if the family is poor, has every chance of succeeding in life.

'Every chance' suggests that every parent and child could or should be expected to conform to one predictable pattern. Field ignores how variables such as 'a healthy pregnancy' depend on an adequate diet and reasonable housing, and therefore an adequate income. He prescribes one pattern of parenting for all, although it is vague: 'positive', 'high quality' and 'improvement' are not defined. Unlike molecules, adults and children are unpredictable, choice-making, intentional agents living in a precarious social world. Far from behaving in fixed patterns and 'constant conjunctions', they interact with many conflicting social influences and, in doing so, they change the world.

DCR therefore analyses social science as open systems that have countless, highly complex, interacting factors and produce only general trends (Bhaskar 1998a: 9, 45, 87). Interpretivists attend to some of these complexities and avoid a superficial search for cause–effect. This may be to the extent that their research is so open that it is descriptive and inconclusive; they show *how* things occur, but less often *why* they do so. That limits their ability to inform and influence public understanding, or policy-makers like Field who rely on positivism's seemingly closed certainties.

Natural necessity in natural science with induction, deduction and retroduction

(Bhaskar 1998a, 1998b, 2008a; Hartwig 2007: 320 ff.)

The three levels of natural necessity are:

1. the empirical
2. the actual
3. the real.

So far, I have often referred to realism, needs, causes and structures. The idea of *natural necessity* is one of DCR's most potent ways to deepen awareness of these concepts and of their interactions and interdependencies. To begin with, natural necessity is most readily accepted in natural science research. It involves *depth realism* at three levels.

(1) At *the empirical level* are the identified experiences and sensed perceptions of knowing subjects, who test and validate data in replicable experiments that have predictable results. Empirical research may be inductive or deductive and involves forming generalisations or hypotheses related to many observations of constant conjunctions/repeated patterns.

Francis Bacon (1561–1626) advocated empirical *induction* to challenge the medieval unquestioning acceptance of Aristotelian science. Induction begins with empirical data, forms general hypotheses, and investigates further cases to search for a negative instance. Scientists reformulate hypotheses to allow for any confounding cases, until the research is exhausted and no new discrepant cases can be found, although these theories are always provisional.

Hume questioned how it is possible to justify induction or 'inference', which works from a finite set of examples to the truth of a universal law. Without a convincing answer to this question, common-sense and scientific belief in a regular, ordered, predictable universe must seem to be indispensible but irrational. Hume's insistence on remaining at the empirical level can confuse and mis-identify effects with causes.

Karl Popper (1902–1994) rejected Hume's objective concept of empiricism. Following Kant, Popper accepted that all descriptions of experience include selection and interpretation, and are shaped by prior theories. He therefore saw induction, and efforts to discover truth and to support and confirm theories, as insoluble problems. Instead, he proposed that science should systematically attempt to falsify or refute imaginative hypotheses through *deduction.* This begins with theory and develops and tests hypotheses, using predictions and observations. Hypotheses are provisional, lasting only until they have been proved to be fallible and are replaced by new, inconclusive theories. Popper recognised that subjective observations and methods also complicate empirical, deductive methods.

(2) In DCR, *the actual level* involves the actual objects and events that occur: many falling objects; subtle genetic changes in birds or peas over generations. Deduction at the actual level explains how, rather than why, objects fall or change, and it stands only as long as there are no exceptions. The hypothesis that all swans are white lasts until a black swan is observed, or that all emeralds are green lasts until a blue emerald is found.

Much research remains at Levels 1 and 2 but these are not sufficient for scientific explanation. One problem of relying on actual examples to prove or disprove general causal theories is that observed examples may seem misleadingly to disprove them. Leaves fly up in the wind against gravity, but that does not disprove it. A second problem is that causes, such as gravity, may endure and obtain while their effects are not observable. Simply because everything stays still in a room does not deny the constant, invisible pressure exerted by gravity: 'Just as a rule [such as gravity] can be broken without being changed, so a natural mechanism may continue to endure, and the law it grounds be both applicable and true (that is, not falsified) though its effect . . . be unrealised' (Bhaskar 1998a: 11).

(3) *The real level* attends to Levels 1 and 2 and to deeper, unseen structures and mechanisms. These generate causes and effects, and make them available to experience. The causes are established, or justified, by their explanatory power. Examples include gravity, or analysis of the emerald's molecular structure and its refraction of light. The analysis demonstrates that, by definition, emeralds must be green; a blue emerald would not be an emerald.

Level 3 transcends (moves beyond) Hume's empiricism/experience, towards Kant's transcendental idealism. But it also draws together abstract ideal and real being in their practical effects. As mentioned earlier, ideas about gravity or evolution illustrate how the imaginative and even speculative Level 3, the real, can be highly respected in the natural sciences. The forces are 'real' in two ways. They cause movement and change, and, while being invisible, they are visible in their real effects.

To emphasise this point, another example is the chemist Dmitri Mendeleev, who published his periodic table in 1869. This grid showed the 65 chemical elements then known, in order of their atomic weight and properties. Mendeleev left spaces for predicted missing elements, and their later discovery confirmed his hypothesis.

Norrie (2010: 8) considers:

> It was the identification of the third domain of the real, the broadest level of being, that drove Bhaskar's original work in the philosophy of science. This was the specifically *ontological* discovery of the natural necessity or real depth of being beyond what was available to experience.

After lengthy critiques of *induction* and *deduction*, Bhaskar (1998a: Chapter 1) asks how we can apprehend or discover unseen, independent, formerly unknown but real structures. Since we cannot create knowledge from nothing, science as a social process depends on adapting former, transitive, transferable knowledge. Bhaskar proposes *retroduction*, which applies models of analogy and metaphor and subjects these to empirical scrutiny. Newton's gravity is like a great pulling down or magnetic force. It is not entirely alien, but is analogous to many common concepts. Retroduction asks what structures, relationships and mechanisms must exist for the events (social or natural) to have occurred. Scientific analysis involves moving between the three levels of natural necessity.

Natural necessity in social science

(Bhaskar 1998a, 1998b, 2008a, 2008b)

Does the three-level concept of natural necessity work in social science? In DCR, it is not only possible but essential to conduct social research at all three levels. This moves beyond the 'flat actualism' of Levels 1 and 2, at which most social positivists and interpretivists work. The first two levels involve collection of empirical data through researchers' observations, questionnaires, interviews, texts and images of actual people and events, followed by organisation of the data to produce patterns, associations, and 'constant conjunctions'. The birth cohort analysis of variables and the policy debates (see Chapter 2) remain at Levels 1 and 2. Intermingled family behaviours are treated as both causes and effects (Dex and Joshi 2005; Feinstein 2003a, 2003b; Hansen *et al.* 2010; and many other cohort analysts). Items in the cohort databanks are atomised, in mix and match analysis, when they lack real organising, unifying, explanatory theories.

Similarly, innumerable small ethnographic studies of children and their activities at home and school, play and work, tend to be descriptive and to avoid overt claims about causes or generalisations. Induction is used in qualitative research, such as in grounded theory (Glaser and Strauss 1967). One version is 'saturation', the point when grounded theorists believe that they have collected all possible examples to illustrate their typologies. They expect only to find repeated types in further data collection (Glaser and Strauss 1967). Yet this is criticised by positivists as subjective and incapable of empirical verification.

To analyse social causes and to 'distinguish a necessary from an accidental sequence of events' (Bhaskar 2008b: 35) involves searching for underlying structures, explanations and generating mechanisms. These are like gravity in being powerful, widely consistent explanations. Natural necessity in social science involves the study of human agency and meaning, and of how knowledge is produced through social processes, including the engagement between knowing subjects and the real world they address. In DCR, retroduction accepts that, like gravity, the social mechanisms are transfactual. That is, they exist in open systems, across time and space, whether we are aware of them or not. They are seen in open tendencies, not in inevitable closed reactions. Chapter 5 will explore these social structures.

Tamaki Yoshida's (2011) critical realist study of physical punishment in two Tanzanian primary schools examined many layers that need to be understood and changed if practices are to alter. These include:

- *Empirical* – adults' and children's accounts and observed behaviours relating to their beliefs and values about education, blame, punishment, bodies.
- *Actual* – the practicalities for teachers who try to control classes of around 100 children in uncomfortable, grossly under-resourced schools; the daily school routines; the pain and humiliation endured by punished children; the surrounding communities. Dar es Salaam is around 95 per cent slums (Davis 2006).
- *Real* – the individuals' motives and reasons; traditional formative relation-ships between adults and children; deeply influential beliefs about childhood and adulthood and correct child–adult relations, about human rights and punishment; broader neo-colonial traditions and neo-liberal global policies and economics, which are shown in their daily effects in the children's and adults' lives (to be reviewed in Chapters 9–12). These enduring, underlying mechanisms generate events and make them available to experience. But the mechanisms are independent of the events, so that complex, interacting open systems work as trends. Like gravity, social and economic influences may be resisted without being refuted, and may be invisible without ceasing to exist.

Seemingly irrational and contradictory behaviours may be clarified when related to agents' intentions and also to social structures. Flat actualism tends to reduce human agency into either predetermined behaviourism, or else unduly free voluntarism, seen in childhood studies' emphasis on 'children as agents'. Natural necessity, however, analyses human nature and activity at every level, from personal beliefs to global structures in a complex structure-agency dialectic. Individuals' intentions connect to reasons, reasons to causes, and causes to social structures. These structures depend on human agency, which reproduces and transforms them. Structure and agency are irreducible to one another; they are interdependent and partly independent. Teachers and students depend on schools, and schools only exist because of them, but neither is reducible to the other.

Structures, systems and powerful normative routines can contradict appear-ances and intentions. In Britain, decades of elaborate national efforts to protect children from the dangers of traffic and strangers were not primarily intended to limit their play and exercise in public spaces. Yet the results include children being confined more at home (unfortunately where adults are most likely to harm and kill them).[4] There are rising problems of reported loneliness and obesity, so that adults' efforts to protect children can paradoxically expose them to new unpredicted risks.

Natural necessity exists in enduring, causal social structures, such as childhood. It also exists in meaning-dependent actions, interactions and interpretations by each agent, which are central topics of interpretivism. When agents' motives, reasons and intentions are real, in the sense of *causal* with the power to produce real effects, they are comparable in DCR to natural causal mechanisms. Their effects include how individuals and groups constantly reproduce childhoods and subtly vary them. However, individual agency is qualified in several ways. First, individuals reconstruct or modify childhood, but they inherit it and so cannot construct or create it. Second, whatever their efforts, few individuals have much effect on altering the numerous social beliefs, behaviours and deep structures that make up childhood. Third, most 'reconstructing' is done inadvertently, and people do not act wholly on deliberate reasons. Adults have children of their own for personal reasons, and not deliberately to reproduce childhood. But the social structure of childhood is both an unintended outcome and the necessary condition that grounds and enables the agency of parents and children. Fourth, interventions may be partly or wholly counterproductive, as in the above 'side-effects' of adults' protection. Fifth, 'the actors' accounts of agency are limited by unacknowledged conditions and unintended consequences, as well as unconscious motivations and tacit understanding and skills' (Bhaskar 2008b: 35). Even so, natural necessity exists as much in the social as in the natural world for researchers to observe, investigate and explain. But it exists in different forms with different subjects, and in social research these include people and society.

Power₁ and power₂

(Bhaskar 1998b: 72–7, 2008b: 402)

DCR recognises positive emancipatory power₁. This transformative capacity enables agents to plan and construct moral systems, to feel and care for others, and to collaborate on promoting justice, solidarity and transformation. In contrast there is negative coercive oppressive *power₂*. The numbering avoids use of the same term for opposing concepts. Steven Lukes's (2005) three forms of power – explicit, concealed and internalised – are all power₂. Power₂ makes both the dominator and the dominated unfree (Bhaskar 2008b: Chapter 3) and this will be discussed in terms of 'master–slave' relations in later chapters.

Power₁ as possibility and power₂ as domination can both be felt as lacks or ills, when the first is absent and the second is present. They may meet in an ontology of ethics, in the dialectical move away from ignorance and absence as social ills, and towards alleviating the causes of harm, and promoting the good in and for itself. Freedom does not involve removing structural determinations of power, which are essential. Instead freedom involves transforming them from unwanted into wanted determinations (Morgan 2007b). Childhood research poses questions about how far children themselves can exercise power$_1$ or power$_2$, how inevitably adult–child relations reflect 'master–slave' relations, and how far adults and children can genuinely transform their power$_2$ into power$_1$ relationships.

Four planar social being

(Bhaskar 2008b: 153 ff.)

Four planar social being consists of:

1. *Material relations with nature* in the physical reality of bodies and of the natural world.
2. *Interpersonal subjective relationships* between individuals and groups.
3. *Broader social relations* and inherited structures.
4. *Inner being*, the stratified personality, subjective agency, and ideas about the good life, the good society.

Deeper, more holistic and coherent analysis and explanations in DCR are possible in the four interacting planes of social being. The planes range from the personal to the international, local to global. The four interacting planes are understood in relationship, shaping and reshaping one another in time and space, history and nature. Chapters 3–6 each cover one plane in turn, and Chapters 9–12 will each enlarge on their political and practical levels. That is why bodies are a main concern in this chapter about the first plane of material relations with nature.

A study of babies in a Brazilian *favela* (slums) illustrates research within one project that relates to the four planes (Scheper-Hughes 1992; Scheper-Hughes and Sargent 1998). The researcher did not know about DCR, but her work ranges across the four planes of social being and illustrates the usefulness of doing so. I will add some comments on how DCR might add to Nancy Scheper-Hughes's analysis.

1 Material relations with nature

Disadvantaged babies are most likely to survive on breast milk but many *favela* babies in the study were fed on formula milk, often over-diluted with dirty water by adults who could not read the language of the printed instructions on the tin. The mothers resorted to sugar and rice water when they could no longer afford to keep buying the tins and their own milk supply had dried up. To restrict the research to this social plane 1 could make the mothers appear foolish or negligent, and blame them for the high infant mortality rates.

2 Interpersonal subjective relationships, individual and group

When mothers survive by doing paid work, it is hard to combine breast-feeding with employment. Many of the mothers were unmarried, and the fathers tended to be unemployed and to have several households. After the baby's birth, if the father appeared to confirm and symbolise paternity with a gift of powdered milk, the mother and baby had a higher social status. The stigma of unmarried mother's milk could attach to a breast-fed baby, in contrast to the higher status of pretty tins of 'man's' milk from fathers and Nestlé. These interpersonal contexts help to make sense of mothers' seemingly irrational and potentially lethal decisions to bottle feed. Scheper-Hughes considered that mothers who could not afford to feed all their children deliberately withheld food from the weakest ones, were resigned to their death and described them as 'angel babies'.

3 Broader social relations and inherited structures

The pressures of poverty and the mothers' precarious efforts to survive in the *favelas* become clearer when seen in political context. Land dispossessions have forced many rural communities into the city slums. The city authorities refused to supply reliable water or electricity services, or to recognise people's tenancy rights, but they did send bulldozers into the *favelas* to destroy homes, and police who shot drug dealers and street children.

There were also the international pressures of advertising by formula milk companies, and in comparison, UNICEF spent tiny sums to promote breast-feeding. Since the 1970s, the UNICEF campaign with leading NGOs (non-governmental organisations) for 'baby-friendly' hospitals that do not promote formula milk has been successful, but UNICEF keeps having to combat Nestlé's renewed promotions.[5] Scheper-Hughes described how philanthropic NGOs funded oral rehydration therapy (ORT) clinics, providing a salt and sugar solution that could save the life of a dehydrated child. She reported that dying babies in the *favelas* were each brought several times for ORT, and each time the NGO recorded another 'life saved'. But the NGOs could not prevent babies from eventually succumbing to starvation; they prolonged the dying, Scheper-Hughes believed.

4 Inner being, agency, freedom, the good life in the good society

By analysing and documenting the 'wars' against children that caused many deaths, Scheper-Hughes worked with other agencies to promote health and justice, in the role of childhood researchers to contribute knowledge that will eventually help to improve children's lives.

How might DCR add to Scheper-Hughes's study and to researchers' plans for similarly comprehensive work in the future? The four planes of social being illustrate and emphasise the importance of connecting the four levels, as Scheper-Hughes did. The advantages include research reports that identify complex, interacting causes; that carefully analyse agency and structure; that show the agents, the mothers, to be resourceful in finding meaning and ways to cope with their hard lives. The multi-plane analysis avoids unduly blaming individuals, which could happen implicitly or explicitly if the analysis ended at the first or second plane of social being. The research provides information for policy-makers and agencies.

The *favela* study might have gained from DCR insights into human natural necessity and human nature. Scheper-Hughes (1992: 201–2) described the mothers as showing calm detachment towards their dying babies, and she concluded that 'maternal bonding' is a western bourgeois construction, and is neither natural nor universal. Yet other researchers reported that the *favela* mothers grieved intensely if their child died and they questioned Scheper-Hughes's interpretation (Nations and Rebhun 1988). Even if mothers withheld food from some of their children in order to feed the others, that can still mean they loved at least some of their children. To manage dire poverty in this way does not necessarily reveal either the real nature of maternal feeling or its absence, any more than starving shipwrecked sailors who resort to cannibalism reveal true human nature. They show how people might feel forced to behave under extreme pressures. It seems likely that parents vary along the spectrum from devoted to detached, harsh to indulgent, as much within each society as between different cultures. Many British mothers say that it is hard for them to 'bond' with their baby, and potential levels of bonding may not be higher or lower in Brazil.

The influences of powerful, interacting, cultural, economic and religious social structures may vary more than the real nature of maternal feelings and relationships. While I was writing this paragraph, David Lammy, a black MP, claimed that the English city riots of 2011 partly occurred because black parents were too afraid of social workers. They could not be 'sovereign in their own homes', free to exercise judgement and chastise or smack their children.[6] Lammy spoke of parents who have to 'raise children on the fifteenth floor of a tower block with knives, gangs and the dangers of violent crime just outside the window'. Four planar social being shows how causal violence, whether in Brazil or Britain, does not simply occur on the first and second planes, when certain mothers smack or starve their children against bourgeois norms. There is violence on the third plane of economic structures that are deeply hostile to certain children and parents. The *favela* study also raises questions about the Church, which by forbidding contraception encouraged large but often hungry families, and provided or supported the notions of 'angel babies'. The *favela* studies illustrate the importance of analysing children's lives critically at all four planes of social being, in order to avoid over-emphasising interpersonal or structural influences to explain human behaviours (see Chapter 5).

Absence and change

(Bhaskar 2008b: 38–203; Hartwig 2007: 9–14)

The nine concepts so far have been mainly about *critical realism* in DCR. The three final concepts bring in movement, change and *dialectic*.

At the heart of natural necessity is *absence*. This might seem an odd and perhaps pointless idea. Why is absence central? Earlier, gravity was mentioned as a universal but hidden force and mover, dragging down objects and holding planets on their course. Absence works rather like this in DCR. Sensed as the almost infinite otherness, absence is everything that has been lost into the past, besides all the infinite potential waiting in the future, of which only a tiny part will ever be realised. Absence is all that we might have, but have not, been or known or done. It is like a great vacuum absorbing almost all around it, and is therefore a prime mover: pushing and pulling everything forward into new times and spaces. The difficulty of thinking about absence is illustrated by the late discovery or invention of the concept zero, not recognised until around the ninth century in India. Yet zero is now at the heart of the 1:0 binary digital technology. Everything is partly defined by what it is not. 'Define' literally means putting an edge around the finite concept to exclude all that it is not. Childhood is largely defined by the supposed absence of adult competencies, and is typically absent from mainstream (adult) society.

Bhaskar traces the denial or avoidance of absence in western philosophy back to Parmenides who was averse to change, which he termed 'generation' and 'perishing'. Plato, another law-giver, vetoed absence in favour of the positive and the actual, the status quo of present control and order. Plato denied that 'non-being' is a crucial part of being. In doing so, Bhaskar contends, Plato denied the possibility of real change. This is because becoming has to involve its opposite, 'begoing', in absence and passing away. Absence as void, empty space, is essential because a world too tightly packed for movement prevents change.

Real determinate absence is part of natural necessity that exists in things. For example, part of accepting new ideas in DCR involves researchers in letting go of former theories, and the power and confidence they associated with them. So in denying absence, Plato denied the reality of independent being, and instead reduced being into his own beliefs and knowing. This *epistemic fallacy* still informs western philosophy and research, which favour empirical and actual, visible levels (1 and 2) over the invisible, and therefore seemingly absent, real Level 3 of natural necessity.

To avoid absence, Plato analysed *difference* rather than the unstable concept of *change*. An example of difference is if one child, Clare, leaves a room and another child, Tim, moves to sit in the chair Clare has left empty. The different child in the chair could be explained in terms of Tim's and Clare's motives to move into *different* places. An example of *change* is if Clare has recently learned to read and, instead of always depending on others, she is keen to read to herself from the page and screen. The change is explained by how she has learned and practised new skills, and taken on a new identity and status as 'a reader'. Change and causal connections are both substantive, really transforming relationships, whereas difference and Hume's constant conjunctions are formal relationships that do not involve real causal change.

Unlike difference, the change in Clare's new skill causes her real becoming (into an independent reader) but also her begoing (in no longer being such a dependent non-reader and listener to stories within closer relationships). DCR emphasises that change into the new depends on losing or absenting the old. If absence is overlooked or denied, change cannot fully be recognised or understood. This is especially vital in childhood research. In order to understand the continual becoming through childhood (and adulthood), we have to see the begoing, loss and absence of many valued as well as difficult aspects of babyhood, early and middle childhood and youth. Denial of absence can regard growth in childhood and youth solely as additional and incremental, acquiring new skills in the ascent towards the perfect endpoint of adulthood. Instead, recognition of change, in becoming and begoing throughout life, can value each age more equally in its own right, and can regret change as well as celebrate it.

Bhaskar (2008b: 400–1) terms the single value of the purely positive present *ontological monovalence*. It denies real negation and absence, whereas DCR involves *ontological polyvalence* or multi-value combinations of presence and absence.

Absence (the noun) can be positive when learning involves the absenting (the verb) and negating of ignorance and error; freedom involves absenting need and desire. Absence is the impetus for dynamic change, and it exists in catalysts for action such as need and want.

Our study with young children with type 1 diabetes found that some children were not diagnosed until they were extremely ill and admitted into intensive care. During the crisis they had to let go of their past identity and freedoms, and accept their new need for lifelong daily treatment. Their accounts suggest their awareness, and the researchers' need to be aware, of a great new absence in their social and personal loss, as well as the absence of the life-giving insulin their bodies no longer secreted. Moogum, diagnosed when she was aged 5 years, told us, 'My sister was at home in bed and she was crying because she thought I was dead.' Guy, diagnosed just after his sixth birthday, remembered being frightened alone in a hospital room and on a drip. 'There was nobody, no one to talk to, there was no little boys. . . I was almost dead' (Alderson *et al.* 2006a, 2006b; see Appendix 1.10).

Emergence

(Bhaskar 2008a; Morgan 2007a)

Emergence is central to movement and change. In emergence, one thing depends on another for its existence. The two are interdependent, and if one changes, so does the other. Yet the second cannot be reduced back into the first, neither can it be explained or predicted by the first. A prime example is how the mind emerges from the brain, which emerged from and with the body. Mind-body dualism can be resolved into complementary interactions by the concept of the emergence. Emotional-hormonal sensations and changes in the body and brain interact with emotions and thoughts of fear or pleasure in the mind. But the mind cannot be reduced back into the body, and in some ways transcends it.

The concept of emergence helps to mediate old dichotomies between the natural and social sciences. It does so by showing how both natural and social realities are stratified and emergent. Naturalism (the use of common methods between natural and social sciences) becomes plausible when, for example, emergent human reasons and motives are seen, like gravity, to be causes with real effects. Disciplines from ecology to geology to astrophysics not only explore the emergence of new entities out of older ones, they also show how new findings depend on, and partly emerge from, the specific knowledge and elaborate processes of each discipline. One example, which could only exist within physics, is the efforts at CERN to find the Higg's boson. Body to mind emergence is especially challenging in that it involves transitions between nature and culture.

Theories of childhood have gradually grown over the centuries through scientific-medical childcare manuals, into developmental psychology, and then slowly into the social study of childhood. Seeming contradictions are partly resolved by tracing the gradual emergence of theories and methods that, in some ways, increase realistic understanding of childhood. This is not to imply that knowledge simply progresses and improves; new misunderstandings also emerge from new contexts.

Children and parents exist in a similar dialectic of intergenerational emergence. As children change so do parents. There is the gradual transfer towards greater sharing of power and control, but the forms, processes and outcomes for the child cannot be reduced into the parents, or predicted by them.

People depend for their existence on society and social structures. Basic changes in people also mean basic changes in society, such as the gradual assertion of human rights and associated changes in social relations and policies. But again, the form, processes and outcomes in people as they become more aware and active in claiming, honouring or resisting justice or human rights cannot be reduced into society.

MELD

(Bhaskar 2008b: 231–79)

Although this final section might seem too philosophical to many childhood researchers, MELD is here briefly introduced and its practical relevance will be explained and explored gradually in later chapters. MELD is a system that emphasises the dynamic movement forward in DCR, driven by the absence of and desire for freedom and justice.

Hegel's three-part dialectic moves through: thesis (identity, statement about the present object of study); antithesis (negativity, contradiction, disagreement, challenging new ideas); and synthesis (totality, new understanding that combines the two earlier stages at a higher level) (Bhaskar 2008b: 15–33). Hegel's dialectic rests on epistemology ('thesis' is grounded in thinking) and logic, and seeks to resolve illogical inconsistencies. To overcome the limitations of this epistemic fallacy, Bhaskar proposed a four-part dialectic, which begins in real ontology and emphasises movement, practical change and transformation, through the four-part acronym MELD. MELD is profoundly influenced by Marx's concepts, including material reality and changing the world.

The four stages or moments of MELD are:

1M first moment (non-identity, absence and the epistemic fallacy)
2E second edge (negativity and power$_2$)
3L third level (totality)
4D fourth dimension (praxis, self-transformative agency and power$_1$, the dialectic that is 'the pulse of freedom')

First moment (1M) involves 'realism in non-identity . . . alterity, sheer other-being . . . whether knowable, known or not', real, irreducible difference that exists in the world in each entity or *product*. 1M has three main motives: (1) to critique anthropism (human-centredness), the epistemic fallacy and, I would add for child-hood studies, adult-centrism; (2) to distinguish between our transitive under-standing, and the intransitive ontology that 1M addresses; and (3) to differentiate between the empirical, the actual and the real.

Our search for real being in natural necessity through not-knowing is partly paradoxical, because we cannot avoid thinking and depending on former knowl-edge.[7] Yet when researchers first approach children, the aim would be to avoid identifying them in terms of naming, defining, classifying, stereotyping or comparing them by imposing our own ideas and values, which can prevent us from recognising reality. To identify the objects-subjects of research translates them into epistemology, and positions them into classified groups with specified causes and functions. The idea of non-identity is, as far as possible, to try to under-stand something anew on its own terms, its own essence, not our attributed defini-tion. This includes approaches to non-human entities, and avoiding anthropism, as mentioned earlier. Instead, the point is to search for their natural necessity, as the independent grounds, but not the guarantee, of our knowledge of their ontology.

DCR begins with absence, 'the simplest and most elemental concept of all' (Bhaskar 2008b: 239) and the effort to imagine the independent, intransitive exist-ence that was there before we observed or knew of it. Children as people really exist in space and in social natural necessity, as do the causal structures we all inherit of language, local forms of childhood and adulthood, and relations between generations. The effort of non-identification in 1M is similar to anthropologists' efforts to treat a new setting as strange and unknown, to avoid attributing their own explanations/epistemology, and to search for the meaning-making rooted in the lives of the local people. The epistemic fallacy is trebly significant in research with children if researchers impose intellectual, adult-centric beliefs and values, first on their own thinking, second on the children they observe, and third on their definitions of problems and possible remedies intended to improve children's lives. Inevitably children will appear to be deficient and dependent and the remedies may be irrelevant. An extreme example is when British colonialists took indigenous children in Canada and Australia into boarding schools and tried to destroy their cultural identity in the name of child-saving. Another example is the way Zambian and other African schools misunderstand and counterproductively erode children's confidence and structures of rural life (Serpell 1993).

Within 1M are the dialectics of individual-general, agency-structure, mind-body, mechanisms-events.[8] The MELD impetus to freedom examines how these dualisms in the social world are permeated by power$_2$ relations, in the epistemic fallacy and in ignoring what the object of study *is not*. This omission (of what is not) moves forward to second edge, 2E and the moment of absence as *process* through desire to absent the lack or need or want in what is not. Absence promises both freedom and alienation. In 2E, absence is negativity, non-being, which brings a moment of becoming/begoing, which is 'thrown' in particular space-time. 'Thrownness' denotes the arbitrary conditions of human life we find ourselves in, and over which we have little control. 3L involves both totalities, and detotalisation when alienating splits or absent connections between mind/body, reason/emotion, agency/structure lead to the possibility of change. In DCR, sociability and reason to act at 2E can transfer individuals' everyday interactions into a network of connections and totalities at 3L. Mediation between self and others relates to human nature, to a concrete universal/singular, in that each individual comprises many aspects of the universal group they belong to. 3L emphasises our capacity to care for others in the open totality that is still not finished but is a *process-in-product*. To understand 3L involves moving towards changing the world at 4D. Individuals are then no longer alienated from their materiality and nature (plane 1) and they become able to act to absent the absence (such as absence of freedom). They do so in contact and harmony with the inner self, with social relations and with nature. They are no longer constrained by power$_2$. Through creative power$_1$, transformative, intentional agents (*product-in-process*) can realise their capacity for freedom.

One example is the emancipatory work of Heidelisa Als (1999), which 'reads' premature babies' 'language' and 'respects their autonomy'. Although conducted without formal reference to DCR, it nevertheless illustrates the four moments of MELD: 1M – to suspend prejudices, to question and patiently observe at great length what (if anything) premature babies might be feeling, experiencing and being; 2E – to see, during many detailed observations, how isolated, misunderstood and distressed the babies can be (amid bright lights and loud noises, sprawling in uncomfortable, exhausting positions, in pain and fear); 3L – to link research findings into detailed observations and practice that develop 'baby-led' structures of care in neonatal unit-wide policies; and 4D – to work through further research, medical and nursing education, and social policy towards more humane neonatal care.

The practical value of DCR in a childhood studies project

This chapter ends with comments on a few of the ways in which I think DCR, if we had known about it then, could have improved our study of the four neonatal units (see Appendix 1.8). I suggest that these comments apply to other ethnographic childhood studies. We were feeling our way uncertainly towards approaches that DCR could have clarified for us besides extending our insights and confidence.

Knowledge of the DCR concepts of *being and knowing*; *transitive and intransitive*; *signifier, signified and referent* could, I believe, have strengthened our certainty about the independent referent, the realities we were researching. They included the being and doing of the babies, their parents and the neonatal staff, and also the neonatal units' structures, routines and policies. Knowledge of *natural necessity*, and its three layers of *the empirical, the actual and the real*, of causal structures and agents, would have been similarly helpful. I think the knowledge could have lessened several negative effects on our work of the epistemic fallacy and the interpretive, social constructionist assumptions that we were trapped inside.

These included our concern that we were projecting our subjective perceptions onto our emotive subject matter. Although this is partly unavoidable, DCR assists in analysing and managing that problem, with the assurance that epistemology does not pervade all ontology.

Social construction theories misled us into thinking that we could not or should not compare the four very different units. We should only describe them and try to understand each on its own distinct and non-transferable terms. Yet we could not help noting great differences between two outstandingly humane units, one quite harsh unit, and one in between. I now think our study should have been more comparative, based on the kind of real and moral *transfactual* criteria that DCR could justify.

Our unnecessary doubts about whether a basic factual reality exists made us hesitant about reporting and validating our findings and recommendations to the medical and nursing staff. I think we tried to base validations of our work too much on sociological analysis and imaginings, on our supposedly unique, original insights (our epistemology). I was also attempting to show that medical sociology is an independent discipline, and not simply a handmaiden of medicine. Like many childhood researchers, I wrote a paper about space, and although it had some potentially useful ideas these were underdeveloped (too epistemological) and the clinicians seemed bemused; some were impatient. Knowing about DCR would, I believe, have given us greater trust in our subject matter and in our ability to analyse underlying natural necessity and causal structures. Our work could have been more directly relevant and useful to neonatal policies and practices. I would then have probably felt less need to try to assert some rather irrelevant sociological credentials.

Understanding *the possibility of naturalism* and *closed and open systems* would also have increased our confidence when working between social and clinical areas of research, and when choosing which theories and methods to apply. There would have been less need to be defensive about sociology in relation to the dominant discipline of medicine. I was nervous about seeming to produce simply common-sense reports that anyone could write. I don't think we were reduced to doing that, but I would have felt less need to 'be sociological' (epistemological), if I had known how it was feasible to examine underlying political and causal structures.

To separate *power$_1$ and power$_2$* opens helpful ways to begin to analyse the immense potential in the units for the positive and negative exertion of power, including the extraordinary efforts made by some babies such as Oludayo to survive.

We researched on a range of personal and political levels. *Four planar social being* would have helped to make our analysis more ambitious, organised, integrated and, I hope, convincing. *Absence and change* and *emergence* are especially relevant to neonatal experiences, and knowing about them would have deepened our understanding and analysis. Finally, dialectic through the four stages of *MELD* would have helped to unify and direct our research in valuable ways that I hope will become evident through this book

The DCR concepts introduced in this chapter will be filled in gradually with explanations and examples in later chapters. The next chapter moves on to the second plane of social being and the second stage of MELD, 2E.

4

SPACE

Interpersonal relations

During rebuilding work in medieval times, like Icarus, an apprentice mason fell from high up in Gloucester Cathedral in western England. A carving in the Cathedral commemorates the event, probably made by the master mason depicting himself reaching out in horror and failing to save the boy. They are both framed within an L-shaped mason's bracket or set square, as if the carving reaffirms faith in their shared vocation despite its dangers.

Marie Curie's father taught maths and physics, and she was the first woman to win a Nobel prize, the first person to win two Nobel prizes, and the only person, so far, to win prizes in separate fields, physics and chemistry. She coined the term radioactivity and isolated radioactive isotopes. Her work benefited countless people who have cancer.

Many real and mythical examples celebrate ambitious adults who help aspiring children. Sometimes there are amazing achievements and sometimes fatal over-reaching in powerful intergenerational bonds of trust, pride in work, soaring imagination and risk-taking. There is the intensive transferring, expanding and refining of knowledge, skill and discovery. Adults often recount how their life-long passion began very early in life. The image of the falling boy symbolises the human position, hanging precariously in the space between infinite abstract thought and finite nature, between the advantages of the aspiring heights of art, science and technology and the dangers they bring.

This chapter moves on to the second plane of social being: interpersonal relationships, here mainly between children and adults, including researchers. For lack of space I have said little about the equally important child–child relationships. There are the countless loving child–adult relationships, as well as times of slight to severe conflict. Bodies and relationships are partly inextricable, and inevitably we observe, hear, imagine and relate to other people's mind-body through our own, so that bodies discussed in Chapter 3 continue to matter.

As considered earlier, ontology and epistemology are irreducible but interdependent and overlapping. Our understanding of their interrelations involves errors, contradictions, and categories such as causality and law and lawfulness. These have their own independent existence. They are in the world and not simply imposed by individuals on the world (Bhaskar 2002a: 83). We can work to separate the objects we experience and perceive, from our experiences and perceptions. This involves, first, accepting the *intransitive* ontology of objects, events and structures that exist independently before and after our encounters with them. Second, it involves accepting that our *transitive* perceptions are partial, provisional, changeable, diverse and partly subconscious. Third, we can then work to be more critically aware of our assumptions, which inform but may also distort our observations. Fourth, we still have to know that our perceptions and values are integral parts of the existence of social phenomena such as childhood, parenting or schools. And our self-awareness is inevitably partial. Bhaskar criticises authors who claim to work reflexively and critically with all their subjective views, or to have set these aside when we cannot wholly fulfil either of these aims and, if we could, we would not need to warn readers about these problems.

The constraints and false divisions inevitable in a two-dimensional, linear book separate the four planes of social being and four moments of MELD. Yet each part relates to the others and to every chapter.[1] This chapter considers further the DCR concepts introduced in Chapter 3, and also explores differing spaces and relationships into which childhood, youth and adulthood are positioned and defined. These include: conceptual space when social science recognises children as social beings and therefore legitimate subjects for social research; comparative space taken up by adults and allowed to children in areas ranging from the physical to the political; metaphorical and intellectual and authoritative spaces, in which adults assess and interact with children's deemed capacities and interests; and emotional space, where children and adults share fear and doubt, trust and hope. Also relevant are geo-historical spaces occupied by each generation, and moral spaces in the distribution of resources, freedoms, respect and control between the generations, discussed in later chapters.

This chapter will consider: MELD 2E; negativity and absence; dialectic as process; negativity and risk; uncertain ontology; trust in research relationships; some thoughts from psychoanalysis about child–adult relations; contradiction and archetypal 'master–slave' relations.

MELD 2E, second edge: negativity and absence

(Bhaskar 2008b: 18–23, 204–58, [1991] 2010b:126 ff.; Norrie 2010: 13ff., 52–60)

Chapter 3 reviewed how 1M involves *non-identity*, and natural necessity (the three levels of empirical, actual, real), and real difference in the world (Bhaskar 2008b: 392). 1M is defined as *product*, as the other, a *state* or *status* of non-identity, what it is not, an intransitive object detached from an observer's transitive identifying and classifying. Chapter 3 also mentioned how Hegel's three-part dialectic, based in epistemology, is expanded into DCR's four-part MELD. Bhaskar contends that Hegel's second stage, antithesis, is insufficiently anti or negative. It adds new ideas rather than radically challenging and transforming the original thesis. This arises, Bhaskar argues, through Hegel's epistemic fallacy and inattention to ontology, to real being and non-being. By remaining within epistemology, Hegel confines contradictions to the illogical or irrational. These can be resolved in stage three of his dialectic, synthesis, through logical clarity. However, DCR emphasises being, with non-being, negativity and absence as part of an essential second stage of dialectic. 2E as *process* is the turning edge towards later ontological transformation.

In 2E *negativity*, being is defined by what it is not: a child is primarily defined as not-adult, an adult as not-child. When assessing a child's competence, it is easier for adults to see absence in terms of obvious incompetence, ignorance and mistakes, than to prove informed competence. Children's mistakes are often created by adults' unhelpful, nerve-wracking questioning. If a child underperforms, adults tend to attribute this to deficiencies in the child, instead of to possibly unskilful, undermining, adult examiners (Allen and Ainley 2007; Donaldson 1978; Holt 1964).

Absence is a determining compulsion-force, a natural necessity in all social and natural existence. First, this is because becoming has to involve begoing away from, and ceasing – loss and negation are part of change. Second, lack of absence and emptiness would mean an immobile world, too tightly packed to allow any movement or change. 2E depends on some kind of physical, social or conceptual empty space if people are to move from ignorance or oppression into the new space of knowledge or freedom, negating their former position-state. Third, absence determines this move when the first space involves need or lack, while movement into the second and formerly vacant space involves the absenting of this lack. Fourth, absence as being and non-being in 2E is negative in its movement away from present unwanted states and objects, its negating of them, and its desire to absent the lack, need or want – what is not. In 2E, each separate, particular entity is seen as 'thrown' in specific time-space-cause contexts, and is subject to negative power$_2$.

The MELD process towards freedom begins by connecting into dialectic the former dualisms, structure/agency, mind/body, reason/emotion. Absence entails possibility, in both the negative liability of alienation from ourselves but also the positive capacity for freedom. Each is part of human natural necessity. We have to experience alienation, which is an absence or splitting away of something essential to our well-being, if we are to become aware of it, and then begin to move towards remedy (see 'master–slave' below).

An example of negativity and absence

Childhood studies are deeply concerned with visible-tangible evidence and, on the whole, with adults' efforts to respect, understand, protect, educate and rescue children. It can be hard to escape *ontological monovalence.* This is the value or dogma that everything has to be seen and understood in positive terms. Positive does not here necessarily mean good, but is about presence, existence, evidence. This attention to the positive can divert attention from negativity and absence, which are essential in understanding childhood and youth.

For example, UNICEF[2] described Afghanistan as one of the most dangerous places in the world to be a child. The continual warfare kills, injures, maims and terrifies countless children and adults; it disrupts and destroys families, communities and everyday life, as well as basic services and amenities. Schools are attacked, and young people are forced to become suicide bombers, to plant munitions, or to sweep for landmines. Warfare leaves deadly vendettas when young and older people are killed by neighbours if they belong to, or are assumed to belong to, or refuse to join, rival armed groups. Over 31,000 Afghani children suffered severe malnutrition in 2011.

Thousands of teenage boys set out for Europe, alone or in small groups (Brothers 2012; UN 2011). On the way they meet people-smugglers and traffickers, soldiers, bandits, thieves and hostile police, and terrible weather as they walk over mountain ranges and arid plains. Girls do not leave, and some are betrothed to older men to raise payments to aid their brothers' escape.

During 2011, over 300 young Afghanis arrived in Paris and queued outside the only, small, 'emergency' night refuge for minors. When turned away, they slept in parks and streets, cold, wet and hungry, until chased off by police dogs. Morteza, aged 13, has white feet, frost-bitten towards the end of his 6,000 km walk. Nearly 5,000 boys claimed asylum in Europe in 2011, and 635 passed through a refuge in Rome. Untold others stayed on city streets, or in prisons, or died on the way. Those who manage to get into a French school work extremely hard and inspire other students, teachers say. Some believe we should educate these young refugees as a diaspora ready to return in future to rebuild Afghanistan. However, the UK and Nordic governments, determined to 'deter' the exodus, as if there were not already enough deterrents, or as if the refugees were too foolish to learn from them, funded a 'repatriation project', despite strong protests from human rights and children's NGOs (non-governmental organisations).

This example involves numberless absences, negativities and begoings. At its heart, and this book's central concern, is the absence of respect for the young people: lack of faith in their judgement that it was better to leave than to stay despite the fearful prospects; lack of admiration for their courage and tenacity to survive their ordeals; non-recognition of the extreme dangers and suffering that would be entailed in their forced return to Afghanistan; denial of European responsibility for the war that caused their flight; refusal to consider any calculation other than the cost of supporting young refugees in Europe; failure to imagine their hard lives and decisions, or how valuable these boys would be, if supported and educated, to help Afghanistan in future. They were to be returned like parcels, non-persons, illustrating 2E in absence, leaving and loss, negative experiences and relationships. In their non-status as citizens, they were helplessly 'thrown' into specific time-space-cause contexts that are overwhelmed by negative power$_2$. 'It puts paid to all our values if we can't take care of those among the world's disinherited children who come to us,' said one NGO spokesman, speaking in extreme negatives (Brothers 2012). There is also the immense transformative power$_1$ of the boys' hope and courage.

Dialectic as process and begoing

2E accentuates *process* rather than *outcome*, illustrated in the Afghanis' unfinished stories, which bequeath decades of future problems and hopes. The boys' emigration enacts the 2E absenting processes, in their lost relationships, and also a moment of beginning, when experiences of real absence move the dialectic forward. Norrie (2010: 139–40) sees 1M and 2E as moments of individual desire and openings towards new trust, solidarity and human interdependence, which the emigrating boys desperately needed.

Mental and social worlds, like the natural world, are in constant flow and flux; air and water currents continually move towards an equilibrium of heat and pressure, and similarly human thinking, feeling and relationships constantly search, change and rebalance through action/reaction, enquiry/response, power/resistance. To recognise absence is an important part of recognising this social flow and the pressure of moving on, through being absorbed away from the emptying-vacated physical, mental or social space and entering into a formerly empty and unknown new space.

Childhood is often seen as movement away from absent non-maturity or immaturity to an end point or apex of adult maturity, modelled on Kantian rational Man, or Darwinan completely evolved Western Man. Yet every age group, including adulthood, has absences, shown by adults' deficient responses to the young Afghanis. We all move and change towards unknown, absent futures, losing some faculties and gaining others.

Among children's early capacities, usually diminished by the second decade, are the abilities easily and quickly to learn new languages, make new friends, and accept other people non-judgmentally. The human brain illustrates loss when the 80 billion neurons we are born with are selectively ablated. Synapses, the links between the neurons, develop during infancy through great 'overproduction' and, crucially, later through 'pruning'. Adults may have 10^{14} cortical synapses, 40 per cent fewer than they had in infancy, and insufficient pruning is associated with learning difficulties (Fischer and Rose 1994). It seems that we are born with innumerable potential capacities and, if we are to develop some, others have to be deleted to make space for them. This absence is a passing away in favour of what is to come, and occurs in daily life through processes of 'negation, contradiction, development, becoming, emergence, finitude' (Bhaskar [1991] 2010b:126).

So growth leaves the absented past, with its infinite lost possibilities. It involves countless entities that change but also last over time (social structures, enduring personalities and relationships). Dialectical thinking about flux and change, beyond dualisms and towards interactions between child–adult, past–future, natural–social, regress–progress, need–fulfilment, depends on seeing negativity-absence as the push–pull power. This both impels and also draws everything forward from former-being to becoming. Central to ontology is active non-being:

> Negativity is the motive of all dialectics [towards freedom] the single most important category, more general than negation because it spans change or force, the consciousness which isolates a positive lack, the absent without a present or positive . . . the negating process [beyond] the outcome or result. Negativity [includes both neutral absence and pejorative ill and is] united in dialectical critical realist explanatory critique, the aim of which is precisely to *absent ills*.
>
> *(Bhaskar 2008b: 238, original emphasis)*

Things may be absent when they are somewhere else in space or time, or they do not yet exist, or have perished, or have never existed. Absence has causal effects. A small example is when a favourite toy is lost and the family searches for it desperately. A severe example is the longed-for baby who is never conceived but who shapes the would-be-parents' daily life and identity. On a huge dimension, Bhaskar ([1991] 2010b: 126) referred to the monsoon that never arrives so that the crops perish, potentially leading to famine, migration and war. In DCR, absence is real negation that works on presence through space and time. It 'brings out the world's dynamic and processual quality, and establishes *change* as integral to it' (Norrie 2010: 14, original emphasis).

Negativity and risk

DCR emphasises that, to apprehend absence, we have to move beyond *ontological monovalence* (the single value of presence that denies absence). Monovalence relies on proof and so is trapped conservatively into evidence of past events. Children may be hostage if their evidence is not heard, or not accurately presented, or they are assumed to be unable to speak. 'Infant' means 'without speech'. In contrast, *polyvalence* accepts absences, omissions, liabilities, open unknown futures and that things can be other than they are. An example is Als's (1999) innovative 'reading' of babies' 'language' in the belief that they have some form of mind, thought, memory and hope (see Chapter 3).

Risk involves and also *is* absence, both of present securities and of unknown but influential futures; if risk predictions come true, risk vanishes into reality. Fear of risk powerfully shapes our relationships (Beck 1992). Risk is particularly relevant to childhood in the numerous, anxious, personal and public measures to protect supposedly vulnerable children, and thereby to protect the hyper-vigilant adults from being blamed or sued if a risk is realised (Katz 2005). Fear of risk is a causal power that can erode trust between generations, as Rose (1999) examined, when mothers internalise psychological ideals of childcare and how mothers ought to ensure their children are always safe, clean, compliant and stimulated to learn. These are partly contradictory aims: learning may involve 'messy, unclean' play or danger, or non-compliant, critical questioning. And mothers find their young children have plenty of energy and ideas and hardly need adult stimulation (Mayall 1993).

However, the mothers' 'souls' and their relationships with their children are 'governed' by these internalised ideals or ideologies, and by anxiety that they will fail to meet them (Rose 1999). They illustrate Lukes's (2005) third level of insidious, pervasive power$_2$ when individuals are persuaded into a worldview that stops them from understanding their real interests and freedoms or the possibility of resistance. Individuals' fears are amplified to political, economic and global scales, when privileged, white, North American (and other) children are increasingly guarded against the world's majority of disadvantaged, threatening, risky children (Nadesan 2010; Wacquant 2008). Wealthier parents worry that their own children, in their gated communities and private schools, might in future provide too little return on lavish investment in their care and education. They are also anxious that disadvantaged children everywhere pose risks of becoming criminals, terrorists, unwanted immigrants, and costly unemployed, sick dependents on the state. Migration, housing redevelopment, and many other disruptions and changes to once stable communities, turn adults and children from neighbours into strangers. They increase fear of 'stranger-danger' and of 'feral' youth. Negative responses range from curfews for young people (youth itself becomes a crime if the curfew is broken) to lethal police culling of street children (Scheper-Hughes and Sargent 1998; Honwana and De Boeck 2005).

Negativity and childhood research

Awareness of negativity and absence can inform practical childhood research in at least five ways. First, children are constantly present in society, yet to many adults they are absent through being excluded, ignored, invisible. So to recognise these often concealed, unnoticed absences is central to the understanding of childhood. Second, children are largely defined negatively, in terms of their deficits or missing attributes by the dominant rhetoric in, for example, education (Allen and Ainley 2007) and social services (Winter 2006), the criminal justice system (Goldson and Muncie 2009), and the mass media.[3] They are measured for the absenting of these absences in their progress towards adult non-deficiencies, and these presumed absences need to be critically reconsidered in research.

Third, childhood and society centrally involve change. The momentum of DCR is its practical attention to realism in the nature and function of driving change. This involves absence, in becoming and begoing/ceasing, in being and not-being. Awareness of absence enables the study of transfers of power and resources through successive, passing generations. Chapter 3 mentioned Plato's functionalist, conservative veto on concepts of radical change. DCR looks back to pre-Platonic concepts, crystallised in Heraclitus's aphorism: 'We step and do not step into the same rivers'. Rivers constantly change and so do we. Exact moments can therefore never be replicated. However, Platonic bias against transformative change deeply influences research about children including: the continuing dominance of outdated child development theory; emphasis on past empirical and actual evidence; reuse of decades-old tests and 'validated' questionnaires; and inattention to hidden structures, movements and causes of change. For example, Baumrind's (1971) 'models of parenting' still dominate research and childcare. The models are *authoritarian* (telling the child exactly what to do); *indulgent* (allowing children to do whatever they wish); the preferred model, *authoritative* (providing rules and guidance without being overbearing); and Baumrind later added *negligent* parenting (disregarding the child). The models assume one-way adult skills rather than relationships between two agents, parent and child. With their 'boundary' setting and punishments, the models ignore the subtle or open negotiations constantly conducted between all pairs and groups at every age, as they try to negotiate towards the centre, away from the extremes of tyranny or weak submission. Relationships are dialectical, not based on Baumrind's dichotomies. High failure rates in schools emerge from a similar problem. Half-formed theories of teaching and learning have, until recently, concentrated on teaching, but have seldom fully understood children and young people to be agents, active learners. And learning involves transformative change, whereas teaching does not necessarily do so. Politicians continue to ignore their agency, except in assuming compliance and treating their resistances as irrational problems to be controlled.[4]

The fourth reason for researchers to attend to absence and negativity is that all research and learning are concerned with absence in their aims to absent ignorance, omissions, deficits and errors, and to attain so-far-absent, future knowledge.

A fifth and, for some researchers, most important reason (discussed later), although it is contested by others, involves the moral agency to absent coercions and injustices and to advance freedom and justice. In childhood studies this mainly takes the somewhat limited forms of supporting children's adult-organised 'participation'.

Uncertain ontology in research about children

This section considers how, when epistemology predominates over ontology, this can diminish meaning in childhood research. Movement and process in MELD 2E relate to research processes as they weave through interpersonal child–adult relationships. Hermeneutic research attends to performance: how children present and manage their bodies, learn and practise healthy behaviours, talk about normality and comparisons with their peers' bodies, respond to minor illness and injury as social events, and deal with the practical embarrassments of puberty, menstruation, sexuality and masculinity (see for example edited collections by Goddard *et al.* 2005; Hörschelman and Colls 2010; Prout 2000; Qvortrup *et al.* 2011). The studies emphasise talk, behaviour, interaction, belief and social feelings such as shame. However, in some studies, children's real embodied ontology can then seem to be lost within social performance.

One constraint is that inevitably the medium of social research is mainly the spoken and written word when gathering and reporting data, and the medium affects the content. A second difficulty, the attempt to find words to express deep physical and emotional feelings, can be compounded when interviewees feel awkward, embarrassed or overwhelmed by experiences they try to describe. Third, interviewee and interviewer may have very different lifestyles that can inhibit mutual understanding. Fourth, researchers want to avoid the risks of undue intrusion or seeming to denigrate children if they ask about physical and emotional problems. Many studies with children who live very hard lives respectfully emphasise their hopes and plans for the future, rather than their ordeals. Fifth, although feelings and thoughts beyond words may be shared intuitively, in ways that we take for granted in everyday life, researchers tend to avoid intuition as too informal and subjective. Yet they sometimes have to rely on intuition if they are to move beyond behaviourism. Otherwise they could not tell, for instance, whether someone is simply kneeling or is also praying (Bhaskar 1998a: 77).

Despite their complexity, in sociological traditions that influence childhood studies, tendencies can be traced, which set culture over nature, and thinking over being. Foucault's (1977) analysis of discipline and punishment of the body emphasised discourses of power, status and control in institutions ranging from schools to prisons. In Goffman's (1969) many varying presentations of the self, the core self seems to be lost into contingent appearances. Bourdieu's (1977: 94) habitas inscribes culture into children's bodies, in their 'dress, bearing, physical and verbal manners . . . treating the body as a memory . . . of the culture . . . beyond the grasp of consciousness [and untouched] by voluntary, deliberate transformation [it] cannot even be made explicit'. Bourdieu allows for change over time when he sees generations of physical experiences being transmitted through subconscious ideas to become re-educated and re-embodied behaviours in the descendants. Beck's (1992) risk society is a context for childhood generally and for healthy living programmes, when children obey or resist adults' injunctions to reduce the risks of maladies that might trouble them in remote middle age, but that have little present physical relevance to them.

In studies where the ontology of children's being and bodies is uncertain, real intentional human agency, which drives practical activity and its tangible effects, can seem to be weak or missing. For example, an ethnography describes how young schoolchildren manage to present their use of an asthma inhaler as 'normal' and how they 'fabricate' friendships through exchanging inhalers occasionally 'but more often . . . demonstrate, through symbolic exchanges and displays, the usual kinds of prowess and controlled access to privileged knowledge which is part of agency' and friendship (Robinson and Delahooke 2001: 95). The actual asthma, the friendships that are 'fabricated' (a word that hints at deception), the mention of 'dissembling behaviours', and how the inhalers differ from the children's other possessions all remain unclear through the paper. The emphasis on presentation and behaviour, in the few, brief sections about the children, gives little sense of individual being.

Children's embodied selves tend to be distanced, as if viewed through the wrong end of a telescope. Lundy (2010) reviewed how childhood researchers seldom address serious illness, suffering or disability, and they favour slight illnesses or accidents primarily as social events. Fairly unusually, one study was set in a hospital (James *et al.* 2008), but the reasons for the children being there, their illness or treatment, were not explained, and they could almost equally well be talking about space and risk in other settings.

Reports about child labour and child soldiers show the researchers' extensive knowledge and concern, but the children's actual experiences are seldom graphically conveyed. In a collection on child labour framed by policy and public health perspectives, an unusually direct account of adversity lists effects of work with pesticides on children's bodies (Osorio 2010: 142), though these are reported in an impersonal list of medical symptoms. Books on child soldiers similarly tend to emphasise background, general reports, respect for children's agency, analysis and remedies (Drumbl 2012; Honwana 2006; Rosen 2005) with occasional accounts of violence, usually told in a child's or a reminiscing adult's seemingly calm, detached voice. Readers of vivid fiction and journalism about extreme events in childhood may feel 'gut-wrenching' concern, disgust or admiration whereas, if sociological accounts evoke detached equanimity, do they realistically convey or misleadingly understate the horrifying experiences and memories that are being researched? The research reports raise questions about the great problems of how to convey real ontology, about how brief or detailed, specific or general, detached or emotive the accounts should be. These questions will be discussed in Volume 2, Chapter 9, showing how Filip De Boeck's (2005) intense, integrated attention to violated bodies, imagination, religion and kinship reveals new insights into child-witches and their society.

When the body adds little to the analysis, body matters almost equate to non-body matters. For example, people can feel similar cultural anxiety about their body shape as about the price and style of their clothing. Some socio-legal analyses of child abuse could almost equally be reviewing any other violent crime, such as in a review of evidence, witnesses and court procedures (Lee 2001). Analysis may float above physical being instead of being grounded in it. Perhaps to avoid humiliating intrusion, Lorraine van Blerk (2010) respectfully reported how young Ethiopian sex workers 'engage in mobility', but this phrase hardly conveys how, often in terror and desperation, they moved to work in different areas, increasing their own and their clients' risk of HIV cross-infection. If physical realities are evaded in bland reports, when young sex workers describe their anxiety about whether clients will use a condom in the same terms as their anxiety about whether clients will pay them, then they might equally be selling vegetables instead of their bodies.

Crucial matters of embodied, lethal power and fear in relationships are then lost or understated. Paradoxically, 'inclusive' respectful reports about selling sex, as if that involves as much autonomy and rational choice as selling any other commodity, could disrespectfully deny the coercion endured by many sex workers. Slippage also appears in the book title *Contested Bodies of Childhood and Youth* (Hörschelmann and Colls 2010). The chapters on child soldiers, alcohol, teenage pregnancy and sex work are about contested (social) behaviours, not about (natural) young bodies, whose existence and functioning are assumed and not contested. Researchers who convey ontology can give deeper, urgent, personal and political meaning to their reports, such as Katz (2004) on the freedoms that children intensely enjoyed in the Sudan in the 1980s before the wars; Winter (2011) on serious child neglect in Northern Ireland; and Yoshida (2011) on physical punishment in Tanzanian schools.

Ontology and trust

The epistemic fallacy in certain kinds of research, when ontology-being becomes lost within epistemology-thinking, can undermine several forms of trust. To be trusted is a main aim of researchers: to be seen as an accurate, reliable and fair source of knowledge. However, if researchers doubt or mistrust or deny the reality they are analysing, the grounds for their own trustworthiness can be undermined, raising the following questions: What is the point of reporting or reading about research on subjects that are too contingent or transient to support any generalisations? If there are no firm tangible realities, how and why should anyone's account of them be preferred to anyone else's account? Without a clear referent (the original reality being discussed, see *The semiotic triangle* in Chapter 3), how can research accounts be grounded or independently validated?

These questions arise in three kinds of relationships: researchers' accountability to themselves; researchers' accountability to sponsors and readers of their work; and the interactions between researchers and their subjects-participants. How can they trust one other and achieve what Habermas (1984) terms 'ideal speech acts', in the mutually respectful exchange of honest information? By 'honest', I do not mean perfectly accurate accounts, because memories, perceptions and contexts shape and reshape them. Accounts are also often misleading, partial, imperfectly expressed or confused. By 'honest' I mean *intending* to be as accurate as possible, and avoiding deliberate deception.

DCR examines how people's accounts and commentaries cannot either stand alone or make up for the missing, essential referent. Over recent decades, research ethics has helped to reduce the numbers of projects conducted without research subjects' knowledge and consent. Yet two social research methods, moral accounts and actor network theory, involve some deception. I suggest that this is linked to the mistrust or uncertainty about ontology that is intrinsic to these methods.

'Moral accounts'

To guard against the risks of active deception by interviewees, ethnomethodolo-gists set aside the content or substance of the talk, and instead examine form: the rhetorical ways in which interviewees construct their accounts. Since ontology-existence combines form with content, the research method evades ontology. In this case, the ontology in people's accounts is their earlier intense experiences. Examples of 'moral accounts' research include interviews with parents whose child has diabetes or a surgical heart condition (Silverman 2009: 138–45).

The interviews are treated as situated, structured accounts, 'local accomplish-ment', used by parents to invoke norms 'aimed at displaying the status of morally adequate [responsible] parenthood'. 'We need not hear or categorise interview responses simply as true or false' or as straightforward reports related to an external reality. Instead, interviews are analysed for how parents present 'atrocity stories' about substandard clinicians, in order to vindicate their own moral responses.

However, several questions are not explained: Why would the parents' priority be to present a moral account of themselves, rather than to talk primarily of their child's potentially fatal illness? Why should the truth or accuracy of their account automatically be seen as irrelevant, and so implicitly dubious? How can the research be useful, or inform policy and practice, when families' actual experiences are ignored? We are not told how parents were informed about the nature and purpose of the interviews, which raises further questions. Why would they agree to take part, if they knew that their substantive points would simply be set aside? If they knew their interview would be analysed as a 'moral account', would that not alter how they presented the account, and so invalidate the research method? Therefore, can such research only be conducted covertly? And if the parents did not know about the research method, how could they give informed consent? And how could research ethics committees approve the research?

Analysis of moral accounts can be very useful when applied, for example, to politicians' devious claims and rhetorical techniques. The analysis can helpfully inform voters, provided the accounts are related to actual policies and activities. However, the value of reducing any interview wholly into a 'moral account', detached from reality, is unclear. Also unclear is the public relevance of reducing into 'atrocity stories', accounts by fairly powerless people about distressing private events. The rather mocking term 'atrocity' (wicked or cruel), implies an irrational over-reaction by parents of children with diabetes and heart conditions. It is a term they would be unlikely to use themselves.

When ethnomethodologists doubt the reality of their interviewees' accounts, and of the original experiences being described, they remove the grounds on which their own analyses may be trusted and believed. There seem to be double standards. Researchers appear to expect, indeed trust, their readers to accept that their research accounts: have valid content; connect reliably to earlier events (the research interviews); can be categorised as true or false; and should not be read simply as rhetorical moral accounts. Yet they deny these standards to their interviewees.

Actor network theory

Although different from the 'moral accounts', ANT or actor network theory also has a complicated concept of ontology. Both approaches are influenced by ethnomethodology and symbolic interactionism. Alan Prout (2005: 57) regards ANT as a way of solving the 'radical disjunction between society and biology' in social interpretivism. He sees the disjunction as unhelpful and 'not a sustainable way forward'. Prout sees childhood as a mixed 'construction' of the 'cultural, biological, social, individual, historical, technological, spatial, material and discursive'. To some extent, DCR would endorse both points: to form closer links between society and biology, and between the many diverse influences on childhood.

Bernard Place used ANT to map relations that are both semiotic (between signs and concepts) and material (between things, bodies, people and machines). This seems to confirm the DCR semiotic triangle with the material as the referent. However, ANT counts all animate and inanimate material things as more or less equal actors or 'actants' in single networks. Place (2000: 183) saw children on ventilators in intensive care as:

> 'quasi-objects' . . . consisting of both 'soft' human flesh and 'hard' technological artefact . . . technomorphic. [Children and machines] are so inextricably linked that it is analytically unfruitful to begin with these two categories (human and non-human) as separate explanatory resources . . . [The difference] is not in principle discernible.

This bionic conflation of metal and plastic machines with vulnerable, sapient, sentient, beloved and irreplaceable children, able to suffer and to flourish, overlooks ontology: the sheer, irreducible, intrinsic, intransitivity of the person within human relationships (Archer 2003; Bhaskar 1998a, [1993] 2008b; Sayer 2011). Child and machine might seem superficially to be fused. Yet reductive ANT raises moral confusion about the comparative value of a child and a machine, which parents like Oludayo's mother (see Chapter 3) most dread to see in staff caring for their child. Despite the 'T' for theory, ANT describes *how*, but does not explain *why*, networks cohere, work, endure or fail. And if people are as mindless and motiveless as machines, there cannot be a 'why' in terms of intentions, choices, decisions, conscious interactions and responses.

ANT, like the 'moral accounts' method, tries to treat events, relations and meanings as if each is newly formed and constructed as a single network or performance. These are seen as unrelated to past events and other realities, which are 'bracketed' off. There is little reference to power, or to any meaning or thing outside the networks. This is remote from everyday social and natural reality, which exists and takes meaning from continuity with the immensely complex past. If ANT events really were disconnected from the past, readers would be unable to make sense of ANT reports. The researchers contradict and refute themselves when they rely on such enduring, transferable realities as language and the internationally transmitted printed word. In doubting or disconnecting episodes from the past, ANT and 'moral accounts' research are bereft of the ontology they need if their reports are to convince and engage readers in the future.

Trust is a moral emotion, and some kinds of interpretive research highlight the question: should social research be objective in terms of being value-free, as advocated by founders such as Comte and Weber? Brian Turner (2008: 9–11) traces his important work on the vulnerable human body back to the German thinkers Nietzsche, Gehlen and Berger. He calls them 'controversial', because of their direct or indirect associations with Nazism. They 'somewhat paradoxically', Turner writes, influenced the development of social constructionism. This includes one view that because we cannot constantly reflect on countless everyday aspects of daily life, we subconsciously project a pragmatic, taken-for-granted, factual but false character onto the social world. To expose this illusion of reality, Harold Garfinkel conducted covert ethnomethodology 'degradation' experiments. He suddenly imposed bizarre situations and watched people's reactions. Alvin Gouldner (1977: 390–5) criticised these as cruel. Later chapters will consider connections between detachments from physical, social and moral forms of ontology-reality.

Ontology and trust: reliable children

When interpretivists in Goffman's and Garfinkle's traditions dismiss the possibility or relevance of truth in interviewees' accounts, this can perhaps make other researchers who trust their interviewees look rather naive and gullible. Yet research and policy lose social relevance if they are too divorced from reality and from their original subject matter. And this could partly account for the transfer of research funding towards positivist social research such as longitudinal studies, evaluations and systematic reviews that initially seem to be more grounded in reality.

Criticising Goffman's relativism, Alvin Gouldner (1977: 384, 487) considered that it loses 'empirical realism and moral sensitivity', as when sincerity or love are reduced to maudlin sentimentality. Although Roger Trigg (1985: 36) was writing about religious faith, his words apply equally to children's and parents' intense accounts, when they talk about crucial personal matters:

> Is Christianity true? Sociologists would immediately say that it was illegitimate for them to deal with such a question. Some would reject the idea of objective truth . . . Others would say they wished to 'bracket off the question' of truth and merely look at the fact of belief . . . [but that] fails to take seriously the fact that to the person holding it, the most important aspect is that *it is true* . . . [An] interpretation which undercuts this, falsifies what it is interpreting . . . [The centre of religion, like] science may well lie in its claim to be an objective reality. [To ignore claims to truth] can appear tantamount to assuming their falsity.
>
> *(Original emphasis)*

Trigg still leaves the problem, for researchers who agree with him, of how to justify and validate their work. DCR is useful to the hesitantly trustful researcher: in its recognition of truth in real ontology; in clarifying the difference between intransitive ontology and researchers' transitive understandings; and in respecting each separately. In contrast, ethnomethodologists and other sceptical relativists appear to try to resolve the problem of the epistemic fallacy, with its missing validity, by denying the existence as well as the relevance of any truth or validity. But that attempt to escape seems to involve burrowing more deeply into the fallacy and absent meaning. A few examples are given here to illustrate relations between trust and truth in accounts drawn from embodied knowledge as a vital referent.

Children can be accurate, reliable witnesses. For example, the head of the Crown Prosecution Service London Homicide Team, lawyer Judith Reed, called a 4-year-old victim of rape to give evidence at the central criminal court, the Old Bailey. Reed (2009) commented:

> Having viewed the video of her interview, I have to say she was really quite remarkable. I'd never seen a child so young give as clear and consistent an account . . . She was one of the best child witnesses of any age I've seen give evidence on video.

During the trial, the child was cross-examined for 45 minutes by video-link. The rapist, who was convicted, had also murdered 'Baby P'. The example illustrates some young children's ability to understand, recall and recount serious problems that affect their body.

Although large numbers are often necessary to support general statements, a few reliable examples can effectively refute generalisations that all young children are incapable. Interpretive, interactive research, which imagines the stand-point of the child (Mayall 2002: Chapter 7), can discover much about how children think, feel, relate and choose (Bluebond-Langner 1978; Donaldson 1978; Winter 2011; Yoshida 2011 among many others). Interviews are partly co-constructed, unique conversations about recalled and recounted experiences. The same person's account may partly vary in each new encounter. And research depends on the inter-viewer–interviewee rapport and the researcher's understanding and later analysis. Even so, there has been growing evidence over the past three decades of researchers' trust and confidence in children. This is overcoming oppressive power[2] traditions of mistrust. The approaches are like increasingly effective telescopes that over-come former optical barriers to open up new vistas of the universe. In DCR terms, this involves 'switching perspectives from the "extrinsic", descriptive and explan-atory viewpoint to the intrinsic, first-person standpoint [when] we can see this moral sentiment is a first order capacity relating to what it means to be human . . . at the core of human agency' (Norrie 2010: 220–1).

Some quite powerful and pragmatic people take children's views very seri-ously. In order to make informed plans for major orthopaedic operations, surgeons whom I have interviewed described relying on children's unique and essential knowledge. This was acquired from *being* the body in question, and experiencing the pain, immobility or deformity that the surgeon hoped to relieve (Alderson 1993; see also Appendix 1.2). Some surgeons would correct a minor spinal curve if children were very distressed about it, but would leave a more serious curve if they were not worried. If treatment was needed quite urgently, whenever possible, certain surgeons would still wait while the child was informed, and prepared, and became willing to consent to surgery. They respected the views of children aged from around 6 years, given the importance of treating willing and not resisting patients. Sue aged 12, and said to have 'a mental age of 2 years' (a concept that underestimates both 2-year-olds' capacities and Sue's 12 years of experience), resisted proposed surgery for a year while her mother and surgeon gradually helped her to understand and become able to agree to undergo the three necessary operations for scoliosis (Alderson 1993: 169–70).

Children described insights and values they believed they had learned through their experiences of serious illness or disability. Amy, aged 10, and Tina, aged 12, had opposite views on treatment for their very short stature, aligned with debates among disabled adult researchers on the medical and the social constructions of the disabled body. Tina was convinced that society should respect and include short people and adapt to their needs, instead of expecting her to spend years of pain trying to adapt her body to fit social norms:

> I was scared of ever being on my own when there weren't no adaptations in the house. I couldn't reach no doors or light switches. I was afraid they'd go out and leave me. I feel much safer now it's adapted. . . . I'd rather stay like me. I don't want false bones and all that stuff.

> *(Alderson 1993: 38)*

When I met Amy, she illustrated Anne Solberg's (1996) experience of interviewing young children who protested that she was infantilising them in an adult–child double hermeneutic (not their words, but their meaning). Together they set up a more equal, respectful relationship. I asked Amy, 'So you are having your legs made longer?' She replied with dignity, 'I suffer from achondroplasia and I am having my femurs lengthened.' She enabled me to realise my approach risked undermining and demeaning her responses, as well as my findings and conclusions, if she had allowed me to continue in this vein. Instead she reversed our roles to show that she was the expert and I was the novice. Amy's challenge opened my study of children's consent to surgery (see Appendix 1.2) and later of younger children with diabetes (see Appendix 1.10) to find that competence to give informed valid consent to major surgery or medical treatment was not related to biological age or stage of development, but to social and physical experience, expectations and relationships. Amy's doctors and parents respected her decision when she was 8 years old and her mother, a physiotherapist who was very aware about the painful treatment, said that only Amy could make the decision. Amy commented:

> When I was eight I asked my parents if the doctors could do anything to make me taller . . . I visited several hospitals and learnt about surgical limb lengthening. The surgeon explained [it] would take 15 to 18 months. He talked about the complications such as infection and how they could treat it, and I saw the apparatus they use.
>
> *(Alderson 1993: 36)*

The 'apparatus' was large metal bars and rings fixed into the leg bones with rows of steel pins. Amy not only heroically endured years of extremely painful treatment on her femurs, when she was 14 she underwent the same treatment on her lower legs with an enduring determination. Amy's parents said they respected Amy's decision and that no one else could decide for her.

The children were deeply informed through their experiences and by what might be termed the wisdom of the body. When my colleague Katy Sutcliffe interviewed children with type 1 diabetes about hypos (low blood sugar) Simba (aged 7) described how, 'I thought I was getting sucked down a hole'. Maisie (aged 3) showed how hypos make her feel 'wobbly', by shaking her arms. Having been very ill with hypos and hypers, the children deeply understood the purpose and effects of their life-sustaining treatment. Nicola, when aged 4, explained that insulin is the 'key that turns sugar into energy' (Alderson *et al.* 2006b; Appendix 1.10). The children's knowledge was vital in their interpersonal relationships. Instead of being ignorant, passive or coerced, they could take an active, informed part in negotiating and managing their painful daily treatment.

Similarly, disabled children and young people aged from 4 to 18 years whom we interviewed (Alderson and Goodey 1998; see also Appendix 1.5) deeply understood social and physical barriers as well as potentials in their lives. Stephen, aged 16, who could not speak, and was so disabled he needed a neck support on his wheelchair, communicated through facial movements and by working along the alphabet on his computer and pressing the bar at each correct letter. He slowly typed jokes for me to read during the many times while he waited for assistance from the staff. He illustrated how human beings live so fully in their imprisoning or liberating bodies. The bodily experiences of serious pain, immobility and deformity informed the children's and young people's sense of identity and their relationships, their values, rights, ambitions and their determination to overcome obstacles, or, in Stephen's case, to manage to accept them, when he overrode the bitterness that might easily have overwhelmed him. Their views were founded in intense physical-social-moral experiences. Disabled young people in one large orthopaedic ward described the understanding and kindness ('kind' originally meaning common identity or nature) they all shared, in contrast to taunts and bullying at school from peers who could not imagine their perspectives (Alderson 1993).

By the 1980s, the new discipline of bioethics was dominated by Kantian concepts of informed consent that respected the (disembodied), autonomous, rational person. Consent was also seen to emerge from a utilitarian weighing of costs and benefits (Beauchamp and Childress 2001). My PhD research question was whether the consent to major surgery given by very anxious parents could be valid or even possible. I found that the parents and (in later studies) the children tended to go through an emotional journey, moving from initial shocked rejection of surgery, through doubt, dawning hope and trust, towards the courage to become committed to the treatment as the least dangerous option. Their tangible journey was informed by moral emotions of hope, trust and courage, and by their relationships when parents intensely imagined their child's bodily experiences. Contrary to Kantian notions of the epistemology of autonomy and consent, that should not be tainted or distracted by relationships, 'emotions and contingencies' (Kant 1972), these realities informed the consent-giving and gave it validity and meaning. Parents and children were shocked and frightened *because* they understood the harms and risks of surgery; in turn their emotions informed their understanding and decision-making (Alderson 1990, 1993; see Appendix 1.1, 1.2).

Positivist research is relevant to consent in recognising actual events and meanings, but its standardised hypotheses, controlled trials and statistical surveys cannot encompass children's diverse, complex and subjective experiences of consent. Tina's and Amy's contrasting decisions showed, for example, that there is no one correct answer; consent is a choice not a duty. Ethnography, months of observing in wards and clinics, taping interviews and talking informally, could follow families' thinking-feeling consent journey, as they gradually became informed and committed to surgery within days or over months. I witnessed many of the events that interviewees later discussed, and I relied on them to trust me and permit me to be present. As trust can only be mutual, I believed their accounts unless there (rarely) seemed to be confusion or misremembering. On one decrepit hospital campus, for instance, too many children mentioned feeling sick after surgery, as their trolley wobbled over broken pathways back to the ward, for their account to be doubted. Underlying the actual and empirical varied examples were deeper realities in the relationships between children, parents and clinical staff, of doubt and fear, hope and trust, that are integral to voluntary consent.

Child–adult relations and psychoanalysis

Psychoanalysts claim that child–adult interpersonal relationships are deeply influenced by the subconscious. Since four planar being is intended to cover a broad range of related ideas, I will mention four theories, which can particularly influence interpersonal aspects of research with children. The first, which young children repeatedly demonstrate, is that they can seldom feel able to blame their parents for neglect or abuse. Instead, they seek moral explanations through guilt and self-blame (Miller 1983; Winter 2011) – the beginnings of deep confusion about adult power and virtue.

A second theory is splitting and projection (Klein 1964) when individuals split off parts of their psyche, and absences that they want to deny and reject – ignorance, incompetence, unreliable volatility – and project these onto others. This particularly involves adults denying strengths and virtues in children – wisdom, experience, stable responsibility – and appropriating all these to adulthood. The Oedipus myth and the drama of Romeo and Juliet are often cited to 'prove' young people's potentially lethal emotions, whereas the strife was actually initiated and exacerbated by the parents and aided by priests.

A third theory is that when children arouse great anger, as well as love, in adults who feel extremely anxious about their dangerous power$_2$ then, like colonialists, adults project their violent feelings onto those they oppress, the children. They thereby try to rationalise and justify their oppression. Parents, children's charities and orphanages, priests and nuns, carers and teachers have a mixed history of very much benefiting children but also greatly harming them.

Fourth are the dangers of sentimental infantilising of children, to excuse protection that can shade into cruel repression. News items frequently hint at these partly subconscious processes. In Bali,[5] there are about 80 'orphanages' mainly filled with children taken from their parents from around Indonesia. In many of the institutions, children are forced to work and 'perform', as the staff call their duty to sing welcoming begging songs to tourists. One mother saved up for six years before she was able to 'buy' her very distressed daughter back for $50 dollars. The staff give little care or food, but hand out severe punishments; the managers keep for themselves most of the donations, largely raised from Australian women who regularly visit with funds and toys.

They illustrate Eric Berne's (1968) Freudian theory of the persecutor-victim-rescuer 'game', which dominates child–adult relations. In the triangle of blaming, punishing or rescuing others, the exploitative managers, oppressed children and ignorant donors enacted one of countless versions of the punitive game. Berne's solution (rather weakened by wording that favours adults against children) was that everyone should behave as a mature, honest adult instead of like an inadequate, devious child. In the orphanages the assumed roles were reversed.

Much childhood research involves one or more of these actual and empirical forms of adult–child relating. Rather than being drawn into them superficially, cautious researchers also critically explore underlying, partly subconscious trends and causes.

Contradictions

(Bhaskar 2008b; Norrie 2010: 65–75)

As mentioned earlier, to Kant and Hegel, dialectic involved resolving contradictions in inconsistent, irrational and illogical *arguments* (epistemology and ontological monovalence that recognises only presence). DCR, however, adds real ontology and polyvalence (that recognises absence), with the aim of resolving contradictions through *transformative change*. Many childhood researchers are disappointed that their 'participative research' ends with the neat reported findings (words) and seldom leads to real, messy, transformative change (deeds). DCR helps to analyse and remedy this problem, in following Marx by identifying five types of practical contradictions to be resolved if real change is to occur.

These begin with (A) *logical inconsistencies* when we are trapped into uncertainties and dilemmas and therefore we cannot act or escape, even if we attempt decision and action. This is like the Afghani boys trying to find peace and prosperity, education and work in European NATO countries, one source of their war, and in the face of growing 'fortress Europe' anti-immigration policies. (B) *Non-dialectical oppositions* such as supply and demand result in uneven over- and under-supply, and great inequalities. They may be fairly independent of external forces, but still result in (C) *structural dialectical contradictions* intrinsic to specific social relations. These arise between two necessarily connected things that presuppose one another but are mutually exclusive, such as parent/child or teacher/student oppositions. They may be diminished and unfulfilled through punitive or oppressive relationships. Contradiction (D) is *geo-historically specific dialectical contradictions* and (E) is *generative separation*. I have begun to introduce contradictions in this chapter, because they are so central to MELD 2E and negativity. However, they also occur at structural levels, the topic of the next chapter, where contradictions will be further reviewed. Meanwhile I will consider the archetypal interpersonal contradiction of the 'master–slave' relationship.

'Master–slave' relations

(Bhaskar 2008b; Norrie 2010: 66–7)

Interpersonal relations include general 'master–slave' relations and are at the centre of oppressive power$_2$ and 2E negativity, uniting several themes in this chapter. They were theorised by Hegel (1770–1831) and Marx (1818–1883). They stand for all unequal oppressive relationships, not only ones of slavery. The absence of mutual respect and freedom allows one person to abuse, exploit and enslave the other. This oppressive abuse of power affects class, gender, ethnic, religious and other inequalities named in human rights conventions (which do not mention age-youth discrimination) (UN 1948, 1966a, 1966b, 1979, 1989; 2006b; European Council 1950). Later chapters will show the vital part that 'master–slave' relations play in the MELD dialectic from absence and alienation towards freedom and justice. I will suggest here how childhood studies can expand the related DCR adult-centric analysis.

A key problem in oppression is moral endorsement. Critical theory emphasises that awareness of being a slave is the first and necessary condition for slaves to begin to work towards freedom. However, history shows that law, religion and public opinion have endorsed many forms of slavery and, as important, of mastery: rulers feel morally entitled and so they relinquish power slowly. The Abolition of Slavery Act was not passed in Britain until 1833. Since the mid-twentieth century, civil rights and anti-colonial movements have taken effect only gradually and still have far to go, with masters arguing the ideology that their rule is in everyone's best interests.

This moral endorsement of mastery overtly or covertly exploits an archetype of benign paternalism: wise masters and ignorant, dependent, childlike slaves. Gradually all adult groups have resisted such infantilising as oppressive and deceitful, but it is still endorsed for children when oppressive master–slave paternalism is confused with caring father–child paternity. Like many adult–adult relations, child–adult ones are often complicated by loving interdependence, which can be used to excuse or mask oppression. Powerful opposition to children's rights (Brighouse 2002; Guggenheim 2005; O'Neill 1988; reviewed by Freeman 2007, 2011) asserts adults' moral power by inaccurately over-stating children's pre-human deficiencies and dependencies. These are assumed to disqualify children from emancipation, and to separate them still further from adults. Until the eighteenth century, most adults and children had few if any recognised rights, and they shared work and leisure activities and spaces. Today, adults increasingly rely on child–adult differences to define their own freedoms. 'We are not children', women protest when claiming equal rights and pay and access to public life. More equal child–adult relations therefore depend on the unravelling of moral differences: between children's dependence being either genuine or else imposed; between adults either caring for children or else oppressively controlling them. Childhood studies provide relevant evidence, analysis and debate about the archetypal paternalism and patriarchy that underlie all oppressions of both children and adults (Franklin 2002; Miller 1983).

A second problem when challenging 'master–slave' relations is the confusion that arises from contradictions (see previous section). Hegel pointed out type A *logical inconsistencies* and type C *structural dialectical contradiction*: masters demand respect from slaves, but masters betray and cannot earn respect because they are oppressive; respect is meaningless if slaves have no choice but to appear to be respectful; and why would masters care about the opinion of people they disrespect? The contradictions create great problems in schools when teachers assume they can demand respect from students instead of meriting it. To punish students for disrespect reinforces the contradiction, when respect can only be given voluntarily. Childhood studies document these problems and show the advantages to adults and children of responsive, mutual respect (the theme of most entries in Appendix 1).

Human rights advocacy, a current major way to challenge 'master–slave' oppressions, raises a third problem, when elitist Kantian rights of the rational man/adult are favoured. In contrast, 'human' rights are justified on the grounds that we are a distinct species with a unique set of capacities, needs, interests, aspirations and relationships and this enfranchises all human beings. Childhood research provides numerous studies[6] of children and young people who are competent rights-holders, and of the dangers of violating their rights in type D *geo-historically specific dialectical contradictions.*

Contradiction E, *generative separation*, means alienation at the core of human being and human relations. A definitive image of oppression is the master beating the slave, and all governments ban such assault on adults but, except for about 20 governments, they allow it on children (UN 2006b). Children are still not able to own property, but they may themselves be treated as property and not persons.

Alienation and flourishing will be considered in later chapters, when the realisation of freedom 'consists in the self-transformation or replacement of unneeded, unwanted and oppressive sources of determination, or structures, by needed, wanted and empowering ones' (Bhaskar [1991] 2010b: 145). This includes adults fairly sharing moral space with children, as well as sharing resources, respect and control, as many childhood researchers aim to do in the methods and content of their work.

MELD 2E and childhood

Power$_2$ negativity in adult–child relations ranges from slight to severe oppressions. These can transform into mutually enabling power$_1$, for example, when adults overcome their mistaken assumptions (epistemology) about children's interests, and learn from children's ontology, their bodily, emotional and relational natural necessity. My involvement with children in hospital began with 2E negativity, absence and power$_2$ in the 1970s, when parents were banned from most children's wards, apart from for short visits. The pretexts to exclude them were that parents spread infection, upset the children, and make them cry. I joined a campaign to allow parents into the wards. As parents were gradually able to stay and to care for their child, they reduced the risks of cross-infection by nurses who had cared fully for all the children. Children felt able to show more of their fear and distress when with their parents, and also to gain support and comfort and so they were generally calmer (Robertson and Robertson 1989).

At all ages of childhood, the process of change partly involves moving from 2E negativity in dichotomies into dialectic. Als (1999) gave the example of premature babies who try to wriggle into the corner of the cot, in order to attain a compact foetal position against the cot sides. Nurses would constantly replace them neatly in the centre of the cot, where they would sprawl, limbs outstretched, stressed, insecure and uncomfortable. Als and colleagues devised uterus-like cotton 'nests', and some baby units use looped towels for the babies to lie in. However, the nests and towels are necessary but not sufficient for the babies' comfort if they are left to sprawl across them. The babies need to be helped individually and interactively by the adults to find and to stay in their preferred position (see Appendix 1.8).

Progress in the understanding and practice of informed consent to medical treatment is partly comparable to progress in children's physical and emotional care. The legal and philosophical epistemology of the Kantian, rational, calculating decision-maker partly contradicts the ontology of extremely anxious and ill patients, and distraught parents. Again, many clinical staff have gradually realised that the consent of children and adults to surgery involves many 'minor' processes too, and involves more than the precious Kantian ideals of respect for persons, and avoidance of the coercion and deception redolent of 'master–slave relations'. Respect also includes valuing and learning from children's feelings, bodies and relationships. When parents began to be present in children's wards, the staff had to take interpersonal levels (level 2 of social planar being) and children's wishes and feelings more seriously. Parents perceived and interpreted subtle and explicit cues about their child's needs, and acted as advocates, trying to ward off harmful or unnecessary interventions and to increase beneficial ones, such as pain relief. Through being present, and observing the clinical routines and other families, parents gained insight into the reality of some of the processes, risks, harms and hoped-for benefits to which they were asked to consent.

Children and adults learn about their needs through their bodily experiences within relationships; they express their needs and views through their bodies; and they are respected or disrespected in the sensitive or casual or harsh ways in which their bodies are treated. In practice, Kantian respect has to enlarge to overcome dualisms, engaging with physical ontology, and awareness of negativity, alienation and power, in order to avoid and absent ills. However, far from the lonely autonomy envisaged by Kant, while respecting his vital concern to prevent unwanted interference, the underlying reality of informed and voluntary consent is about feelings and relationships. The patient's or parent's emotional journey moves from doubt and fear to informed confidence and trust in the treatment and in the clinicians who provide it. Children's relationships with other adults such as parents and teachers involve similar physical-emotional-social-moral complexities, and veer between their doubt or trust, power$_1$ or power$_2$. Childhood researchers learn about children's lives through engaging in mutually trusting relationships with them. Chapter 5 moves on from interpersonal to social structural aspects of these individual and group relationships.

5

TIME

Social relations and structures

In Atlanta, Georgia, in 2011, Raquel Nelson was convicted of 'reckless conduct' and jaywalking.[1] She and her three children had been shopping, and they had to wait 90 minutes between the two buses on their journey home. They alighted from the bus opposite their flat, but in between was a five-lane highway, with the nearest safe crossing half a mile away. While they tried to cross the highway, Raquel's 4-year-old son was killed by a driver who admitted to being partially blind and under the influence of alcohol and pain medication. Although this was his third hit-and-run conviction, the driver received a shorter prison sentence than Raquel Nelson's three years. She was convicted of 'vehicular homicide', though she has never had a car, and of 'crossing the street other than at a crosswalk'. The authorities had ignored local residents' repeated requests for a marked crossing and a lower speed limit. As an African-American, Raquel Nelson was not convicted by her peers, but by middle-class, white jurors who did not use buses.

The third plane of social being concerns general social relations and structures, which endure over time and cause and shape events. The example of Raquel Nelson illustrates the inexorable power and timing of the social structures of urban planning, transport, criminal justice, class and ethnicity. Increasingly, the convenience of car-owners is respected, and inevitably they are not children. There are covert structural inequalities of age and income, when children's safety is perceived to be a private matter for parents, not a public or neighbourly concern, and when a child's life and prevention of dangers to children are assumed to have little worth. The judge later altered Raquel Nelson's sentence to probation, but the problems and dangers of being a poor, black, young family continue (Wacquant 2008, 2009; Nadesan 2010). If she had not had children, Raquel Nelson might have been carrying less shopping, have had less need to travel so far to a discount store, and could more easily have walked to the crossing or dashed across the highway lanes. Her initial sentence would only increase the distress of her two other children, ignored in the court case and the news report. In Britain each year, the mothers of 17,000 children are imprisoned, with scant attention to how their mother's sentence might be even worse for the children.[2] In DCR terms of natural necessity, the courts deal with the *empirical* report of the *actual* crash, but set aside *real*, underlying, causal structures. Causes are less about making things happen than about the integral powers, capacities and potential of each causal entity.

Road transport highlights children's uneasy place in adult-centred societies and structures. In Britain, road safety has steadily improved from when around 1,000 children were killed in 1970, to 221 children in 2000 (80 per cent while walking to school), to 131 children in 2008.[3] This great progress has been won at the cost of children's freedoms, with dramatic decreases between 1971 and 1990 in the numbers of children aged 7–11 allowed to cross the road, walk to the park or catch a bus on their own (Hillman *et al.* 1990). Children in disadvantaged families, those least likely to have a car or a garden to play in, suffer 80 per cent of traffic injuries. In 2010, of the 22,660 people killed or seriously injured on British roads, 19,569 casualties were aged 0–15. After decades of laborious effort, road safety campaigners still blame 'hostile roads, bad driving and weak law enforcement' that surround the events. These are misnamed 'accidents' (Green 1997).

More majority world children aged 5–14 years die each day on the roads than through AIDS, tuberculosis and malaria combined.[4] Some children have to cross six-lane highways to get to primary school, and road death rates are spiralling because of rapidly increasing traffic. When families work and live on the streets, the youngest children who wander into the roads have a double jeopardy: they are least likely to be seen by drivers until it is too late, but are most likely to be severely injured by vehicles.

Commercial investments and loans to the majority world favour trade and transport and therefore road-building. There are often no safety plans or pavements. Poor design and materials, and corrupt sub-contraction, leave many roads potholed and dangerous. Lack of seat belts, air bags, adequately maintained cars, of cycle helmets, sufficient training for new drivers, road safety laws, law enforcement and regulation on speed and alcohol limits, all increase the hazards. With many other factors they illustrate the power of social structures that resist change.

Social research raises questions of how power and causes work between structure and agency. This chapter will review childhood and social structures, first, through concepts of MELD 3L. Then theories of structure and voluntary agency, of social construction and structuration, and of childhood itself as a social structure within determining social structures will be discussed. I will contrast 'alongside' versus dialectical approaches to structures including the transformational model of social activity. After considering contradictions further, as these are at the heart of structural inequalities, I will review meanings of 'generation' in childhood and adulthood research, and end with some comments on the importance of structures in childhood research, and some researchers' approaches to them.

MELD 3L, third level

MELD 3L moves to resolve 1M *non-identity* and 2E real, determining *absence* into a complex *totality*. Hegel's dialectical drive towards totality was aimed towards greater, more inclusive explanation, to overcome the wrongs of exclusion and omission in society, nature and reasoning. However, Hegel's dialectic ends in a final synthesis, when illogical or irrational arguments are resolved by reason (epistemology) into a totality.

DCR's totality is instead whole but open and, further, it involves ontology and transformation. Real, material, stratified (layered) presences co-exist with absence, which includes absented pasts besides open unknown futures, to work in deeper, more powerful forms. These forms are understood in their working and changing relations, both internal and external. An example is an internally total book. Yet the book relates to other totalities. It may be in a total shelf of books in a library (Bhaskar [1975] 2008a: 123). Each total letter and word counts towards the whole book. Language, among other structures, works through and between the books, and so do all the ideas in one book drawn from earlier books. Also the readers will bring untold new responses to the open totality of the book.

An example of totality in social research is the case study. Like framing a photograph, boundaries are set to the case: a child, a family, a school or a district, each a totality among other totalities. Case studies aim to reveal inner connections and workings, and also interactions with external entities. Christopher Goodey and I researched special education policy in two areas: one semi-rural, the other in a city (Alderson and Goodey 1998; Appendix 1.5). We began with the disabled school students in their homes, and then with their permission we observed their schools: in the semi-rural area numerous segregated state and private schools; in the city, all inclusive, integrated, state schools. We interviewed teachers, and local authority councillors and staff whose policies pervaded the schools. Schools influenced one another in a flow of internal and external relations, while reshaping the perceptions and values of all concerned about social inclusion or segregation. Inclusive education can only work when all schools serve all their local children, unless, for example, certain groups such as deaf children attend a fairly nearby mainstream school with extra resources, where they have deaf and 'non-deaf' friends and everyone learns some signing.

Beyond *describing*, knowledge involves *accounting* for the events observed in terms of the underlying causal structures that generate them, as when school policies reproduce local politics: social inclusion in the multi-ethnic, Labour council, inner-city area; social segregation in the mainly white, Conservative council, semi-rural area. The politics of inclusion/exclusion worked at every level. For example, in the city, a boy in a wheelchair was in the street playing with friends when Chris arrived to interview him. His mother described his streetwise, confident humour. When a market trader asked her why her son was in a wheelchair, the boy replied, 'What's he think? That it's a Christmas present?' In the rural area, I met a girl who seemed 'normal' despite her strange family and special school. All the curtains at her home were closed, her family sat inside in fear of neighbours' taunts, she travelled many miles each day on the school bus, and had no nearby friends at home. All the schools were training all their students towards being adult members of either inclusive or segregating neighbourhoods and workplaces. 'Normal' children were learning to see their disabled peers either as future co-workers, employees and friends or as segregated strangers.

DCR's open *totality*, such as of each total child or neighbourhood, recognises the world's dynamic complexity. Different totalities co-exist and are held together, like stars, in *constellations*. For example, each school affected the other local schools: in the schools' self-identity (specialised or inclusive); in how they identified disabled children (primarily as disabled and in need of special schools, or else as part of the spectrum of local children). The schools interacted as individual totalities that cooperated or competed.

To respect each child, teacher or school as a totality sees each one as a *concrete universal↔singular*. Each is distinct and unique and also part of a universal – of childhood, of all teachers, or all schools. To 'identify' anyone or anything involves the contradiction of recognising both their unique differences and also their shared universal features. Each individual presupposes the whole. To identify anyone as a child assumes many complicated common features of total childhood. In this way, negative splits and absences at 2E lead on to a network of connections at 3L. Socially, these connections mediate between self and others, when human nature and our capacity to care for others are seen as part of the *concrete universal↔singular* of being human.

DCR sees everything contained or *constellated* within an *open totality* as a *process-in-product* (Bhaskar [1993] 2008b: 305–7). This accepts that closed systems with a single dominant force are very rare: gravity is counteracted by wind currents, bird flight and jet engines. Open social systems even more involve the real, constant, dialectical interacting of different forces and structures. Similarly, complete totalities are also rare. Totalities are usually partial, 'finite, limited and conditioned . . . constituted by their geo-histories and their contexts in open potentially disjointed process' (Bhaskar [1993] 2008b: 126).

A larger example of a social constellation involves protests from multi-millionaire philanthropists about tax changes during 2012. Their donations to charities were partly a method of tax avoidance, generated within tightly-knit structures. These included: the aristocracy as patrons who reward philanthropists with prestigious and powerful networking and lobbying contacts; the churches, universities and high-status arts and (children's and disability) charities as recipients of the donations; the financial advisers; the sources of wealth; and the millions of people who have to cope with the effects of the lost taxation.[5] Pleas for deserving charities were intended to obscure or justify the tax avoidance. Yet tax avoidance depletes democratic, accountable, coordinated state services, for example for children, more than the charities might benefit them.[6] Understanding change involves understanding the internal and external processes of interacting totalities, including childhood and adulthood, and their porous boundaries.

Concepts of totality and of dialectic become *diffracted* (Bhaskar [1993] 2008b; Norrie 2010: 50–85), broken up as light in a prism fractures into different shapes and colours, or torchlight reveals the fracturing, the bumps and grooves on a dark path. Diffraction refers to differentiation and also to fracturing, although not in the sense of fragmenting or splitting completely apart, but within totality, unity-in-diversity, and emergence (Hartwig 2007: 141).

The concept and method of diffraction are thereby adapted to explore complex realities, rather than simplistic ideals. Childhood studies have opened up childhood to include much more than developmental age-stage structures, or models of pre-social learning, or genetic or economic determinism. They combine knowledge from these and many other approaches through a complex range of disciplines, perspectives, methods and sites.

Childhood studies examine *holistic causality*, when each totality (such as the child) interacts with numerous other surrounding and interacting totalities through the life-course and the lifeworld. The *holistic causality* concept fits the mysterious social-natural growth of each unique child in his or her social-natural context. This occurs not simply through one thing causing another, but through many elements interacting and interchanging. Each new experience is an emergence and over-reaching from an earlier state. Similarly, the global structure of childhood gradually changes, as the state and status of billions of children advance or regress in time and place.

The next sections review the main themes in childhood studies: social construction, social structure and structuration.

Structure and voluntary agency: social construction and structuration

Childhoods vary greatly as they are reconstructed and renegotiated by agents across the world, and over time. Elaborate cultural, historical and social imaginings, experiences and rituals of childhood, as a stage before adulthood, are inherited and transferred between generations. Many varied structures that relate to childhood include: different social groupings; buildings and institutions; villages, towns and cities; transport and communication networks; markets and states; social and political systems; cultural structures of language, education, the arts and religion; collective memory and myth; social effects of physical bodies and the natural world. These all interact within open systems.

There is also an immensely powerful absent or non-structure: *luck, chance or 'thrownness'* (Bhaskar [1993] 2008b). We are born, and keep entering, and being 'thrown' into pre-existing time-space-cause contexts that are like fast-moving vehicles. Helpless thrownness is especially apparent to people who join a new group or area, or who experience sudden luck or misfortune. Babies and young children are least prepared and least able to choose, or alter, or control their social-natural contexts, and they can be most deeply and permanently affected by the chance of being born into a fortunate or disadvantaged family with all the subsequent opportunities. The Victorian colonel's daughter, fêted as 'a little princess' when she was rich and despised as a skivvy when she was a pauper, illustrated how attributed identity and merit are part of children's changing fortunes (Hodgson-Burnett [1905] 2008). Meritocratic claims that success results wholly from individual agency deny the luck of cultural and genetic family structures, and can encourage illusions that success or failure, reward or blame, are always morally deserved. Such beliefs deter efforts to promote social justice, while disbelief in chance and over-confidence in reason and mathematical predictions led to the 2008 banking, insurance and housing crashes, and Ed Smith (2012) advocated more realistic humility and respect for fortune or, in DCR terms, for the thrownness and absences of human power and knowledge.

Social constructionists reject the *determinist* structural functionalism of Talcott Parsons and Piaget, which, they argue, attributes too much power to external social structures or internal bio-psychological ones. Parsons (1951: 208) assumed that socialisation of the 'barbarian invasion of the stream of newborn infants' was essential. Jenks (1982: 16–17) considered that such determinism transformed living people into machines through a 'theoretic violence, particularly on the child' and a 'mortification'. Instead, many childhood researchers favour *voluntarism*, which attributes much power and free choice to agency. That has promoted respectful research with and about children as intentional actors, their experiences, views and capacities, their influence over people and events, and their share in reshaping childhood. The research has remedied sociology's former exclusion of children as pre-social, future beings.

Some interpretive childhood researchers favour structuration, Giddens's theory (1984: 25) that 'structural properties of social systems are both medium [context, process] and outcome of the practices they recursively organise'. Rather than attend either to individual actors or to societal totalities, Giddens examined networks of concepts. Each is a 'medium whereby truth as a relation between statements and the object-world is made possible, but does not provide the substance of that relation itself'. Structures include rules and resources that are available to agents. They also include structuring properties, which bind time-space in social systems, and give them form and existence when they are reproduced in cycles of structure-agency duality.

If structure and agency are, however, overly-turned into abstractions, there is a risk of losing crucial differences between living, intentional agents and inanimate structures and things. Structuration also risks underestimating the immense power and potential of structures to benefit or harm, shown in the above example of Raquel Nelson. The tendency of childhood studies to separate childhood from the 'adult' world has been mentioned earlier. Partly in reaction to the former neglect of childhood in social science, some researchers highlight questions that they see as unique to childhood. 'Once we start questioning the absence of equivalent concepts such as "adult abuse" or "adult poverty" we start to think of features that are intrinsic to children rather than any other group in society' (Wyness 2006: 21). Concern with unique, intrinsic features, however, also tends to separate children from many social structures, including politics and economics, which affect both children and adults. Wyness (2006: 206), for example, comments: 'the children's needs discourse makes it difficult to think of children as political'. Yet the ontology of needs, such as the hunger of millions of children, is the basis of human rights and justice. The structures of childhood and of rights exist in interactions with economic and political structures.

Giddens challenged both positivism that reifies structures beyond human control, and also interpretivism that more or less overstates individuals' power and agency to create society. Instead he saw structure and agency as equal partners in creating social order, not in conflicting dualism but in complementary duality. His concept of structures includes rules and frames that provide predictable routines in 'ontological security'. Agents can trust and apply these to make sense of their lives through constantly performing and accomplishing them as, for example, Goffman analysed. He treated the self as a reflexively constructed phenomenon, and structures as the medium and the outcome of social intercourse, and the rules and resources that actors reproduce through social interaction. Bodies are counted as structures, the medium and outcome of human labour, which constrain human action and are the means of altering daily life.

James and James (2004: 39–40), summarising structuration theory, refer to 'fluid' social contexts, when every reflexive individual actively contributes to social reproduction, by resisting or conforming to social norms and structures, using the available rules and resources in particular contexts and ways:

> Routinised over time, this social phenomenon takes on the reality that sociologists have reified by the concept of a 'thing' called 'social structure' [although it] is no more nor less than the culminated means and outcomes of people's social practices enduring over time.

Yet if social structures are reduced into concepts (in agents' minds), this repeats the epistemic fallacy. Structures without some independent existence, which appear to emerge from agency, can seem arbitrary, transient, malleable and potentially meaningless, simply a passing, expendable collection of cultural habits. Structures may then be reduced into flat actualism, and acknowledged only in their visible effects, which are mistaken for causes, when their effects in actions are assumed directly to cause structures. Agency may then be over-stated. For example, research with young children dying of cancer has been cited to show that they initiate and sustain the social order (James 2011). Yet the children with cancer were powerless to initiate or change hospital routines, adult-led relationships and secrecy, and the course of their disease and painful treatment. Although children share in constructing their own lives, they are mainly confined to rearranging familiar, inherited, tight parameters and structures, within given repertoires of rules and roles, behaviours and relationships.

One instance of a balanced view about agency and structure is David Buckingham's (2000, 2011) evaluation of evidence about children's interactions with the vast and powerful structures of the mass media. He has challenged moral panics about commercial adult pressures causing the 'death of childhood'. He concluded that children and young people tend to be sensible, critical viewers of television, although better education could increase children's and adults' critical powers. Buckingham contends that anxieties about children's vulnerability to advertising and other commercial pressures would better be understood in relation to influences on the whole of society, instead of being diverted into concern about only the youngest generations. He lists techniques and technologies that powerfully influence children and adults to form their loyalties to brands with their associated emotions and values. There are online programmes: to track and target the child market; to develop and test brands along with children's dreams and choices; to present products as if they express personal choices instead of impersonal, mass-marketed items; to gather and use personal data about family and friends from children at ever younger ages; to nurture active, desiring, 'autonomous' consumers although 'empowerment' mainly involves spending power.

However, Sharon Beder (2009) describes immensely powerful structures active through technologies that involve digital recording and data-mining of billions of responses from children and adults, gathered through: online games and competitions that ask them to create personal profiles, blogs and videos; cookies that covertly track users' online movements; the fan culture; peer-to-peer marketing and 'cool hunting' in research with children at home and online. Computer technologies pervade children's daily activities, while multiplying the databases and analyses about them (Crouch 2011; Davies 2008; Dean 2012; Green *et al.* 2005; Klein 2000; Leveson 2012; Polman 2010; Rusbridger 2011; Savage and Burrows 2007).

Among others, Mayall (2002: 32–3) considers that structuration theory overlooks the power and present constraints of historical forces and traditions, besides the inequities in extra, inexorable pressures of structures on the least powerful individuals, such as children. Giddens has been criticised for oscillating between voluntaristic and deterministic views of the body and behaviour, nature and culture, and of being uncertain about the conditions in which bodies enable or constrain action (Turner 2008). Shilling (2012) contends that Giddens gradually moved from the body in nature to the constructed, malleable body in modernity, colonised by society, and towards the reflexively mobilised self. Giddens (1984: 231) proposed general 'sensitising' theories, not intended for detailed empirical work, as if his work has uncertain relevance to everyday life and research. (For further critiques see Archer 1995; Smith 2011: 380–2.)

Alan Prout (2011) aimed to move beyond modernist certainties and dichotomies of agency/structure, being/becoming, nature/culture in a postmodern fluid, plural, fragmenting, disorganised and diverse world. I found his paper compelling while reading it on a train speeding past the London city-scape, home of deregulated capitalism. And yet the London towers still stand, and the commuters with their mobiles enjoy formerly unimaginable control over their health, food, dress, transport, communication, time and space. Compared with medieval plague, famine, war, lawless violence, feudalism and superstition, are our agency and structures really so much less controlled? Wanting to move beyond the myth of the autonomous, independent person, Prout usually called for more multidisciplinary work. He aimed to open up the excluded middle, between the dichtomies of child/adult or agency/structures. However, what exactly lies between them, an entity or an empty space? One middle form is the human-technical hybrid (which I criticised in Chapter 4), another is network, in which a person is both a point and a network of all influences and contacts so far. Does this mean our minds and bodies are like stations with trains rushing through them? If so, who or what is the 'I' who experiences and remembers, generates and reacts to the network traffic? And can we see structures not only as fluid networks but also as enduring and powerful, as Raquel Nelson found?

There are risks in overestimating individuals' freedoms and responsibilities, and then assuming they can and should shape their own lives, and bear all the blame when they fail. This model denies great inequalities in people's skill, knowledge, status and resources.[7] Childhood as a structure is more than the sum of all the agents; it interacts with other totalities and structures formed by the political, economic and social past and present. Reference to 'childhood' and 'children' as if they are interchangeable confuses structure with individual agents. Agents can achieve little direct social change, and they often cause inadvertent and unintended effects. Having reviewed some of the advantages and limitations of attention to structures in relation to *voluntary* agency, I will next consider *determining* (though not determinist) structures.

Childhood and determining social structures

Qvortrup and colleagues (1994, 2011) studied intergenerational distributive justice and the draining of wealth away from younger to older generations. While he was researching changes in family patterns, Qvortrup was amazed to find the economist researchers saw children only as problems for parents (costs, burdens and barriers to adults' free lives) (Mayall in press), views still dominant among some economists (Hansen *et al.* 2010; Vleminckx and Smeeding 2001). This led him to plan a sociology of childhood and to set up the 16-state European study conducted during 1987–1992 of the sociography of childhood, distributive justice, and the activities, economics and legal status of childhood.

Qvortrup (1985) used a Marxist, macro-historical analysis of children's contributions as workers to the division of labour in modern industrialised societies. He saw European children as agents, who in the past worked in households and streets, fields and factories, and who now contribute to national economies by their school work, in learning to become future adult workers. Many children are both paid or unpaid workers and school students. The concept of schooling as active, contributive work challenges the Durkheimian view that schooling is mainly passive socialisation. It also questions assumptions that teachers are the main workers in schools. Qvortrup and colleagues show how children serve the adult workforce, first, by attending schools, which are centres for childcare and thereby free parents to do paid work. Schools greatly expanded around 1900, with the mass movement of women from the home into factories and offices. Second, children are the clients of countless employed adults (teachers, play, care and youth workers, psychologists, social workers and many others). Third, by far the majority group in schools, the students are crucial agents in creating and maintaining school and other adult-led structures in such policies as social inclusion (Alderson 1999b; Appendix 1.6), and peaceful, creative cooperation (Highfield School 1997; Appendix 1.4). These policies only work when everyone, from the oldest to the youngest person, is actively involved, although children's positive agency is often overlooked or seen as passive compliance.

With colleagues, Qvortrup showed how childhood is an important, permanent-though-changing, biological-social structure. It is integral to every society, whether it lasts for a brief infancy or for two decades. As a social space and time in which children and adults interact, childhood is worthy of dedicated research, particularly in how economics specifically affects children and young people. Children are usually concealed within adult-led structures of the family or the school, whereas separate data on childhood reveal children's often relatively meagre share of space and resources (Qvortrup *et al.* 1994, 2011). Qvortrup (1991; Qvortrup *et al.* 2011) have argued that the great and rising structural inequalities between children and adults, rich and poor are vital topics for childhood research. Oldman (1994) regarded childhood as a politically oppressed *minority group*. In Britain, children are about one-fifth of the population. They have no vote, and younger parents are in the demographic group least likely to vote. Critics analyse how governments' austerity measures since around 2010 have most affected the youngest and poorest groups (see Volume 2, Chapter 10).

Qvortrup and colleagues (2011: 28) contended that study of the life worlds and structure of childhood should be 'abstracted from individual children [and] does not necessarily demand that children are directly observed or asked . . . most powerful parameters influencing children's lives are set in motion without having children or childhood in mind at all'. Similarly, we can discuss class and gender 'without necessarily knowing anything about' individuals.

The firm separation of structure from (child) agency has helped to redress the former neglect of political structures, conditions, circumstances and transformations, and to move beyond personal research with children to political research about them. Avoidance of individual children also possibly emphasises that childhood research is serious, demanding, 'adult' work. Qvortrup and colleagues produce crucial evidence about historical changes in the economy and polity, including the dwindling proportion of children and of households with a child in the minority world.

The past century has seen the immense fall in childhood mortality and morbidity rates in the minority world. Recently, several European countries have seen a marked fall in 'non-accidental injury' of children. This may be due to the police taking cases of child abuse much more seriously in the earlier stages, before they escalate to lethal levels.[8]

In Qvortrup's structure/agency dichotomy, inattention to individual children does, however, raise problems. First, it could repeat the habit, that Qvortrup criticised, of the movers of 'most powerful parameters' to ignore children themselves, despite aiming to redress their oversights. Second, it claims expertise but does not say how we can know about childhood without knowing something about children, besides what adults do to them. Gender, for instance, is partly understood through specific discriminations against women, and also through women's experiences of discrimination. The power and meaning of parameters around childhood similarly inhere not only in external structures, but also in how they impinge on children, and are variously experienced and sustained, resisted or reconstructed by children. Otherwise, schooling, for example, could be assessed solely by educators' own measures that exclude the experiences of satisfied and dissatisfied students. As DCR analyses, transitive human meaning always mediates intransitive social structures.

Third, the dichotomy ignores the unique problem in almost every report on childhood: they are virtually all by adults. Feminist authors are usually women. Law books are by lawyers. Yet children are so remote that they can scarcely ever speak as authors in the childhood literature. When their views and voices are missing, there can seem to be a kind of empty, missing ontology, seldom possible (thanks to feminism) when today's adults write about one another. Fourth, the reality of social structures ('structure' literally meaning 'built') is at times underplayed. Structures can only exist through human agency, and are better understood through dialectic and integration (see MELD section above) than through dichotomy and separation. The partly biological and relatively intransitive origins of social structures in relationships involving sex, age, (dis)ability, ethnicity, generational order and kinship, matter in how they are reconstructed through transitive human interpretations and agency, cooperation and conflict.

Qvortrup (2008) also has the important aim of establishing childhood's essential place in every society by emphasising its universal features, and by opposing pluralist approaches as unduly social constructionist or postmodern. We cannot understand a multiplicity of childhoods, he contends, until we grasp that childhood is 'a collectivity set aside from adults'. Yet is childhood 'set aside' from adults or largely interacting with and constituted through adults' as well as children's activities? The DCR theory of the *concrete universal↔singular* (see MELD section above) can help here by illuminating relations between the universal and individual through their interactions, as well as reconsidering internal and external structural interactions. Open, not closed, totalities are defined less by separation and difference and more by determining structures that interact with partially voluntary agents.

'Alongside' structures: class and age

'*Alongside*' concepts of structure will now be considered, to be contrasted later with *dialectical* concepts. By 'along-sidedness', I refer to concepts such as structure and agency, body and mind, and different agents as individuals or groups, which are set next to one another, but without showing clear causal connections or power relations between them. People may be sorted by some characteristic: age, status, colour, employment. An example is the I–V socioeconomic class system. Despite the advantages in efforts to recognise and respond to inequality when everyone is allocated to a social class, there are difficulties. People can too easily be moved around into different groups; definitions and boundaries of the groups may be debated and modified; individuals may seem to fit more than one class, such as if they have a low income but splendid housing. All these variations do not much alter either the groups or the relations between them. The groups may be described in relation to one another, by higher or lower income, but reasons or causes for the differences are not offered.

Uncertainties about classifying adults can be doubled or trebled for children. Their parents including step-parents may fit into different income and occupation groups, different inheritance and lifestyles. Class can be defined and subdivided in numerous ways, and for children and young people, especially salient though not necessarily congruent class differences include: household income and expenditure and how these are shared among family members; type of housing and neighbourhood; type of school, post-16 education or employment or lack of these; cultural and ethnic identity especially for migrant children and those seeking a lifestyle that differs from their parents' values; their prospects through their parents' networks and influence; their ability to afford higher education fees and careers that begin with months of unpaid work. Inequalities between privileged and disadvantaged children and their differing prospects are rapidly increasing, but class is seldom cited as a concept that could explain or cause these inequalities. Scambler (2012) argued that sociological analysis urgently needs to examine class but that, the more extreme class differences become, the less they are acknowledged. Part of the along-sidedness of current concepts of class is the profusion of fragmenting cultural identities, and class as a descriptive but not a causal concept. However, recently the debates have changed. The rapid increase in inequalities in recent years have evoked protests, such as the Occupy movements with the slogan of the privileged '1% versus the 99%', with more mention in the media of the 'political class' and the 'ruling class' (Haddad 2012; Henry 2012; Mason 2012; Mount 2012; Shaxson 2011).

Along-sidedness also occurs with age-based structural groupings, when the mention of 'childhood' presupposes its defining opposite, adulthood, but the nature of adulthood, its relationship to childhood, and its presumed differences from childhood may not be analysed. There is frequently what might be termed the *myth of the perfect polar opposite*: talk of irresponsible children implies wholly responsible adults. Unless the myth is explicitly stated and analysed it can easily and subconsciously confirm popular stereotypes, which deny how all age groups are partly responsible and irresponsible. Unreal polar opposites are part of along-sidedness, which can confuse rather than clarify understanding of structures.

Interacting dialectical structures

In contrast to alongside relations, DCR analyses mutually defined, dialectical dualisms. DCR positions structures in *constellations*, set in causal, interlocking interaction with one another. And besides comparing and describing social structures, DCR also examines causes of how and why resources and power are drawn away from one social group and towards the other through innumerable processes. Bhaskar (1998a: 32–6) found both Weber's voluntarism (actions that underplay structural conditions) and Durkheim's determinism (structural conditions that underplay actions) inadequate. Without structural conditions, people are reduced into helplessly making vague, free-floating choices that lack real meaning and, therefore, lack the agency of rational choice. Conversely, if scientific laws determine human behaviour, then free will cannot exist and behaviours are simply automatic reactions. Instead, DCR acknowledges the real, underlying power of social structures, comparable to gravity in their immense, enduring, often unacknowledged influences, which generate causes, and become visible and available to experience, in their effects in events and relationships

Retroductive reasoning explains (does not simply describe) recurring patterns and effects (Bhaskar 1998a: 44). Raquel Nelson's trial for example (see opening example in this chapter) emerged from unseen, determining policies and structures of urban design, transport, commerce and law, class, gender and ethnicity, which are reproduced more, or less, or much less, voluntarily by the agents involved. She chose to cross the highway, but within many more constraints than the car drivers experienced. The determining structures fit DCR criteria in that they exist over time and space, provide reliable, consistent explanations of events, are associated with constant power and change whether their effects are observable or not, and they are known through their effects.

The demand for direct evidence of social structures (such as class) is like the scepticism that would dismiss gravity because it is invisible, and would look only at the falling objects and try to find causes of their falling within them. Variable analysis in the birth cohorts, and the politicians' responses (see Chapter 2) does just this, in trying to track meaning between different effects of disadvantages, such as styles of parenting, instead of also looking at deeper causes. Rather than defining class by individuals' actual attributes such as income or lifestyle, DCR like critical theory defines class by the deeper structural nature of the relationship between classes, such as employer–employee, or 'master–slave relations'.

Critics who dismiss structural social causes argue that some disadvantaged children succeed well in adult life, and therefore everyone could succeed if they chose to (Field 2010; the American dream). Overemphasis on either structure or agency can underestimate the power of the other, and the dialectic between them and between structures in open systems. As gravity can appear to be disproved by bird flight but really endures, structures of inequality can appear to be disproved by individual success, but poverty or privilege still have immense, enduring, general effects. Underestimation of structures can underestimate the great efforts of agents who succeed against structural pressures, and can detract from study of how to change oppressive structures.

Paradoxically, uncertain open results may be accepted more readily in the natural than in the social sciences. In biochemical, randomised, clinical trials (an artificially closed system) doctors accept results that show only a tiny relative difference. When chemotherapy for breast cancer achieved only a 3 per cent higher rate of survival than other treatments, it became the treatment of choice,[9] although it was not known which patients would benefit or exactly why. Yet much higher, simplistic standards of proof and explanation are required by critics of class analysis, when they demand unanimous results or proof, despite social structures and interactions existing in far more complicated open systems of structural inequalities.

Scambler (2012) criticises Marmot (2010) and Wilkinson and Pickett (2009), respected experts on health inequalities, for their inattention to causal economic structures. The experts meticulously document extensive social and economic inequalities. Yet instead of attributing the direct causes of ill health to these *political* structures and to their everyday *material* effects (such as poor housing and diet), they attribute ill health primarily to the *interpersonal, psychological* effects of the stress of being in subordinate, less successful social positions. Their evolutionary psycho-biological explanation is derived from hormone studies of stress in subordinate monkeys. Wilkinson and Pickett (2012) explained the 2010 English city riots in terms of rioters' personal feelings of worthlessness and insecurity and anger, citing psycho-biological research on stress levels and mortality rates. Incidentally, Marmot identified the most stressful, unhealthy employment conditions that induce heart disease and diabetes as: not being in control; having to meet high demands; not being allowed to talk to colleagues; having to ask permission to go to the toilet – in other words being treated like a child during a routine day at school.

This public health theory reflects the psychological theory, devised by Julian Rotter (1954), of an 'internal locus of control' and a personal sense of being able to act effectively. The converse, an 'external locus of control', perceives luck or chance as the source of power, and was later extended to include 'powerful others' such as teachers or doctors. The 'internal locus' has repeatedly been found to be associated with better health. Rotter's theory sets aside causal social and economic structures of inequality, and concentrates on psychological agency or non-agency, mainly in the form of beliefs and stories that people tell themselves about their own seeming power or powerlessness. The theory logically supports cognitive behaviour therapy (CBT) as the favoured psychological treatment for unhealthy beliefs and behaviours, since CBT involves retelling stories about self-esteem and self-control, to counter 'learned helplessness'. The beliefs and the therapies can strongly influence behaviour, with beneficial effects. CBT is promoted for being more cost-effective and speedy than psychotherapy, although evaluations have been criticised for lacking clear definitions and methods, for being too short-term, and for usually being conducted by the therapists concerned (Whitfield and Williams 2003). Yet it is unclear whether CBT reconciles unhappy people to their lot by suppressing anomie, or really addresses social conditions that alienate them from themselves, when it sets aside economic and political causes of unhappiness.

A report from the London School of Economics (LSE 2012) deplored poor mental health services for the estimated 6 million adults and 700,000 children with crippling anxiety and depression in England, and urged better healthcare for them including CBT and medication. The 34-page report, chaired by an econo-mist, did not mention causes of ill health or social structures although, without having first established the causes, it seems premature to prescribe the treatments. There are dangers in ignoring social contexts, and also in defining all children's 'hyperactive' and other 'disorders' as 'illnesses'. Their behaviours can then be dismissed as symptoms and evidence of disordered, irrational minds, when sickness is identified within the child. However, children's behaviours might be legitimate, rational protests against pathogenic and unjust social structures and unresolved contradictions and alienations, which could continue to damage children unchecked. In some cases, political remedies might be more relevant than psychiatric ones. Nevertheless, the report and CBT, in their epistemic fallacy, reduce physical and political realities into words and perceptions, reduce struc-tures into personal stories. If, or when, causes of distress are external, and begin in interpersonal relations or social structures, then by seeking to internalise them, medical and psychological treatments could only increase alienation

DCR analyses interacting dialectical structures, which set the necessary condi-tions for social events. Structures powerfully influence and transform events, but do not completely determine them. Open systems, those of coordinating and competing structures, produce tendencies but not inevitabilities. DCR treats inter-acting human agency and social structures as interdependent. Neither can produce the other out of nothing, but they are not necessarily balanced or equal. Structures can only work actively through human agency when individuals and groups teach and learn, trade, heal the sick or commit crimes. And agents can only do all these things when they presuppose and act within social structures of meaning, resources and traditions of education (language, recorded knowledge, teaching younger generations), markets, politics, law and order systems.

TMSA, the transformational model of social activity

Individuals, groups, social structures and social relations within societies are constantly being reproduced and transformed through *TMSA, the transformational model of social activity* (see Figure 5.1).

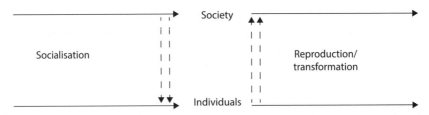

FIGURE 5.1   TMSA: transformational model of social activity
Source: Adapted from Bhaskar 1998a.

TMSA critiques methodological individualism, and instead sees individuals interacting with social structures in the dialectic of constant movement, change, transformation, absenting and negating being and becoming. All this occurs in space–time, which is a 'relational property of the meshwork of material beings' (Bhaskar [1993] 2008b: 53). TMSA is *tensed* in that it inevitably moves from past to future, never backwards. This understanding begins very early in the life of finite human beings, when babies aged 6 months show surprise if they observe effect seeming to precede cause (Siegal 1997). Children can have especially ambivalent and vulnerable positions in TMSA unless they are respected as agents and members of society, without being exploited. Everything is also tensed in being largely constituted by its past and geo-history, and it exists through many overlapping, converging or contradicting *rhythmics*. Bhaskar ([1993] 2008b: 55) describes these rhythmics in great cities where buildings, ceremonies, conflicts, 'electric cables, motor cars, television sets, rickshaws, scavengers and disposable cans coalesce in a locale'. Space, time, cause, structure and agency all interact as product-in-process, process-in-product.

The critical realist Margaret Archer (1995) sees structure and agency as each ontologically and analytically distinct to allow for dialectic and causal relations between them, which unfold over time and within cultures. She identified dualism (rather than Giddens's duality) of structure and agency; structural frameworks set conditions and limits on human action in a realist ontology; and structure precedes agency in cycles of social structural and interpersonal reproduction in social analysis. Archer explored concepts of 'I', 'me' and 'ego', and of the person as subject and object. She analysed how her 20 interviewees mediated structure and agency through their internal conversations, working through contradictions towards understanding what they really cared about. She divided time, and her social analysis, into four stages: structural conditioning and emergent causal powers and properties; social interactions between agents; immediate outcomes; outcomes that elaborate, reproduce or change structures.

Chapter 4 reviewed how Hegel explained inequalities and power$_2$ relations between the dualisms in terms of universal *'master–slave' relations*. These are structural as well as interpersonal, and were developed by Marx towards *material generation in social processes*. The dualisms have layers of conflict and contradictions. Each element is distinct yet presupposes and depends on the other one for its existence. A person can only exist as a master or slave, a teacher or student, a father or son, in relation to the other. The *telos* (function and purpose) of each are at least partly opposed, and cannot both be recognised, when one enslaves and the other wants freedom. Conflict may be latent or overt; the relationship is self-defeating and self-negating (Bhaskar [1993] 2008b: 70–1, 90–5, 345; Norrie 2010: 66–7). 'Master–slave' relations involve Marx's understanding of concepts that are central to DCR. These include: a real, intransitive, ontology beyond thought (and beyond Hegel's epistemology); a materially structured world that generates the forms of the actual existing order; forms that have immanent contradictions that can suggest an ideal and misleading representation of the world; and also a real world that can be described, classified and explained in various, changing, developing ways. Marx, as a scientific realist, believed that explanatory structures or essential relations are not only distinct from, but are often, and even normally, in opposition to the phenomena they generate. Examples include the way many schools fail many of their students (Allen and Ainley 2007; Serpell 1993), or how healthcare services distract attention from real underlying causes of alienating ill health, offer palliation instead of effective prevention, and perhaps inadvertently help to sustain pathogenic systems and prevent much-needed transformative change (LSE 2012; Coppock 2002). This 'material generation in social processes' can be examined through four planar social being, and three-layered natural necessity, and TMSA.

The dialectical tensions, interactions, momentum and change in DCR draw on Marx's 'causal, not conceptual, necessity'. This means that, unlike the fairly arbitrary, *conceptual*, alongside relations between, say, social class IV and V, the dialectical relationship is locked into *causal* dyads, which powerfully influence what is done, said or thought. The interacting pair may be amicable or hostile. Until both are emancipated into more equally respectful power relations, there will still be essential inequality, involuntary 'slavery' and oppressive power$_2$ forces.

In Bhaskar's view, Marx also 'limits teleology [purpose, function] to its proper place in human affairs' to the intentional human agency and causality that reproduce and transform society. These alone invest the world and its structures with meaning and purpose. This is a vital concept in DCR: structures can be causal because they derive ultimately from human intention and purposeful agency. They are central to Marx's 'concrete science of geopolitical history' and the eventual hope of transformative agency. Structures have their own partially independent reality, teleology and causal necessity. These cannot be reduced, as Hegel believed, to 'alienations of spirit, thought, or any kind of mind' (Bhaskar [1993] 2008b: 70–1, 90–5, 345; Norrie 2010: 66–7). That would be like explaining inequality simply by disadvantaged people's attitudes towards success, trying hard or giving up, while ignoring all the material, practical barriers.

Further critical realist approaches to structure

The critical realist sociologist Douglas Porpora (2007) identified four concepts of social structure held by social scientists. Aggregate behaviour stable over time is the atomistic view held mainly in economics (see Volume 2, Chapter 10). Law-like regularities, which govern social facts with rigid agent/structure separation, support positivist, causal explanations, such as in the birth cohort studies (see Chapter 2). Structuralist analysis treats structures as determining rules and resources that affect relatively weak agents. In DCR, structures are complex enduring systems of human relations among social positions. DCR's ontology of emergence and of deeper underlying causal, structural realities combines structure and human agency so that each is neither separate nor autonomous. This moves beyond rigid notions of causes in laws and rules (concepts that Porpora listed second and third) because these conclude that human agency, freedom, responsibility and 'free will' have no causal explanation and are simply unpredictable, free-floating choices and behaviours.

Another critical realist sociologist, Christian Smith (2011: 317) contends that 'a thick [complex] notion of *persons*' (see Chapter 7) 'is essential for rightly understanding what social structures are and why and how they come to exist and change'. The characteristics he gives for social structures fit childhood: actively sustained by human agency and bodily practices; having specific dynamic historical existences; always implicating inanimate material objects (from toys to schools, for example); constituted in part by cultural mental categories (such as the ignorant, dependent child); and always involving normative and moral dimensions and normalising sanctions (especially relevant to education and socialisation) (Smith 2011: 322–9). Smith thinks that social structures usually encourage passive acquiescence if not agreeable adherence. Persons and structures exist and interact in stratified reality (at the empirical, actual and real levels) and they are emergent. They develop from, but cannot be reduced back into, the units from which they have emerged, any more than water can endure if it is deconstructed back into oxygen and hydrogen molecules.

Having reviewed critical realist emphases on the importance of understanding structure and agency in relation to one another, I will now return to the theme of contradictions.

Contradictions continued

The dialectic of structure–agency centrally involves *contradictions*, which began to be introduced in Chapter 4. Contradiction (A) *logical inconsistencies* underlies (B) *non-dialectical oppositions*, such as supply and demand that result in uneven, over- and under-supply. For example, Julian Tudor Hart's (1971) inverse care law contends that the people most in need of healthcare tend to be least likely to receive it. A similar contradiction is when the children with most learning difficulties and in greatest need of skilled teachers are assigned to untrained assistants (Blatchford *et al.* 2012). Children tend to be especially affected by these oppositions,[10] associated with contradiction (C) *structural dialectical contradictions*, the theme of this chapter and epitomised in 'master–slave relations'. These set the conditions for (D) *geo-historically specific dialectical contradictions*, which emerge from (C) and lead to crises, changes or transformations in particular contexts. Contradictions within unstable inequalities eventually erupt in time and space into, for example, protests about rocketing prices, or youth unemployment, or political repression. These reactions cannot precisely be predicted, because many interacting open systems influence change, but the trends can generally be foretold (Bhaskar [1993] 2008b: 59).[11]

Contradiction (E) *generative separation* involves deeper structural oppositions and alienation[12] at the core of human being and relations. Alienation involves the absence of ties or bonds and this is illustrated in many schools. Young children are highly enthusiastic and self-organised learners: babies work out that sounds have meaning, they quickly learn one or more languages and by 4 years of age, and earlier, children have mapped out their basic lifelong concepts about self/others, time/space, art, science and technology (Gardner 1993). When they begin formal education, many children retain this enthusiasm and initiative, but others lose it. Noddings (2002: 216) poignantly commented: 'I have never encountered a child under, say, seven who does not love poetry. But I almost never encounter a teen-ager who likes it . . . in our schools . . . we have wrecked the experience of poetry' by emphasising dissection instead of pleasure. Noddings cited examples of joy and happiness, such as in natural spaces, learning and companionship, which she considered schools 'wreck' by devaluing them or by turning direct experiences (ontology) into dry theory (epistemology). Donaldson (1978) and many others have shown how, in effect, children learn primarily through ontology, through being and doing, whereas schools concentrate on verbal instruction – epistemology.[13]

When they are around 15 years old, in some East Asian countries (Cho 1995; Field 1995), school students study for up to 18 hours a day, largely through rote and memory learning. Their exhaustion and disaffection relate to five additional splits identified by Marx. They are split from: (a) the means and materials of production (control over their learning resources, processes and outcomes) and (b) their labour, when they cannot choose or organise their own topics, methods and timing of learning; (c) their material transactions with nature, and their own bodily and health needs; (d) their social relations with others – peers, teachers, parents, when they are fixed into relations of extreme, anxious competition rather than cooperation. In (e) they are ultimately split from themselves. Stress, obesity, lethargy, depression, self-harming and rising suicide rates are symptoms of this splitting away from how young people might otherwise be living, learning and relating.

Beyond documenting these problems, Field and Cho consider the underlying contradictions, such as: the extreme shortage of university places; very high failure and rejections rates; lifelong (down)grading of non-graduate workers' abilities fixed by their final school exam marks that never recognise later personal development; dissatisfaction among university students whose degree course is chosen by their scores and not by their preferences; students' loss of creative, critical thinking; and the way their (also alienated) mothers and teachers, fixed on the future rather than the present, feel compelled to enforce these regimes. There is great anxiety about economic survival, and students' chances of obtaining reasonably well-paid, secure employment so that they can support dependent and ageing family members where there is little state welfare. Further layers of analysis involve government education policies, school management and resources that are ever more firmly squeezed, and the pressures of international league tables. Scott's (2010) critical realist analysis reveals how league tables do not simply assess what is taught. They reduce teaching and learning into easily tested processes, and into alienating, fragmented, correct/incorrect information (see also Beder 2009). Politicians cite international school league tables all aiming for their country's score to be high, without perhaps realising the cost to students in some high-scoring countries.

Absences in highly pressured schools, families and policies, and in children's and adults' free agency, connect with the TINA denial of reality. TINA ironically refers to the prime minister, Mrs Thatcher's, deceptive claim 'there **is no** alternative' to monetarism (Bhaskar [1993] 2008b: 114–18). TINA is sustained, bolstered and legitimated by a set of mystifying, misinforming contradictions of power$_2$ forces, false arguments, laws, practices and structures. An example is the TINA argument that schooling must be compulsory.[14] In England, this supports policies to make school attendance compulsory up to 18 years of age, 'truancy sweeps' by the police, fines and imprisonment for parents whose children miss school, and deeply held TINA assumptions that many children have to be forced and punished into learning. This can result in alienated students feeling 'separated, split, torn and estranged from oneself, or what is essential and intrinsic to one's nature or identity . . . to be alienated is to lose part of one's autonomy' (Bhaskar [1993] 2008b: 114) in the 'dialectic of malaise' (p. 287) in one's knowing and being on all four planes of social being. The alternative would be to reconsider the natural necessity of young children's avid learning and how schools could nurture this more fully through the dialectic of equity and de-alienation (pp. 287–92) to avoid the splits and alienation in education, explored in great detail, for example, by John Holt (1964) and many others. Child–adult relations have destructive as well as creative and life-giving potential within larger economic and political structures and contradictions.

Generation in childhood studies

Childhood studies, by establishing childhood as a distinct social structure, enabled *intergenerational relations* to be theorised in adulthood–childhood dualisms. Leena Alanen (1994) was concerned that large studies risk producing overly economic and essentialist analyses, which attribute too much to biological age and too little to social contexts and constructions of childhood. Alanen (2011: 167) recalled how she advocated 'empirical study to find out what actually is the constitutive principle in the social ordering, and organising, of child-adult relations'. She built on feminist concepts of gendering in order to theorise 'generationing' in how child/adult relations, positions and practices are produced, maintained, and occasionally transformed, in each different context. Youth is seen as 'a social category constituted in relation to, and indeed in opposition to, the category adult, as is feminine to masculine' (Fitz and Hood-Williams 1982: 65, cited in Alanen 2011: 160). Alanen planned micro studies of and with children to examine the circumscribing generational order, within which children 'construct' their social lives, relationships and life trajectories (Alanen 2011: 161). Childhood and adulthood are seen as mutually constituted and interdependent, reproduced through intergenerational interactions, through which a particular social structure or organisation of social relations recurrently emerges.

Alanen and Mayall (2001), Mayall (2002, 2011), Punch (2005) and others have empirically researched how people variously 'do' parenting, childing and generationing, in terms of social questions and not natural givens. They have reflected with children about their own views and roles, and the structures and rules in their lives, finding, for example, how much more autonomy children enjoy at home than at school.

Feminists analyse how basic but narrow biological, sexual differences (intransitive ones in DCR terms) are greatly amplified and broadened by (transitive and questionable) socially constructed, patriarchal, ruling relations of gender. Childhood studies similarly show how intransitive, biological age differences are exaggerated by transitive, socially constructed, adult-centric, ruling relations between generations. 'The social order is also always a generational order' (Alanen 2011: 171), although underlying power discrepancies in relations of age (or sex) are not natural, given or inevitable. Detailed analyses reveal and challenge the hermeneutics, when adult/child dyads are seen to reconstruct old stereotypes, such as victim child/rescuing adult. These are held consciously and subconsciously, when processes of emancipating $power_1$ and more commonly restricting $power_2$ relations, of older over younger generations seem standard, 'normal' and inexorable through being constantly reinforced.

Alanen (1994, 2011), Zeiher (2003, 2010), and Mayall (2002; Mayall and Zeiher 2003) have drawn on Karl Mannheim's concept that each generation forms specific internal alliances in its responses to social and political movements.[15] For Mannheim ([1928] 1952) each age cohort consciously shares a cultural life stage, significant events and historical emergence during their youth. They also share potential for intellectual and social change. One example is the generation of *Thatcher's Children* (Pilcher and Wagg 1996). In another, Zeiher (2003) examined the 1930s German depression, the 1930s–40s war and defeat, with the effects on families and children when women were swept into factories for the war effort, then back into the home and kitchen, and later in the 1970s when they returned into the expanding industries. Mayall (in press) comments that German sociologists were perhaps the first to connect empirical work on children's daily lives and perspectives to social structures.

Alanen (2011: 161) saw the concept of 'generational order' as a tool to analyse adult–child interactions: 'For social practice the implication is that childhood and adulthood are produced and reproduced interdependently, mutually, reciprocally constituted in their social roles and interactions and recurring intergenerational practices'. She quoted Mannheim on:

> specifying the structure within which and through which location groups emerge in historical-social reality. Class-position was based upon the existence of a changing economic and power structure in society . . . Generation location is based on [biological rhythms and] a common location in the historical dimension of the social process.
>
> *(Mannheim [1928] 1952: 289–90)*

Alanen considers that Mannheim takes a Weberian situational, relational view of class and generation (in my terms 'alongside') in the probability of each class or group of people enjoying relatively more or fewer material and social goods and life chances as a result of their relative control over goods and skills. Alanen (2011: 170–1) mentions that children's powers or lack of them 'derive' from structures, which reveal 'the range and nature of the agency of concrete, living children'. 'The source of their agency in their capacity as children is to be found in the social organisation of generational relations.'

Generation is complicated, like gender, in being personal as well as political. Men and women, adults and children (usually when in the same class) live together and interact, communicate and know one another far more fully than members of different classes tend to do. Intimate, reciprocal, loving relationships and kinship ties can nurture empathy and equality. Power$_2$ patriarchy in families is endemic but not inevitable.

Uniquely, unlike social class or gender, generation involves total movement from one group into the other: children become adults; adults have been children and they continue in some sense to be the children of their parents. Moreover, when adults age they rely increasingly on younger people, and power relations may be reversed. It is therefore in adults' future interests not to abuse their power. Children's position is weakened when those with most skill and knowledge constantly become adults, and are replaced by less experienced younger ones.[16] In the Children's Parliament in Rajasthan where working children aged 6–14 years organise their night schools, girls who are expert prime ministers and other senior officers have to leave when they are about 14 to get married (John 2003). However, these groups demonstrate young people's great achievements.

Ruling classes claim that their enduring power, far from being abuse, is their right and duty (like the colonial 'white man's burden') and is also in everyone's best interests. This Marxian concept of 'false-consciousness', or *mystifying* of the reality, is propagated as a routine part of class power (Bhaskar [1993] 2008b: 71). It entails complicated similarities to the 'master–slave' paternalism on which the mystifying is modelled. Parents and teachers can truly claim that their power$_1$ nurtures, educates and protects children. The difficulty lies in knowing when necessary, creative power$_1$ becomes oppressive power$_2$, which usurps and unnecessarily delays the emerging equality between growing children and their adult carers.

Between the extremes of determinism and voluntarism, as mentioned, DCR theorises structures that powerfully influence but do not necessarily determine human agency. And this raises questions about how and why structure–agency interaction occurs in different times and places and age groups. Childhood studies extensively research these questions, and DCR's contribution is to clarify the underlying philosophical concepts and debates about the necessary conditions for childhood – and for childhood research – to exist. Bhaskar contends that people often sustain, reinforce or resist social structures unintentionally. They work, marry and have children for personal reasons, while inadvertently reproducing structures of capitalism, marriage, family, childhood and generation. Babies are the inadvertent agents of generation who alter everyone's identity and status, transforming adults into parents and grandparents, aunts and uncles, and other children into siblings and cousins. Babies perpetuate families and indeed humanity and, as reviewed earlier, they soon begin to consolidate and interact within increasingly interdependent, intergenerational relationships. In embodying the genetic fusion and regeneration of different families, often of different ethnicities, babies are the visible glue of society.

Childhood and youth researchers deconstruct oppressive power$_2$ assumptions through emancipatory empirical research about children's and young people's 'mature, adult-like' activities: employment and labour movements (Boyden and Bourdillon 2012; Fassa *et al.* 2010; Heesterman 2005; Invernizzi 2008; Kemp 2005; Liebel 2004; Mizen *et al.* 2001; Nieuwenhuis 2011; Vandenhole *et al.* 2010); civil rights (de Schweinitz 2005; Reynolds 1995); organising schools (Alderson 1999a, 1999b; Apple 2012; Highfield School 1997; John 2003); being a parent (Rolfe 2005); heading a household (Meintjes *et al.* 2010); living in deprived, violent inner cities (Butler 1998; Katz 2005; Nadesan 2010) and on the streets (Biaya 2005; Glauser 1997; Goldstein 2003); political journalism (Acharya 2011; Headliners 2012 – see www.headliners.org); active use of the social media (de Block and Buckingham 2007); criminal justice (Goldson and Muncie 2009); armed conflict (Brett and Specht 2004; Drumbl 2012; Honwana 2006; Rosen 2005); holding views on nuclear power (Stephens 1996); migration (Bailey 2011; Han 2006) asylum-seeking (Pinson *et al.* 2010); and as 'makers and breakers' of their societies (Honwana and De Boeck 2005). Monica Barry's (2005) collection on experiences such as being a young carer and being homeless includes commentaries by young people. Within the seemingly inexorable structures of age-generation, few essential differences between the generations are easily identified. Uncertainty about the end of childhood is shown in the differing legal age of marriage, usually 18, though in the UK 16 years, and young people aged 16 can vote in Austria, Brazil, Ecuador, Iran and other countries. Many children and young people are less constrained by intransitive lack of capacity than by transitive prejudices, barriers and laws. Like women, children may have to be extra-competent to overcome these barriers. Those who are the main carer of a sick or disabled adult say that the hardest part is to cope without the respect and support that adult carers can expect (Evans and Becker 2009).

Emancipatory research attends to children's and young people's own views about age-related roles. In South Africa, in 2006, an estimated 122,000 children lived in child-headed households. One study found that most of them had at least one living parent, and most of them adamantly wanted to live with their siblings, and not in foster care or orphanages. They were responsible and resilient and behaved 'like adults'; their maturity being less related to their age than to their social context and experience (Meintjes *et al.* 2010). They showed the importance of research that, first, separates the intransitive ontology of children's capacities from the transitive, intergenerational social concepts about children's needs and immaturity and, second, examines how the two interact and reconstruct one another.

The adult and child generations have moved apart over the past century in the minority world. The legal, cultural and economic emancipation of adults has moved many women and working men, black, disabled and gay adults away from the subordinate state they once partly shared with children. Their move into greater adult freedom and equality has inevitably distanced children from mainstream society, in symbolic and practical exclusions. Moves towards desired (adult) freedom involve moving away from somewhere, and this absented, deficient, un-free area often relates to childhood generally, or to adults' own former childhood, or to how children limit women's lives, careers and income.[17] 'Adult' and 'grownup' are terms of respect; whereas 'childish' is one of denigration, variously and paradoxically used (in news reports during 2012) to describe bankers' irresponsible greed and politicians' feuds, vanity and futile war-making, although such behaviours are adults' prerogative.

Early research on adolescence (which means 'becoming adult') treated youth primarily as a medical-psychological state. Adolescence was partly invented by Stanley Hall (1904) in his great tome with its long chapters on puberty. Hall wrote amid concern in the USA about how to meld the many new immigrants into a unified nation, and he lent scientific validity to economic policies to extend schooling. In industrial countries, a second formative decade of education and socialisation after childhood came to be deemed necessary, to produce a skilled workforce. This expanded the 'scholarisation' of childhood (Denzin 1977), adults' power and status as the guardians of knowledge, and the supposed division between the generations, who are primarily either learning or else labouring, although in reality many do both activities throughout life.

Structures of generation in adulthood studies

Mannheim's theory is generally applied to generational cohorts, of younger and older adults, and although children are also centrally involved, their part is seldom mentioned. Two adult-centred examples are given here to illustrate the kind of broad-ranging analysis which childhood studies could develop. The examples explain how the 'baby boomers' have cheated later generations. Francis Beckett (2010) follows the British baby boomers, born between 1945 and 1955, through each decade of their lives. In 1948, despite enormous national debt following World War II, the British government implemented the great Acts, such as on social security and the National Health Service (NHS). The aim was to defeat the giants of want, ignorance, disease, squalor and idleness, which had tormented every previous generation. So successful was the new welfare state, Beckett argues, that the baby boomers never knew the terrible force of the five giants. Neither did they care, which is partly why, he believes, they are dismantling universal benefits and health services now. The 1950s saw the end of the British Empire and growing social division and public cynicism in Britain about politics, religion and society. Beckett dismisses the baby boomers' famous student protest movements in the 1960s as cynical, vacuous and pleasure-seeking, vague about what they were against, and what they were for. The best year to be alive in Britain is estimated to be 1976. Since then there have been increases in crime, family breakdown, inequality, benefit cuts, cost of living and pollution (Garnett 2007: 1). Beckett details trends since the 1970s that are gradually demolishing the welfare state. The baby boomers are still a most powerful force in Britain. Often on generous pensions, they are most likely to vote, to spend on luxuries, and to protest vociferously in their own interests (Demos 2004).[18] Politicians' dependence on their votes is shown by the austerity cuts from 2012 onwards to benefits, services and future pensions, which mainly affect younger age groups, but leave pensioners' benefits, such as free travel, untouched. Given the rapid rise in longevity, many baby boomers might live to be 110 or older and exert their generation's power for another 40 years or more.

There are 16.7 million British baby boomers, born 1945–52, but their children, born 1979–94, the so-called 'jilted generation', consist of only 13 million. They are outweighed by their parents' numbers and even more by their political and economic clout. Ed Howker and Shiv Malik (2010) reviewed intergenerational impacts on their own jilted age group. They were the first generation to incur huge debts through having to repay higher education fees, just when house prices were rocketing, and employment prospects were falling. Howker and Malik traced the origins of present problems back to the 1980s. Although the housing crisis has become ever more severe since council houses were sold off during the 1980s and were never replaced, fewer, smaller and poorly insulated new houses and flats are being built. Most are unsuitable for young families, and housing is likely to be bought and let out for rent on six-month contracts by older householders, to young people who cannot afford a deposit. Being homeless, or in short-term tenancies, or being unable to move out of their parents' home, affects young people's whole life, as does short-term, agency and casual employment. They are less able to have a permanent address, live with a partner in a stable relationship, start a family, develop a career, fulfil hopes and ambitions, save and invest generally in their long-term future and identity. Young people anxiously drift (Sennett 1998). During the prosperous year 2005, one-quarter of 16–17-year-olds were unemployed, and young people's wages stagnated, while other workers enjoyed soaring pay rises. Since then unemployment among young people and young adults has been increasing, with ever widening gaps between higher paid (usually older) and lower paid (usually younger) workers. To avoid paying out pensions and to continue collecting taxes, governments encourage higher-paid older people's continued employment rather than supporting youth employment. Politicians blame young people's lack of skills, rather than the lack of jobs, and employ older people to train and support unemployed young people rather than finding or creating fairly paid work for them.

During the 1980s and 1990s, most people in the richer minority world lived in unprecedented luxury, increasingly subsidised by outsourced labour, and goods and services supplied by exploited minority world workers. Despite all their current wealth, the baby boomers also borrowed from the future, such as by remortgaging their homes to subsidise their spending, because they assumed the price of housing would always rise. In 2008, the bubble of housing and banking finances, lending and debt, burst, while public and private debts continued at all time highs.

Howker and Malik also analyse the economic and societal inheritance, including national assets and the welfare state, formerly carefully preserved and enriched and passed on to succeeding generations but, since the 1970s, filched, sold or destroyed by the baby boomers in new short-term politics. Mainly concerned to win the next election, politicians appeal to the wavering views of floating voters, not to their own supporters, so that policies and mandates have become hollowed out or concealed. The authors connect all the debt, quick profit-making and short-termism to new, collective, dysfunctional attitudes towards time, which put intergeneration relationships out of joint.

These lucid, broad-ranging, interdisciplinary, detailed books about social structures analyse how older generations are damaging the lives of younger adults. Children and young people are as much if not more affected, but so far there is no equivalent work about them. Multi-authored collections lack the sustained argument. Qvortrup and colleagues (2011: 6) wonder if children's 'smallness' conceptually incarcerates 'them in a micro world . . . of particularism' when they 'are seldom studied as people who are part of a universal, cosmopolitan or global orbit'. They consider it vital to study 'whether, how and to what extent they are differently impacted [on] than adults'.

Missing social structures in childhood research

This closing section considers researchers' problems with positioning children within social structures. Critical realists such as the sociologist Christian Smith argue that social structures, and their latent and evident causal powers, need to be understood for their subjective, transitive, expressive components, and for their objective, intransitive realities. He is committed to discovering generalisable theories, abstract knowledge, and comparisons from empirical instances when, he considers, attention to structures is crucial. He accepts, however, DCR's retroductive analysis, that open structures and totalities cannot yield unanimous, uniform results in either the social or natural sciences. Smith (2011: 329) searches for 'real, general, underlying and manifest entities, principles, properties, mechanisms, and processes that exist and operate across a range of historical and empirical types of facts, circumstances and events'. This fits DCR's aim, reviewed in earlier chapters, to involve social science in *explaining* as well as *describing* society.

Jens Qvortrup and others are concerned that childhood studies attend fairly seldom to vital social structures, and I will suggest possible reasons for this neglect. The reasons are connected to researchers' concern with children's agency, their inductive research methods, their use of qualitative and of quantitative methods, the concealed nature of many structures in minority world settings, and types of specialist knowledge.

First, there is childhood researchers' welcome respect for children as competent and worthy research participants, which tends to set agency and social constructionist approaches before structural ones. Linked to this concern with agency is children's seeming absence from social structures. For example, in economics, minority world children tend to be seen as liabilities not assets, rarely or never as earners, owners, investors, entrepreneurs, managers of budgets, householders, debtors, or as people who could or should work their way out of poverty. Trapped in their parents' poverty, they inadvertently increase it in two main ways: as expensive dependants, and as depriving parents, who take time away from paid work to care for their children, of 'foregone' income, career, and pension opportunities (Davies and Joshi 2001; Dex and Joshi 2005; Hansen *et al.* 2010; Vleminckx and Smeeding 2001).[19] Even researchers with positive approaches towards children still attend mainly to their relatively passive experiences of having poor or wealthier parents (Pantazis *et al.* 2006; Qvortrup 1991, 2011; Qvortrup *et al.* 1994, 2011; Ridge 2002). For example, Pantazis *et al.* (2006: 206–7) note increased rates of mental illness among British debtors aged 'under 60' (and incidentally over 16, in other words they mean adults) but they do not discuss children's mental illness or the care that children provide for their mentally ill parents. And those who research child carers tend to take personal rather than structural approaches (Becker *et al.* 2001; Evans and Becker 2009). In these ways, children tend to be passive or elusive in research about social structures.

A second reason for childhood studies' relative inattention to structures is when researchers begin with children's observed experiences and use inductive methods such as grounded theory. This postpones the difficult task of searching for generalisations, and of relating examples to broader structures. In contrast, deductive methods common in quantitative research, and less used in childhood studies, start from general hypotheses often linked to structures.

This is linked to the third reason, the preferred qualitative research methods.[20] The time-consuming data collection methods, ethnographies, lengthy observations and detailed interviews limit the size of samples, and thereby reduce the scope for making generalisations. However, even a small study can produce thousands of pages of notes and transcripts about diverse and unique childhoods. I have found that the rewarding stages of collecting and then becoming immersed in what I regarded as my precious data could deter the analytical processes of ruthlessly selecting, editing, dissecting and grouping the complicated examples, especially when I had enjoyed quite close relationships with my generous young interviewees. When analysing their experiences of major surgery (Alderson 1993), I felt that I was almost re-subjecting them to a quasi-surgical experience, by disrespectfully slicing through their narratives, retaining fragments and discarding most of their data. And unlike surgery, my work was not even intended to benefit those children and young people directly, when I aimed to process their experiences into impersonal generalisations.

Fourth, quantitative research can raise similar problems in attempts to generalise, when covariate analysis breaks down the whole sample into many subsections. One effect can be to seem to treat structural concepts, such as types of poverty, parenting styles or housing tenure, not as structures but as variables and, implicitly, as personal attributes. Agency can then seem to be unrealistically powerful. For instance, mothers who become unemployed are said 'to move into poverty' (Hansen *et al.* 2010), whereas the mothers may neither choose nor control such moves, and the powers that do so are not explained. Causal structures become hazy or invisible when the carousel of covariates vaguely appears to spread equal power and causal effects among all the variables. For example:

> Mothers who reported being happier with their relationships had children with significantly higher vocabulary scores. This relationship was reduced, although it remained statistically significant, by the addition of the other covariates, suggesting that it is partly explained by the parent, family and child variables.
>
> *(Hansen et al. 2010: 68)*

Although the authors tentatively admit stronger associations between all the collective variables of either advantage or disadvantage, they immediately add that there are exceptions and some disadvantaged children do well. They may wish to avoid stigmatising and overly rigid, pessimistic warnings, although they imply, perhaps inadvertently, that agency can unquestioningly overpower the (unexplained) structures. This can raise doubts about families who fail to overcome and achieve, and can divert concern away from their structural disadvantages. Hansen *et al.* (p. 269) admit that from their data 'it is not self-evident why children of richer parents do better', while the benefits of government policies are uncertain. When causes and mechanisms of disadvantage remain uncertain, so do policy recommendations; instead of practical transformation, they may dwindle, for instance, into proposals to advise mothers more on childcare (epistemology). When health research concentrates on adults' and children's deficits and dysfunctions, it underestimates their positive assets, agency, achievements and potential to interact strongly with structures (Morgan *et al.* 2010).

A fifth reason for inattention to structures could be that, especially in the minority world where most childhood research is conducted, children's confined lives tend to highlight empirical interpersonal levels and to miss concealed, underlying structures. A comparison between studies in Europe and in Africa illustrates this point. William Corsaro's decades of research vividly record young children's creative preoccupation with interactions and relationships. Corsaro (2011) described an Italian nursery where for weeks 2- to 3-year-olds played a game of walking and jumping on a line of chairs, not exactly forbidden by the staff but certainly not encouraged. Corsaro wrote of the Italian children 'challenging' the staff, and in a Finnish preschool of escalating 'mischief', play with forbidden 'smuggled' toys, 'sly' smiles, and 'avoiding or delaying' tactics when play was interrupted and restricted. Corsaro implies an adult judgement, though he also conveys children's irritation with fussy rules and adult micromanagement: 'Clean up time is dumb, dumb, dumb. We could just leave our trucks here and play with them after snack time!' (p. 306).

Cindy Katz (2004) conducted very different research in a Sudanese village around 1980. The children helped at home, cared for younger children, tended fields, herded animals, hauled water, collected wood and helped to make charcoal, besides attending school. One day they walked, without adults (except for the researcher), for over an hour to a distant wood where they picked berries, made fires and collected buckets of ash. Young children made their own elaborate games, with toys and dolls modelled out of natural and discarded objects. They created detailed farms and tools, while playing about their real agricultural and domestic life and work. Games followed the seasons, from sowing seeds to marketing harvests. Children played in mixed age groups, when younger ones show much greater skill than they can in narrowly age-banded groups (Gardner 1993; Dunn 2004). They also played without adult supervision, sharing, negotiating, resolving disputes and avoiding danger. Katz showed the pressures on Sudanese children of poverty and hard work. Yet the children enjoyed freedom of movement, of friendships and play, of the natural world, as well as responsible work and agency; boys played games of skill and chance and went swimming while they herded goats. They knew about realities such as seasonal change. The community was safe (then) with close contacts between all the children and adults.

In these remarkably different childhoods, children had different relationships with structures. European children tend to be researched within educational institutions, separated from mainstream society, in highly organised and equipped indoor and outdoor spaces, often with little scope for free, vigorous movement, and with tightly organised timetables. The most apparent structure here is of generation, of adult control and children's subtle or open resistance. Other structures are concealed or absent: global agriculture, industry, trade and transport that supply the consumer goods to the preschools; the division of labour that separates children from adult workplaces; piped utilities and invisible waste disposal services; the many layers of management, training and inspection to organise children's centres in England (HM Treasury *et al.* 2003; DfE 2007); the massive debts of the public-private children's centres and schools building programme (Ball 2007). The children may rarely walk around local streets and shops or see how neighbourhoods work. They are under-informed to the extent of being misinformed about all the structures, the labour, policies, resources and finances that support them. These absent or invisible structures, with the agents' highly visible interactions, have perhaps led minority world childhood researchers to concentrate on interpersonal agency over structure.

Katz's work reflects how the Sudanese children were in touch with deep structures and the natural necessity of human being: agriculture, the seasons and the great effort of producing and selling food; multi-task subsistence work in an interdependent community; relationships between every age group over the life course instead of narrow age-banding; personal friendships and conflicts, which children learned to manage themselves; scarcity so that resources were highly valued. Corsaro (2011: 312) considered that children's play is similar across the world but that poor children 'often adapt their play routines more closely to the often harsh and challenging realities of their daily lives'. They also deal with teasing and conflict more easily than 'middle-class children in western societies' do, when adults' prompt interventions prevent them from learning how to resolve disagreements. In other words, many children in the majority world directly experience, and are more aware of, human social and natural necessity within powerful structures.

Child autonomy raises contradictions between talk (epistemology) and practice (ontology). Very broadly, middle-class, wealthier adults talk of offering choices and respect to children, but their intense managing of their children enforces a fairly helpless dependence or resistance. Children may be allowed to choose the colour of their felt-pens, but not whether to attend the children's centre or wander around their neighbourhood, or where to be, or whom to be with. Conversely, disadvantaged adults may expect unquestioning obedience and hard work from children, but in practice may trust them to be very responsible and independent in much of their unsupervised work, play and relationships. Childhood itself is then structured in different intergenerational relationships of (in)dependence. It may be harder to research structures within 'child-centred' spaces, away from the 'adult', real working and natural worlds.

A final possible reason for neglect of structures might be childhood researchers' specialist knowledge. This tends to be about childhood and youth with a broad sociology or psychology background. 'Adult' researchers, however, tend to specialise in their topic and may therefore be more aware of its structures, whether urban planning or politics, economics or physics, as might their adult interviewees too. One example is law. Michael Freeman (2007, 2011, 2012) is unusual in being a lawyer who studies childhood from a legal perspective, whereas childhood researchers generally start with observing children and then applying law. They often miss basic legal concepts, such as that a right is something specific that can be willed and enforced, and can ultimately be sanctioned in the courts. No one has an (unenforceable) right to love or to health, 'to a childhood' (UNICEF 2010)[21] or 'to childhoods' (Hartas 2008), or to be 'properly researched' (Beazley *et al.* 2009). The idea that 'developing a positive identity is fundamental to realising every child's rights' (Brooker and Woodhead 2008: Preface)[22] could imply that children need 'a positive identity', with subjective high self-esteem and praise from others, if their rights to clean water, healthcare, education and freedom from unjust, cruel, humiliating or degrading treatment are to be respected. Yet rights are realised through social and political structures and are for everyone, not only for the well-adjusted. These are instances of structures being overlooked in childhood studies.

Studies of children's competent agency have challenged negative stereotypes and helped to promote respect for children. They need to be complemented by research that examines structural causes, explanations and mechanisms of change, and obstructions to it, beyond empirical, actual and interpersonal levels. In DCR, to summarise points in this chapter: structures and mechanisms *generate tendencies*, but not inevitable effects, because they work in complex open systems. Invisible, causal social structures and mechanisms (the third deep layer of natural necessity) exist whether or not they become evident in the two higher layers of the empirical and the actual. They become evident through the events and experiences they generate. Events emerge both from causal structures and through agents' causal intentions and reasons. Structures can contradict, conflict, and also cohere in constellations. Structures, events and agents are constrained by time and space, and social structures involve inherited knowledge and technologies, material and cultural resources.

6

INNER BEING

Alienation and flourishing

Interviews with children aged four to seven years, who had been severely neglected and abused, involved them in decorating a small box with craft materials. On the outside they showed what kind of person they felt they were, and on the inside they expressed their wishes and feelings.[1]

'Crystal' aged five seemed cheerful and confident on the outside of her box. 'It says that I am happy and kind and I love visiting my friends.' Later on, the inside about her baby sister was sad. 'My baby who died, this is the baby's eyes and teeth and that is a wee hat and hair.' Asked what she would tell her mother, Crystal said, 'You's[2] stop arguing 'cos the kids is trying and the kids is missing you.'

'Connor', her brother aged seven, said: 'Me wishes is um, er, to keep people happy . . . On this bit of card, er, write me the word "sad" and I'm gonna glue it down in my box so no-one can see it . . . One more not nice feeling and that is, er, what's that word with "m" [pause] miserable. Could you do that on card for me? [Long pause while he makes a fence of sellotape and lollipop sticks.] I put a fence round my feelings; that's why I don't want no-one to see them.'

(Winter 2010)

Crystal and Connor were aware of painful contradictions between their public behaviour and their private states of mind. Secure and academically able children are expected to show the most advanced mental development, but adversity is a powerful educator as these young children showed. Across the world, despite many benign policies and interventions, the youngest children are at highest risk of experiencing extreme neglect, abuse and injury, malnutrition and illness. Yet they are the least listened to, in the common misbelief that those aged under 8 years cannot form or express reliable views, and neither need nor want to be informed or listened to (Winter 2006, 2011). There is an absence of interest in young children as persons with complicated self-awareness. The neglect may be part of adults' own self-protective evasions, when they feel unable to help the children, or to bear the pain of listening to their distress.

Given the previous chapter on the importance of structures, it might seem odd to return here to individuals. Yet structure and individual agency exist and are understood through the dialectic between them. DCR re-emphasises this old idea. After embodied, interpersonal and social structural being (in Chapters 3 to 5) inner being (in this chapter) covers all the other aspects of human life. Also referred to as the person or mind, the soul or self, it is the fourth plane of social being. Although not often mentioned in childhood studies, the inner self is so central to the more usually researched concerns of agency, learning, developing, relating, need, ethics, citizenship and welfare that it needs to be critically examined, rather than taken for granted. Personal inner being underlies the meaning and processes of misery and alienation and the transformation towards the well-being or flourishing of individuals and of whole societies. These are the concern of MELD 4D, the fourth dimension, to complement and fulfil the first three moments of MELD.

I will begin by considering concepts of flourishing and the complications of researching them. Then I will review the debates about whether the social sciences can and should be value-free and neutral, and I will aim to make the case that they are inevitably moral and value-informed. This prepares for the section that outlines MELD 4D, followed by an example of a DCR approach to freedom. The main part of the chapter is a review of the history of ideas about the human person, soul or self, ideas which are partly religious, philosophical, scientific, psychological, social, theoretical and empirical. These ideas have become increasingly split apart and contradictory. The final section begins to consider how to interpret the contradictions in order to make sense of the young inner self, of alienation, misery and flourishing in childhood today. These themes will be continued into Chapter 7.

Some DCR concepts introduced earlier will reappear, to show different ways and contexts in which they apply, and to assist readers who are new to DCR to digest and remember their meaning. Once more I have attempted to summarise and condense intricate and lengthy discussions in the DCR and other literature. I have aimed to highlight a few of the ideas that seem to be most relevant to practical childhood research. I can only aim to provide very brief, though I hope reasonably accurate, summaries and introductions, and to refer readers to the background literature.

Flourishing

Since the aims of DCR and MELD are to promote flourishing in individuals and societies, this section considers theories of human flourishing. Does flourishing only exist in adults or in children too? Might it even depend on experiences in early childhood? The 'flourishing' person and society are controversial concepts about what human beings are, or could, or should be like, and what they need in order to flourish and to lead the good or happy life. Beliefs about the good life have been highlighted in resurrection or reincarnation myths. These relate the meaning, purpose and value of this present life to an idealised afterlife that may be more fulfilling (or tormenting) and possibly more deserved than the present one. The early Egyptians' *Book of the Dead* about the afterlife was thought to have inspired the later Greek ideas of Elysium (Faulkner 1990). On average, people lived only 34 years and their poignant, vividly depicted idea of eternal bliss was to paddle on the Nile in small boats and to grow corn for the gods, activities enjoyed by adults and children alike.

The prospect of judgement, reward or punishment in an afterlife invested new meaning in present actions. It offered incentives for moral striving, hope of future happiness for the presently disadvantaged, or else threats and bribes to quell their present discontent. In parallel, children are pacified, bribed or threatened while they also prepare for their 'afterlife' of adulthood. A multiple complication in attempts to define well-being, even if a definition is agreed for adults, is doubt about whether children too can or should enjoy well-being. Does it consist of certain rational, responsible adult freedoms that children must somehow earn or develop towards?

Happiness is variously sought along the spectrum from self-indulgence to Stoic, Christian and Buddhist self-denial and freedom from desire. For the wealthy, happiness has included having beautiful possessions and homes, paradise-like gardens, attentive servants or slaves, enjoyment of companionship, the arts and of power (for example, Diamond and Glynn 2008). Aristotle favoured intellectual and political engagement and friendship, the flourishing virtue in the power and excellence of fulfilled human nature and purpose. He believed that youths aged under 30, slaves, and many others could not attain *eudaimonia*, although he thought 'generous' youths were better at friendship than 'sour-tempered' old people (Aristotle 2004: 209–11). While some philosophers included in *eudaimonia* health, wealth, beauty and being a parent, others stressed aesthetic denial, virtuous thought and practical wisdom. Greek philosophers agreed that human beings want *eudaimonia* more than anything else (Martin and Baressi 2006).

Socrates associated a happy life with the virtues of self-control, courage, justice, piety and wisdom in mind and soul. He argued that 'everything the human spirit undertakes or suffers will lead to happiness when it is guided by wisdom, but to the opposite, when guided by folly' (Plato 1964: 142/88c). Stoicism, around 200 BCE, promoted equality of race, sex, age and class, with everyone being responsible for their own self and for the community. Stoicism identified well-being, first, with detachment from physical and emotional needs, pleasures, pains and anxieties, and second, at times, with concern for others (Martin and Baressi 2006). Significantly, much later, Freud associated childhood with egoism and lack of altruism, in secular echoes of the Puritan belief that children are born in original sin, while Piaget (1932) and Kohlberg (1981) aimed to prove, in scientific experiments, Kant's and Freud's theories about childhood's gradual ascent towards adult morality (Bradley 1989).

Derived from 'happenstance' or fate, the word 'happiness' signifies an elusive goal. Some believe that it is only a secondary, potential effect of other aims, such as to love or serve, to work or own. The US *Declaration of Independence* (US 1776) grants the right to 'the pursuit of happiness', suggesting a Kantian open freedom to follow one's own fate and values, but not to possess happiness itself as a specific or factual good. Similarly, the UNCRC (UN 1989: Preamble) cannot assure a 'right to happiness' but recognises 'that the child, for the full and harmonious development of his or her personality, should grow up in a family environment, in an atmosphere of happiness, love and understanding', and that all children's rights can contribute towards promoting and protecting this happiness.

Today's debates concern which goods, services, opportunities and capabilities every adult and child basically needs for a reasonably happy life. Economists varyingly emphasise either parents' obligations to provide adequate care and income for their children, or support from the state through benefits, amenities and services for all children, or at least for ensuring that no child falls below a certain level of relative poverty (Dex and Joshi 2005; Gordon *et al.* 2002; Hansen *et al.* 2010; Layard and Dunn 2009; Pantazis *et al.* 2006; Ridge 2002; Sen 1999; Townsend 1979; Townsend and Gordon 2002; Vleminckx and Smeeding 2001). Measures of well-being are derived from deficit evidence of the severe effects, to be avoided, of poverty, ill health, crime, failure, inequality and social exclusion. Alternatively, measures are drawn from 'ordinary' and disadvantaged people's views about the 'essential' things they need to have and to do. For many, well-being includes the basic social inclusion of being able to give presents and to have meals with friends (Pantazis *et al.* 2006; Townsend and Gordon 2002). Sayer (2011) proposes that, along with distributive rights, well-being is promoted when everyone's contributive rights to worthwhile, challenging work that benefits society are recognised.

Different weight is given to happiness as: material well-being; an emotion or relationship; an experience or activity; common or rare; a process or outcome; something found through self-interest or through altruism, and through public policy or individual endeavour. Even if the measures can be agreed, there are disagreements about whether they are best researched when measures are generated by investigators or by respondents, are objective or subjective, absolute or relative, personal accounts or assessed by others.

Richard Douthwaite (1999) criticised how the national gross domestic product (GDP) measures economic success in ways that counter people's well-being. All income and expenditure are counted positively in the GDP, whether they are 'goods' (services, products) or 'bads' (waste, clearing up after traffic crashes or oil spills). To buy a hamburger is better for the GDP than to grow and cook your own food. Sixteen adverse social health measures in the USA, including infant mortality, child abuse, child poverty, teenage suicides, drug use, mental illness and high-school drop-out rates, rose steadily from 1977 alongside rising GDP economic growth. Richard Layard (2006) was also dissatisfied with the GDP as the only measure of national well-being. He proposed a happiness index,[3] so that people's assessments of their satisfaction with life can influence policy.

Such thoughts on relations and obligations between individuals and society move towards political ideas of well-being. Aristotle (2004) believed that individuals can flourish only in the good or *eudaimonic* (though hierarchical) society. Millennia later, the similar though far more equitable vision of Marx and Engels ([1848] 1998) was that 'the free development of each is the condition for the free development of all'. These views have been developed by Nussbaum and Sen (1993), among others, into international, political theories of (mainly adult-centred) standards of living and well-being.

Given the diverging concepts and origins, forms and contexts of happiness or flourishing, how can researchers agree on its meaning, on how it might be perceived, experienced and described by either interviewees or researchers, and on which research methods and tools to use? Some researchers argue that well-being is too complex, subjective and elusive to fit into objective totals that can be measured, compared and replicated. Many others, especially in health and economics, are involved in measuring and assessing happiness and well-being.[4] In one example, children were asked, 'Which best describes how you feel about your life as a whole?' And they were invited to choose among seven faces with captions ranging from 'completely happy' to 'completely unhappy' (Layard and Dunn 2009: 8). The question overlooked the reality of ambivalent or fluctuating views, or mixed feelings when a child is happy about some things and not others. It assumes that children (and adults) know how they feel, and that they are able and willing to report something as mysterious as a passing mood accurately. International comparisons of children's well-being, such as UNICEF (2007), have extra problems of explicit language differences and subtle cultural ones (Morrow and Mayall 2010).

And yet to set aside children's flourishing, because of researchers' uncertainties and disagreements, would deprive childhood studies, and their potential contribution to policy-making, of perhaps its most vital concern.[5] Many concepts, such as childhood itself, are complex, but that invites rich multidisciplinary research on these topics, rather than exempting them from inquiry. And directly or indirectly, explicitly or not, most childhood research is designed to contribute towards improving children's lives and reducing unhappiness. This aim is based on beliefs about children's nature and well-being. Nevertheless, these beliefs are too often assumed and too seldom examined and debated critically. The theme of this chapter therefore is to examine underlying beliefs about children's nature and well-being.

One practical way forward could be to combine many research reports, whether positivist or interpretive, into critical overviews. These could go beyond the Cochrane Collaboration reviews on happiness, which attend to research methods and outcomes, and often dismiss all but a few papers that meet a required standard. Instead, the overviews might include theoretical discussions about the immense range and depth of children's flourishing or happiness. Overviews could show how many of the reports each contribute a tiny part towards the whole, acknowledging the partial limitations of each research method, and the need for cooperative, interdisciplinary research. To draw the different studies into some kind of cohesive union, frameworks could include happiness at the four planes of social being and the four moments of MELD. Transitive perceptions of happiness could be complemented with the partly intransitive, embodied, moral, social and political ontology of children's and young people's flourishing and its converse, misery.

An example awaiting interdisciplinary resolution occurred in a discussion between the economist Richard Layard and the philosopher Julian Baginni.[6] Layard was caught in a liberal and methodological trap. He felt that he must leave to individuals the freedom each to define their own source of happiness, while still claiming a factual, scientific basis for his well-being index and his measurements, such as by referring to hormonal cortisol levels. Baginni was equally trapped by insisting that happiness is not at all about facts, but only about immeasurable, abstract values. A way forward could be to explore, beyond their epistemic fallacies, how well-being and values have real, intransitive ontology in causes, structures and agency, as well as transitive interpretations.

One interpretation of inner health, quoting a 1974 paper in Norwegian by Siri Naess, sees the person as 'active, having good interpersonal relations, feeling self-esteem, and having a basic mood of joy'. Although 'joy' might seem to be an unrealistic and even oppressive requirement for well-being, it is shown to involve generally valued qualities:

> rich intense feelings of beauty, feeling close to nature, open and receptive, secure, harmonious, the absence of worry, anxiety and restlessness, a state of joy and compassion, finding life rich and rewarding, the absence of emptiness, depression, pain and discomfort . . .
>
> *(Lindstrom and Erikson 2010: 26–7)*

Young children often show these qualities. They can feel intense distress, which perhaps is an inevitable part of their capacity for joy and pleasure. Possibly our later emotions through life echo and are intensified by subconscious memories of emotions in babyhood. Lindstrom and Erikson contend that society gains more from allocating resources to children than to other age groups, not only to benefit their whole lifetime, but also their influence on future generations. Other researchers have added solidarity and further social concerns to Siri Naess's list, including 'ethics, equity, sustainable human settlements and ecology [to] create societies where we all can live well' (Lindstrom and Erikson 2010: 27).

Mozart, Schubert, Keats and Van Gogh are among many people who worked supremely well while being extremely ill. So while being desirable, good physical and mental health are not essential for certain kinds of flourishing. Instead, a far more inclusive view of people who live with severe illness, disability, disadvantage or adversity is that we might flourish, primarily, when we can manage the lack of control over our lives and bodies. Although money, knowledge, experience, culture and tradition immensely help to structure healthy lives, our ability to use them, and our sense of coherence (SOC),[7] could be more important than the actual resources. SOC involves the ability to manage many complex stressors, to cope with and resolve many tensions:

> People have to understand their lives and they have to be understood by others, perceive that they are able to manage the situation and, most importantly, perceive that it is meaningful enough to find motivation to continue [with] a feeling of an inner trust that things will be in order, independent of whatever happens . . . If we create processes where people perceive they are able to live the life they want to live, people will not only feel better but will also lead better lives.
>
> *(Lindstrom and Erikson 2010: 32–6 summarising*
> *Antonovsky 1979, 1987)*

This strong, purposeful autonomy might at first seem to be at odds with early childhood. Alternatively, it could be seen as central to young children's desire to be active and independent – such as to feed themselves as soon as they are able to – and central to their preoccupation with making sense of relationships, language, rules, meaning and order in their daily life. Antonovsky thought that SOC is formed in the first three decades of life. Like Archer's (2003) internal conversations, SOC raises vital questions for research about how it begins and can be nurtured in childhood.

Value-free social science?

Can and should the social sciences be either value-free or else morally informed? Comte's original aim to create a neutral social science modelled on the natural sciences, Hume's edict 'not to derive an ought from an is' and Kant's (1972: 90) wish to be 'wholly free from' inclinations, emotions, needs and contingent values have had lasting influence on social science (Sayer 2011; Seidler 1986). Positivists still eschew the 'bias' of values. Many social constructionists see all moralities as local and contingent and believe that researchers should scrutinise them but neither impose them nor adhere to them in their work (Lukes 2008).

The education sociologist Martyn Hammersley (1995: 18) believes that empiricism, which refuses to be subordinate to philosophy and positivism which 'abandons ethics and politics', should remain the 'primary model' for social research. Hammersley (2009) warns against critical realists' claims to derive values from observed facts, such as if they assume that starving people who might die therefore (morally) need to be fed. Hammersley (2009: 5–6) contends:

> 'need' is a quasi-evaluative term: it concerns an actual or potential gap between what is and what ought to be . . . there is a difference between what exists and what *would be* desirable or necessary, or undesirable or fundamentally unethical . . . [W]hat should or should not be done [cannot] be logically derived solely from social science evidence about the matter . . .

neither the social scientist nor the philosopher has any superior expertise or authority in [judging appropriate action] and very often there will be scope for disagreement.

(Original emphasis)

The starving people might be an oppressive army, he adds, and therefore researchers 'should strive to be value neutral or objective' in their own work, while accepting 'that value argument ... is essential to governance and to everyday life' (1995: 14).

The medical sociologist Clive Seale (1999) agrees with Hammersley in defending (neutral) liberalism against the ideologies of Marxism and feminism, which he sees as value-led, biased and overtly political. Seale (p. 3) also follows Norman Denzin (1988) in refuting the idea of objective study of an empirical world, when we now 'live in a postmodern world of multiple selves and endless fragmentation of experience', so that the grounds for truth, reliability, validity and agreed values have been lost. Instead, Seale (1999: 6) concentrates on methods, the craft of research, and he supports fallibilistic, 'genuinely self-critical research, so that something of originality and value is created, with which, of course, people are then free to disagree'.

However, in defence of explicitly value-informed research, Lukes (2008) comments that relativism reduces all values to local norms except the value of universal tolerance, prized above all other values including justice and respect. Yet tolerance hardly counts as a major value, and it is fairly meaningless and empty in that we 'tolerate' things we do not really respect or agree with.

The difficulty with disclaiming any grounds for truth and other values is to raise doubts about all comments (including the disclaimer), besides doubts about the grounds to justify any research reports and, therefore, the point of doing research at all. Even attempts to contribute to knowledge seem pointless if knowledge is simply, like fiction, sets of stories with which anyone is 'free to disagree', and when invention is easier and cheaper than data collection. In DCR terms, critics of values in research have collapsed intransitive ontology and the existence of real values as causes, into transitive epistemology. They have also removed the referent from the semiotic triangle (see Chapter 3).

Critics of explicit values in research are themselves unable to escape from making value judgements. Their supposedly neutral liberalism is as ideological as any other politics (Callinicos 2010; Fine 2010; Harvey 2005; O'Neill 1998). Hammersley argues against researchers jumping to moral conclusions (that the army should be fed). Critical realists would agree that research involves carefully working towards conclusions through argument and evidence, and not jumping to them. Nevertheless, by introducing the dilemma (should an oppressive army be fed?), far from proving a correct avoidance of values, Hammersley illustrates that social research is unavoidably value-laden. He thereby undermines his case that morality can be ignored, or deleted, or is irrelevant. Instead of being falsely inserted, moral values are integral to social facts.

Critical researchers are likely to agree with Hammersley that they are no more expert than anyone else about 'what is wrong and what ought to be done', and that simple answers are beyond their expertise. Their skill lies in collecting and analysing the evidence, the background details and participants' views as fairly and fully as possible, in pointing out ignorance and inconsistency and in making connections, perhaps by exploring future options and their potential short- and long-term effects. During their analysis, critical researchers will be informed by their own moral views and will question these. They do not necessarily have either more expertise than other people – or less expertise. Moral values are integral not only to social research but, as Hammersley agreed, to everyday human thinking. The critical realist Andrew Sayer (2011) questions why researchers are supposed to suspend their humanity when at work. He notes a double standard if social researchers attempt to delete values from their research, on which they depend in their daily lives and relationships. If they do suspend values in the content and processes of their work, they risk breaking the golden rule of always treating others with the same justice and respect as you would expect to be treated yourself.

'Objectivity' involves the important aims, vital to all researchers, of being fair and impartial when openly listening and trying to understand and report every side. But these distinct concepts have all been bundled into 'objectivity', which has been hijacked also to mean valuing everything neutrally, evenly, and inconclusively (unless an experiment seems to provide self-evident proof). If 'objectivity' extends into moral neutrality between, say, justice or injustice, flourishing or misery, then it has been loaded with unnecessary and unviable meanings.

Even 'value-free' researchers still rely on such values as veracity, accuracy and impartiality; on the trust they expect their participants, sponsors and readers to invest in fiduciary relationships with them; and also on their right to freedom to research, comment and publish. They can expect their reports, however seemingly neutral, to be understood, used and possibly manipulated by their readers in value-driven ways. There is the further difficulty, when researching unequal relationships, that there is no neutral central ground. Attempts at neutrality tend inadvertently to side with and reinforce the more powerful status quo. Chapter 5 mentioned the problems for children that researchers are almost always adults. They are usually also women, and Alanen (1994, 2011) and Oakley (1994) have discussed the hostility and physical and emotional uneasiness of many women towards children, linked to values that need to be examined and not ignored.

The two main problems for those who contend that social research 'should not' be value-laden are, first, that they are making exactly the kind of moral assertion that they are trying to veto. Second, their anxious need to make such assertions shows that social research is prone to be value-laden, and so they seem to be trying to derive an 'ought not' from an inaccurate 'is not'. Despite areas of agreement, to reach total agreement between those who support value-informed social research and those who do not is unlikely. This is because their arguments are based on values rather than facts.

Value-informed research

Having set out some general arguments to support value-informed research, I will turn to the DCR view, that truth and freedom are central to research and to everyday interactions and relationships.

Habermas (2006) contended that ideal speech acts (when each person is equally informed) have to presuppose the possibility of truth, associated with freedom and justice. If untruths are told, they can still only be understood and defined as such in the context of accepted, normative truth. Bhaskar expands Habermas's defence of truth in language and knowledge (epistemology), to truth in ontology, in being, doing and relating, when truth guides humans who are trying to find their way and their place in the world (Norrie 2010: 128, 132). Besides truth, freedom and justice, 'every transaction and material exchange' also involves the latent ethics of equality, liberty and solidarity, of respect and recognition (or lack of these), when humans are both desiring, acting creatures and also judging, speaking beings (Bhaskar 1986, quoted in Norrie 2010: 132).

Unlike Rawls's 'veil of ignorance' that seeks justice by withdrawing from the world, DCR looks to social science to explore the many complex meanings and activities of justice and truth in the world (Bhaskar [1993] 2008b: Chapter 3; Norrie 2010: Chapter 5). Among the criteria for true, sound judgements (also relevant to research reports) are that they should: correspond with reality, evidence and a referent (see semiotic triangle); be truthful in the light of universal standards; be given in good faith and trust; be grounded in the concrete singularity of the particular persons and contexts concerned (for example, each addresses the other as the known person and not suddenly as if they were someone else); be practical and worth acting on; and be reasonable and warranted. The criteria for true judgements and reports are integral to the inevitably moral relationships that people have with knowledge and with one another.

Bhaskar ([1993] 2008b:261) contends that social science is 'value-saturated'. Its subject matter, social ontology, is 'value-impregnated' on all four planes of social being. Its explanations are morally implicated, whether they are critical and emancipatory or are not. Children's generally vulnerable, subordinate status reveals researchers' moral motives, which are primarily to further understanding and protection of children, or appropriate provision for their needs, or respect for their competencies and agency (Alderson 2008, 2011). Research is also value-saturated in the practical, ethical questions posed by every stage of a project from first plans to final dissemination, and in how researchers respond to these questions (Alderson and Morrow 2011).

Sayer (2011) continues Bhaskar's argument that morality is integral to real human nature, relationships and societies. Sayer asserts that the typical avoidance of values in social science drains away the real meaning found in human beings and their relationships. Although critical social scientists are evaluative, Sayer (p. 11) considers that they lack 'an adequate account of human capacities and vulnerabilities, generally through an exaggerated fear of ethnocentricism' and so they are too cautious and inward-looking. I suggested in Chapter 2 that concern to avoid arrogant, post-colonial, ethnocentrism could discourage confidence in babies' universal nature and needs (their ontology), to the extent of a dehumanising denial that is unhelpful to babies everywhere.

Sociologists speak too often in the third person, Sayer considers, and too seldom in the direct first person. They rarely invite readers to check accounts against their own experience from the inside, and instead treat them as if they should be detached observers who avoid identifying with others. Sayer connects values to our profound human reasoning, our experienced wisdom and natural necessity, and our constant need and hope to flourish and to avoid suffering. Reason informs emotions and emotions inform reason (Chapter 4 traced these interactions in the emotional journey towards voluntary consent to surgery). If reason and values are mistakenly separated, both lose their power, meaning and relevance.

Far from being scientific, social science that tries to delete values is like attempts to describe a landscape without colour, even black or white, because morality is so integral to the human landscape, Sayer argues. He examines how our lives are value-laden in the smallest details of daily concern. We live along the dimensions of actual to potential, flourishing to suffering, well-being to ill-being, from doing good to doing harm to ourselves and others, and we interpret all events and relationships along these dimensions. Even if we discuss the weather, the point is not meteorology but morality, and concern about its harm–benefit portent for human plans. Sayer illustrates how our moral sentiments are formed through our sense of harm or flourishing, by analysing how we work out our relationships with others, and with ourselves and our self-identity, through constant, anxious, reflexive, moral self-assessment. He writes mainly about adults, and seldom mentions children. Yet these preoccupations begin in the early weeks of life. Premature babies quickly learn to flinch in anticipation when a doctor holds their foot before jabbing in a needle, whereas they trustingly relax when they are stroked (Alderson *et al.* 2005a). Dignity is one example of our highly socialised morality that is so sensitive to how others treat us with respect or indifference. Sayer contends that over the past 40 years critical social science has become cautious and detached, whereas it requires stronger conceptions of human suffering and flourishing, which inform and can be informed by studies of these social processes.

Sayer applies his first-person comment by asking the sceptical reader to recall feeling a strong sense of outrage against some injustice or wrong, and to remember why it mattered so much. (Some readers may feel strongly about values in social science.) He would like social science to grasp these powerful, complex, partly elusive experiences, to overcome its aversion to normativity, and to engage with realism. His reply to Hammersley's army example would be, 'a politics without ethics can embrace genocide as easily as democracy' (Sayer 2011: 248). Sayer would like to see a social science that is more like therapeutic medicine, aiming to identify society's ills in order to promote social alternatives and well-being, while paying great attention and respect to the different as well as common ways in which different groups and individuals across the world experience well-being. Explicitly or not, this aim drives childhood studies at macro and micro levels, when they address children's (value-laden) disadvantages, problems, preferences and competencies, and seek to inform and improve knowledge, policies and practices that affect them.

MELD 4D, fourth dimension

(Bhaskar 2002b, [1993] 2008b: Chapter 3, [1994] 2010a: Chapters 5–7, [1991] 2010b; Norrie 2010: Chapter 5)

Having reviewed support for value-informed social research, I will now summarise MELD 4D, fourth dimension, where values are central. Previous chapters summarised the traditional three-part dialectic, thesis-antithesis-synthesis towards (epistemological) logical, consistent completeness. This was contrasted with the four-part MELD. To include real being (ontology) and real transformation, MELD 1M first moment begins with non-identity and absence; 2E second edge involves negativity and oppressive power$_2$; 3L, third level, concerns open, dynamic totalities, which move on to 4D, fourth dimension, of praxis, transformative agency in ethical practice and liberating power$_1$, the dialectic that is 'the pulse of freedom'. I hope that this chapter, by showing all the MELD moments, will help to clarify the meaning and relevance of some earlier parts of this book. They all relate to the DCR logic that human beings inevitably desire and move towards freedom and justice, and that this is or should be the central concern of social science. Given the extensive DCR literature, and the many critics, even of the idea that values are central to social science, my attempts to select, explain and justify DCR arguments have to be quite extended.

The DCR confidence in moral values as part of human natural necessity is also explained in the four planes of social being. The embodied identity, interpersonal and social structural relationships are completed on the fourth plane of *inner being*, which involves subjective agency, and ideas about the good life, the good society and unfinished moral evolution. Assuming that ought can be derived from is, Bhaskar ([1993] 2008b: 98) reasons from what we are, to what we could be, in our desire to absent 'constraints on well-being and possibilities'. When individuals are out of touch and alienated from their body and nature (plane 1), from other people (plane 2), and from structures and institutions (plane 3) they can become unable to act in order to absent the absences and power$_2$ relations, and they are denied the capacity for transformation at MELD 4D. However, transformative agents (*product-in-process*) are capable of intentional actions to transform the world in order to realise their capacity for freedom. According to Hartwig (2007: 32), '[w]e humans have a fundamental desire and need (hence right) to experience at-oneness with the natural world and our labour process', with other people and our social relations, and 'our essential selves, inner and outer . . .'.

Positivist, empirical and interpretive research miss these underlying realities when they end in disagreements about the origins, nature and purpose of values, and are locked into fallacies of western philosophy (see Chapter 7), so that 'when [Enlightenment] fundamentalism was finally abandoned in the second half of the twentieth century, acceptance of [postmodern] epistemic relativism led to the intrinsic irrationalisms that dot our philosophical landscape' (Bhaskar [1993] 2008b: 111–12).

DCR's attention to realism involves *concrete reality*. 'Concrete' means not rigid or abstract, but ' "well-rounded" . . . balanced, appropriate, complete' and fit for purpose (Bhaskar [1993] 2008b: 128). The concrete exists at a deeper level than the actual and empirical. Individuals are referred to as the *concrete universal* ↔ *singular*, to emphasise that, although they share universal common humanity, each is also unique and specific, and cannot be lost within abstract, over-generalised Kantian ethics or fragmented postmodernism. Practical *concrete utopianism* stands in contrast to abstract, intellectual utopianism; to be practical involves absenting constraining absences as, each in their own way, human beings try to overcome power$_2$ and 'master–slave relations' in society and nature. In *Dialectic: The Pulse of Freedom*, Bhaskar ([1993] 2008b: 298) sees dialectic as an 'inner urge that flows universally from the logic of elemental absence (lack, need, want or desire) . . . [against] power$_2$ relations [towards] freedom as flourishing . . .'. DCR assumes an inevitable *alethia* (truth) in the realistic, intransitive ontology of human being and human nature, of freedom and of 'morality [as] an objective real property' (p. 259), besides accepting the infinite, transitive ways in which they all interact and are critically perceived and experienced. Morality guides action, but great uncertainties and conflicts include those between: the actual and the ideal; intentions and outcomes; different values and interests; and many interpretations of values. Human nature and morality are determining, open structures, not determinist, closed ones.

Social ties and duties as part of human nature were unfashionable concepts during the 1980s era of Thatcherism and the atomised 'selfish gene' (Dawkins 1976). Since then, more sympathetic understanding of essential cooperation and adaptive interdependence has slowly gained ground: in human social evolution (Rose and Rose 2001); in psychology (Gilligan 1982); in anthropology (Hrdy 2009); in philosophy (Midgley 1979, 1996, [1985] 2002, 2010); in the interplay of culture with biology and genetics (Gould 2007; Rose *et al.* 1984); and in the study of fragile, interactive, natural ecosystems following Carson (1962) and Van Valen (1973)[8] (S. Jones 2008; Lovelock 2009; Lynas 2008), among many authors. Marx and Engels shared older beliefs in an original, cooperative solidarity in primitive societies (at structural though not necessarily interpersonal levels) before ownership of private property developed and incited class inequalities and oppressions, a belief recently confirmed by anthropologists (Graebner 2011). Growing economic crises have reawakened general interest in Marxian predictions of the dangers of voracious capitalism, and in a concern with human protest and solidarity (for example, Beder 2009; Callinicos 2010; Chang 2011; Harvey 2005,

2011; Klein 2000, 2007; Mason 2012; among many others), which are central to DCR theories of moral realism, and the ethical naturalism of integral human impulses towards freedom.

Bhaskar ([1993] 2008b: 176) considers that the goal in MELD 4D is 'not to an end state, but to an objective process of human self-realisation, eudaimonia or flourishing (– in nature)'. He proposes that these impulses in all human being begin with the baby's 'primal scream', a moment of fear of absence, desire for needs to be met, but also of trust and solidarity in the infant's reliance on others to meet those needs as partners in human relationships – early impulses which others have researched (Alderson et al. 2005a, 2005b; Dunn 1988, 2004; Murray and Andrews 2000; Stern 1977). I would add that the intense dialectic between self-orientated need–desire and other-orientated trust–solidarity, between interdependence and longing for freedom, is seen from the first weeks, in children's determined efforts to explore and express themselves, often against adults' determined constraints. The two most generally castigated age groups, the 'terrible twos' and the teenage years, are times when children and young people most urgently want and need to develop and enjoy their new capacities, and when adults tend to feel most anxious and inconvenienced by the rapid changes.

So, MELD 4D is not a final endpoint for individuals or society but a goal that keeps recurring in open totalities. Freedom might seem to be both too limited but also perhaps too complex and vague to be a useful goal, and the next section addresses such concerns, besides continuing to illustrate DCR analyses.

Freedom

(Bhaskar [1993] 2008b: 282–4)

The seven forms of freedom combine different meanings of freedom, usually thought to be in conflict. The seven forms or levels of *constellated ethics* respond to criticisms that, without consensus, moral values cannot be established. The seven forms help to create a consensus to explain and support the DCR dynamic, which moves from basic personal freedoms up to the highest level of universal but also personal freedoms.

The first level is *the agent's capacity to do otherwise*, necessary for choice and freedom of expression, for realising new potential, and for certain legal freedoms. This first freedom is highly valued by all age groups, although its intense importance to the youngest children is often subordinated by adults to their real or perceived needs for guidance and protection. The second form is Isaiah Berlin's (2002) *negative freedoms* (lack of constraints), which are tantamount to *positive enabling freedoms* to act. Third is *emancipation from specific oppressive constraints* and the transformation into wanted, liberating states of affairs and structures. This third level may be individual, collective or universal, and it transfers the concepts of freedom from individual to include dialectical, universal concerns and 'the remoralisation of the world' (Bhaskar [1993] 2008b: 282).

The fourth form is Kantian, *self-determining, rational autonomy*, which corresponds to the universal respect for human rights, with added concern for nature and other species, and future generations (see Chapters 9 to 12 of these volumes). Freedom becomes stretched to consider universal, absolute and also relative, concrete ↔ singular needs. At the fifth level, *well-being* includes a utilitarian absence of ills and satisfaction of needs. Again this applies to the concrete singular individual or group, and to universal well-being, 'with the possibility of developing four-planar social being as *rights* and . . . *grounded freedoms*' (Bhaskar [1993] 2008b: 284, original emphasis), in universally reciprocated rights that do not transgress on the freedoms of others. This reflects movement away from concepts of rights as selfish individualism, towards 'recognition of the inherent dignity and of the equal and inalienable rights of all members of the human family [that] is the foundation of freedom, justice and peace in the world' (UN 1989: Preamble). The sixth level is Aristotelian *flourishing*, informed by the just and equal sharing of goods and possibilities (including Sen's capabilities). This leads to the seventh form and the goal of DCR and MELD: *universal human flourishing* or the *eudaimonic* society. This level links to the personal first level in the idea, mentioned earlier, of a just community as 'an association in which the free development of each is the condition for the free development of all' (Marx and Engels [1848] 1998). Until power$_2$ and 'master–slave relations' are overcome, no one can really enjoy freedom, if it is not only denied to others, but also depends on that denial, such as the freedom to consume goods because they are subsidised by others' low-waged or unpaid labour.

The DCR concept of personal and collective freedom is *concrete utopian*; it outlines a potential and ideal society with real possibilities for *concrete universal ↔ singular* individuals to search for their own, as well as for collective, fulfilment. This responds to Layard's concern quoted earlier to promote a good such as happiness or freedom by researching it, yet not to prescribe it narrowly. And it is *meta-critical* (Bhaskar [1993] 2008b: 279), 'meta' meaning that the constellated ethics stands beyond or before actual societies and facts, on the level of people's potential judgement. It also stands at deeper levels of their being and natural necessity, and beyond innumerable actual conflicts and constraints. Tensions and contradictions between freedom and relationships, the ideal and the actual, have been deeply explored by feminism in terms of relationships between women and men, but so far less with children and young people who experience similar challenges in relationships with adults.

Theories of the self: religious origins

The following sections summarise the history of changing ideas about the self, how they led up to present theories in childhood research, and how the changing ideas respect or exclude children. Ideas about the self also illuminate the fourth plane of social being, the inner self, and MELD 4D on flourishing and its converse misery.

Much theorising about the inner self or soul could seem to be outside the bounds of sociology. First, the theories are partly too abstract and lacking in evidence to fit empirical research. Second, they are partly too individualist, psychological or spiritual to fit the scientific study of social structures, systems and relationships.

However, DCR explores unseen deeper realities, and shows the problems in social research that ignores them. Childhood research, without some explicit theories of human nature and the young self, either has to ignore concepts of harm and benefit to children, or else will base the concepts on vague, contested uncertainties. It is then hard to explain or justify any conclusions or policy recommendations. For example, the sociologist Majia Nadesan commented that conditions such as autism raise deep philosophical questions about the nature of being a child, about mind and consciousness and their relationship to the body and society, about normalcy and difference within and across cultures. She continued:

> We attempt to answer these questions with socially constructed philosophical ideas about what it means to be human. The ideas change over time in response to institutions and everyday life. Our ways of knowing are always socially and historical situated, and do not necessarily evolve towards an essential and transcendent essence.
>
> *(Nadesan 2005: 134)*

Although they might seem remote from social science, ideas from religion and philosophy seep into common imaginings about the self (the pure, innocent child or the bearer of original sin, the isolated or the interactive baby), and so they need to be examined. For millennia, philosophers have shaped and freed or restricted public thinking and values, such as when they value reason over emotions and feelings.

Anthropologists and archaeologists report how early peoples had magical beliefs about life after death, ghosts, spirits and ancestors, and sometimes human resurrection, like the new life that emerges from the seemingly dead seed or egg. The mysteries of birth and of each infant's very early, distinct and unique personality have similarly inspired ideas about a prenatal existence of the enduring soul-spirit. Socrates and Meno gave a slave boy a maths test, which the boy confidently passed. He only became confused when Socrates tried explicit instruction. Amazed at the boy's seemingly innate and untaught ability, Socrates concluded that to teach by questioning was better than by instruction, and that learning consists in remembering 'the truth about reality' which is always in our immortal soul (Plato 1964: 139). Teresa Nunes and Peter Bryant (1996) found that Brazilian street traders aged from 9 years are better at mathematics because money has emotional and social meaning for them, than their peers are in British schools where learning is more abstract. Curiously, they echoed Socrates in thinking that children might have some implicit knowledge of negative numbers, and become confused if they are asked to make this knowledge explicit before solving problems (Borba and Nunes 2000). Noam Chomsky (1986) expounded nativist concepts of an extensive, innate capacity to understand language, and Jean Piaget's (1928, 1932) concept of 'readiness' denotes innate, universal, unfolding stages of children's intellectual and moral development, which Piaget believed had to precede their capacity to learn.

Jesus, following many earlier prophets, Buddha and Gandhi were examples of charismatic initiators of subversive movements of peaceful revolution for social justice and spiritual virtues. They exemplified 'childlike' humility, poverty, vulnerability, willingness to admit ignorance and to learn, with obedience to transcendent goodness and an innocent (literally harmless) detachment from worldly power. Their successors rapidly inverted their teaching back towards promoting 'adult', hierarchical, worldly power (Armstrong 1993; Nisbet 1967; Weber [1922] 1978). The differences are epitomised in images of the child. Whereas Jesus is quoted as exhorting his disciplines to 'become as little children' if they hoped to 'enter into the kingdom of heaven' (Matthew 18:3), only a generation later, Paul valued 'completeness'. 'When I was a child, I spoke as a child, I understood as a child, I thought as a child. When I became a man, I put away childish things', like seeing in a mirror darkly and, Paul believed, in the afterlife like adults we will 'see face to face' and know fully (Corinthians 13: 9–12).

Robert Nisbet (1967: 221–63) considered that sociology is the only social science to examine how religio-sacred myth, ritual and sacrament inform secular life, and to perceive human nature and society as intrinsically moral, instead of assuming that secular, economic, utilitarian, self-interested and competitive doctrines are 'the essential and sufficing pillars of social analysis' (p. 221). Nisbet reviewed classical (and usually atheist) sociologists' contentions that religions implant a deep sense of unity and meaning, social order and duty, the sacred bonds of the social contract, together with respect for individuality and true human nature, wisdom and virtue. These are safeguards from paralysing fear, disorder and tyranny. Many religions do so partly by investing individuals and communities with supernatural dimensions, such as a divinely-ordained heredity monarchy, when even a very young heir is recognised as a rightful sovereign.

When religions profess that human life is sacred, created in God's image, blessed and valued, and possibly having an immortal soul, in theory they encourage equal respect for everyone from birth. Today's secular version is respect for 'the inherent dignity and . . . the equal and inalienable rights of all members of the human family' (UN 1948). This is partly derived according to the American *Declaration of Independence* from the 'self-evident' truth 'that all men are created equal [and] endowed by their Creator with certain unalienable Rights' (US 1776). 'Men' referred ambivalently to all humankind, and latterly women (UN 1979), children (UN 1989) and disabled people (UN 2006a) have been increasingly recognised as persons with rights.

The following summary draws on *The Rise and Fall of the Soul and Self*, by the philosopher Raymond Martin and the psychologist John Barresi (2006). They trace signs of the concept of an enduring, more-than-physical self that might matter after death back to Neolithic grave stones. Pre-Socratic debates, that have continued for millennia, question whether the immaterial soul is separate from or integrated into the mortal body and, either way, how two such different entities might interact. Does the soul or self or personality exist in the body, brain or mind, the consciousness, or else through social interactions? Is it unified, or does it have separate parts? From Pythagoras and Plato to Freud there have been images of a three-part soul or self. Plato's (1952) charioteer of reason tried to harmonise with the white horse of emotions and the black horse of passions. Freud's similar triad has been described in popular psychology as the impulsive, instinctive child (id), who is supposed to grow away from parental domination (super-ego) towards conscious adult freedom (ego) (Berne 1968). Bhaskar (2002a: 68) theorised an embodied personality, a psychic being or soul or anima, and a ground state, all three striving for harmony.

Key philosophical theories

Martin and Barresi (2006) analyse the gradual transition over 2,500 years from spiritual to scientific concepts of the self. The moves included growing interest in the body and anatomy, mental and physical illness, similarities and differences between human and other animals, in consciousness, introspection, and by the fifth century CE Augustine's innovative, tormented autobiography. A perennial problem was the assumption that each unique soul somehow relates and reacts to everyday life, and yet is like the Platonic Forms, Aristotelian *nous*, and the Judaeo-Christian God, in being complete, indivisible, unchanging and therefore eternal. The twelfth century saw growing religious introspection into sinful desire and personal conscience, into idealised courtly and Platonic love, which celebrated individualised, self-conscious subjectivity. Penetrating introspective regimes, such as the religious confessional, led later to the clinic with medical and psychological supervision particularly of women and children (Donzelot 1977; Foucault 1977, 1993; Rose 1999). The fourteenth century celebration of human excellence, success and wealth accelerated transitions from spiritual to secular, material and scientific concerns.

During the sixteenth century, Martin Luther challenged theological traditions and Francis Bacon challenged scientific ones, subjecting them to the critical scrutiny of direct human experience. The natural replaced the spiritual in many ways. Mental illness, for example, began to be attributed to physiological disturbance instead of to demonic possession. Bacon wrote about subjectivity, sincerity and dissembling in presenting the self, while Michel de Montaigne, through intense self-examination, felt himself to be not whole and constant but fragmented and changeable. He struggled to find an authentic, united, permanent self-identity through faith in God's permanence.

Although, by the seventeenth century, René Descartes centred human understanding in the thinking mind, he still accepted changeless God and souls, although these concepts were losing relevance in the drive towards empiricism. Gradually this dualism (soul versus material body) would be wholly replaced by materialism: Thomas Hobbes believed that souls and even God were not spiritual but material, and he began to write about the changing, relational, insubstantial personal identity. The debate continues in today's scientism, which assumes that everything can be explained by empirical science. Through the seventeenth century, nature came to be seen as a mindless machine and animals as soulless automata like clocks, functioning through means but without ends, purpose or spirit. Galileo Galilei, gazing through the telescope and microscope, divided actual objects from our subjective perceptions of them, and advocated atomic research into the mathematics underlying nature. Science and nature began to be separated from religion, metaphysics and epistemology, with stress on: efficient, mechanical, clockwork-like function; avoidance of the invisible and spiritual; trust in the objective, expert observer instead of the observed subject; and concern to measure rather than to analyse. The foundations were being laid of modern psychology, neuroscience and child development, with the child's mind today being imagined in computer instead of clock imagery.

Descartes contended that all thought is self-aware and reflexive – in order to think, we have to know that we are thinking – and he excluded animals from having thoughts and motives. The greater the divide between humans and animals, the greater the ambiguity of young children's human or pre-human/animal status. Descartes also demoted 'animal spirits' or 'soul-spirits' (Goodey 2011), from Aristotle's animating, life-giving spirit, the *anima* or soul, down into the idea that animals' sense organs are mechanically stimulated by the size, shape and movement of matter that impinges on their brain. 'Animal spirits' were further degraded until today they are associated with financiers' greedy, reckless gambling.

The fragmenting self

Loss of faith, during the seventeenth century, in the enduring soul or self led John Locke and Gottfried Leibnitz to consider that human identity depends on and is unified by memory (Martin and Barresi 2006: 138–41). Leibnitz believed that each moment sees a tiny slice of the whole person who is an aggregate of them all. These views are likely to devalue childhood, as the least complete state, furthest away from the final aggregate of experience and memory.

Locke and the empiricists regarded young children's minds as empty until they were supplied by the sensed experience that precedes thought, although it remains uncertain how thought can emerge from experience, and how experience can exist before thought. Locke ([1690] 1997: 2.27, 16.341) considered that experiences of pleasure and pain give rise to the child's initial idea of a self with needs and the ability to compare experiences and, through memory, to acquire a self-consciousness that is morally accountable for actions. The concept of a process of creating identity through consciousness encouraged the idea of selves as inventions and fictions, proposed by Locke (and in later centuries asserted by David Hume, William Hazlitt, Auguste Comte, Frederick Nietzsche and others) (Martin and Barresi 2006). Jean-Jacques Rousseau and Denis Diderot were deeply interested in how children gradually acquire human thoughts, emotions and self-concepts, and they began to map age–stage child development.

Into the eighteenth century, the growing materialism opened human nature to scientific analysis, just as Isaac Newton opened the physical world to scientific analysis. Unable to discover a soul, empiricists such as Hume thought that the idea of personal continuity was an illusion, and Hazlitt thought it was absurd. Hume considered in detail how we sustain the fiction of an enduring self to ourselves and others through a series of performances, when we mistake resemblance for an imagined persistence and unity (Martin and Barresi 2006: 152–3).

This discontinuity raises still unresolved questions about moral values and why, if we keep changing, we should care about our present or future transient selves, and why anything should matter. Crucially, the eighteenth century saw the transfer from general faith in a divinely ordained, meaningful moral order towards efforts to justify a constructed, human moral order. In response to Hume's empirical scepticism, Immanuel Kant (1781/1965) proposed a phenomenal (known, actual, possible) world of experiences in space and time, along with a noumenal (unknown) world. We cannot experience the noumenal, transcendental world, or know that immortal souls, or God, or values such as freedom, exist or are real. And yet, Kant thought, we *need to assume* that they exist as the necessary basis for moral action, and for the human faith and knowledge which structure and interpret experience. Rousseau believed in God, immortal souls and inner conscience, which Kant reframed as human reason. Rousseau opposed Hobbes's notion of men as brutes who, through self-interest, allow society to civilise them. Instead, Rousseau thought that 'savage man is at peace with nature and the friend of all his fellow creatures', that each human self is unique, innocent, benevolent and free, and is only corrupted and enchained when 'civilised' by society (Martin and Baressi 2006: 180).

Kant (1972) advocated respect for persons as rational beings, with the right to make their own decisions without interference. Martin and Baressi consider that Kant's view marked a great transition from classical and feudal honour systems and hierarchies towards modern equality. However, I suggest five ways in which Kant's crucial work on democracy was not original or comprehensive. First, as I have already noted, the great religions had originally centred on justice and equity (despite being later subverted to serve the powerful). And for centuries, people had rebelled against oppressions and had fought for freedoms that very gradually came to be recognised and enshrined as modern human rights. These rights were explained and refined by philosophers, but were not invented by them. Second, Kant retained hierarchies by reserving respect for rational, autonomous men, but he excluded women, children and employees (Kennedy and Mendus 1987). Third, whereas Rousseau valued each individual as equal and as unique, Kant was influenced by the first insight but not the second. And this led him to overlook specific reasons why people are valued or disrespected, honoured or denigrated. Kant's respect has been judged to be so abstract that it could serve to support disrespect and injustice (Seidler 1986) and fascism (MacIntyre 2002).

Fourth, Kant shared in perpetuating older hierarchies within modern systems. Christopher Goodey (2011) examined how classical Greek and medieval ideals of aristocratic honour were transferred into religious concepts of divine grace for a chosen elite, and then later into the hierarchy based on intelligence. These transitions occurred over the centuries, filtering through countless details of social life: the religious catechism, for example, developed into the modern IQ (intelligence quotient) test. Goodey argues that measures of ability and disability, like honour and grace, are social constructs, which preserve the interests of the powerful. Kant's elevation of man's reason helped to consolidate the modern, undemocratic IQ-based meritocracy. And fifth, this elevation contributed to the further distancing of children from the supposedly rational, adult world.

By the nineteenth century, dynamic and social concepts of the self had emerged. The poet Samuel Taylor Coleridge perceived in his own children the origins of their human identity in their emotional relationships. He wrote, 'Ere yet a conscious self exists, the [baby's] love begins' of the mother's face and body, quoted in Martin and Barresi (2006: 184) who describe this as 'one of the earliest expressions of the view that self-consciousness follows the discovery of self *in the other*' (original emphasis).[9] Georg Hegel similarly considered that self-consciousness realises itself through interaction in one's recognition of others' awareness of oneself. His 'master–slave relations' (see previous chapters) explore the contradiction that the master may come to depend on the slave's opinion of the master, and he assumes that domination and struggle have to precede harmony and interdependence (Martin and Barresi 2006: 188–9).

Through the nineteenth century, belief that humans are made in the image of God altered into belief that humans are made 'in the image of biology and society', largely through the influence of Darwin and Marx (Martin and Barresi 2006: 201). The scientific study of physical human nature, neurology and consciousness led to complex, multiple concepts of the self.

Darwin's theory of evolution, as a mechanism of adaptation among species while they compete for scarce resources and for survival, was followed by many comparisons between animals, primitive people, early human history and children (Kessen 1965: 115) in the 'biologising' of childhood (Morss 1990). Critics of Darwin, who believed that God created each distinct, complete species on the fifth and sixth days of creation, rejected his theories of evolution and 'the descent of man' from the apes. However, Midgley (1979, [1985] 2002, 2010) analyses how, rather than lowering humans, Darwin was elevating apes (later found to share almost all human genes) by respecting their immense social and natural complexity and interdependence.

Herbert Spencer developed (some say distorted) Darwin's theory into the evolutionary social psychology of inevitably selfish, human competition. The model is still influential today in public opinion, the mass media, politics and economics (Dawkins 1976; Dorling 2011; Mason 2009, 2012; Midgley 2010; Rose and Rose 2001). Also, as Ian Burkitt (2008: 32–46) reviewed, evolutionary psychology still influences the sociology of the self, following George Herbert

Mead (1934), and influences education, following the pragmatists John Dewey and William James. It is evident in the education market, set up in Britain in 1988, in which schools are intended to improve through competing against one another (Scott 2010). Evolutionary concepts of ruthless human competition can leave children in invidious positions: as needy dependents without emotionally committed adult care; as naive, potential victims who must be taught to survive and compete; as developing beings who demonstrate functional, biological, evolutionary determinism with each additionally acquired skill.

Marx's contention that conscious life reflects underlying material and social relations of production, and that social being determines consciousness, furthered transitions away from the idea of a real, stable, essential self into a fluctuating, socially constructed one. William James ([1890] 1981: 462), the last philosopher-psychologist,[10] who famously commented that babies know only 'one great blooming buzzing confusion', was interested in the empirical, material, social, emotional and spiritual study of the self, consciousness and personhood.

Martin and Barresi (2006: 230, original emphasis) summarise:

> *The twentieth century began in grand ideologies and ended in narrow specialisations* [which thought] of the self more as a product of culture than its creator. The last half of the century witnessed rampant, unintegrated scientific specialisation; the withering philosophical critiques of deconstruction and postmodernism; the penetrating attack in analytical philosophy on the very concept and importance of personal identity . . . and a newfound awareness of gender, sexual and ethnic identities . . . [T]he self, which began the century looking unified – the master of its own house – ended it looking fragmented – a byproduct of social and psychological conditions . . . that mirrored the growing complexity and fragmentation in theory.

And so the study of theory, empirical research, mind, brain, consciousness, the self, ego, I and me, the unconscious, the social and the developing self came to be scattered around many university departments. In philosophy, the phenomenology of Edmund Husserl, Martin Heidegger and Jean-Paul Sartre denied human nature as an entity. The logic of G.E. Moore, Bertrand Russell, Ludwig Wittgenstein and A.J. Ayer took reality to be subjective conscious episodes. In psychoanalysis, Sigmund Freud and Carl Jung searched for evidence, through listening to personal accounts, to support Schopenhauer's and Nietzsche's theories that the irrational, unconscious mind dominates human development and consciousness. Symbolic interactionists such as Mead (1934) and developmental psychologists such as Lev Vygotsky ([1934] 1986), considered that the mind and self gradually emerge as products of social interaction and experience, language, games and play.

In contrast, the psychologists J.B. Watson and B.F. Skinner examined child development in behavioural experiments, confined within lab-based theories and methods, with self-fulfilling results. Abraham Maslow (1943) claimed that human developmental needs ascend from basic physiological needs, to security, to love, to self-esteem, to adult self-actualisation. However, young children show that the needs are integrated rather than hierarchical; their early attempts to feed themselves can involve every level. And Maslow appears to imply implausibly that the billion hungry people who live on subsistence levels cannot experience love, morality and creativity.[11] Unmet needs can inform people's values, solidarity and political protests, whereas emotional and social lethargy may follow over-prosperity (Porpora 2001). Researching with very deprived children in Ethiopia, Tatek Abebe (2009: 461) gave food and gifts to the children, and was surprised to receive their gifts in return. He commented: 'reciprocal relationships have nurtured the research space in many fruitful ways ... dominant ethical principles are actually lived in, reproduced and experienced by research participants through interactions'.

From the 1930s onwards, the influences of fascism and communism, of Nietzsche and Freud, overshadowed and 'darkened' views of human nature (Martin and Barresi 2006: 253). A founder of the current philosophy of education wrote of the 'barbarian' child (Peters 1966: 43, 49), who inhabits a twilight world, where the ' "mind" is ruled perhaps by bizarre and formless wishes', by 'passions and self-love', until teachers later can 'sustain and cultivate a crust of civilisation over the volcanic core of atavistic emotions' (Peters 1972: 87).[12] Such beliefs still underlie the contradictory claims about schoolchildren having to 'learn how to think', and 'learn how to learn', although it is impossible to learn these skills without already performing them, which babies do avidly from birth.

The Frankfurt School 'trashed the Kantian ideal of a rational, autonomous self' and of historical progress (Martin and Barresi 2006: 255). Despite becoming fragmented across disciplines, the self remained intact within each discipline until the 1950s, when Claude Lévi-Strauss, Rolande Barthes and Jacques Lacan developed Ferdinand de Saussure's theories of language and semiotics (see semiotic triangle). The self became decentred and the ego dwindled into an illusion that children acquire, according to Lacan, through shifting chains of signifiers and fantasies. Lacan speculated whether reflexive consciousness, developed through negotiated narratives, is not an intrinsic property of mind. Instead, it may only be a theoretical construct. The mind itself may be a fiction, and reflexive consciousness a theory that children in western culture acquire in order to explain human behaviour (Martin and Barresi 2006: 274).

Foucault's (1967, 1977, 1993) poststructuralism reduced the knowing subject into a function of discourse and a product of power, while Jacques Derrida deconstructed and decentred the self. Ethnic, gender and post-colonial identity politics, and international research, emphasise differences between people, whereas in previous centuries similarities had been stressed. In sociology, Erving Goffman (1969) conceived of the self as a series of social roles and presented performances. Social constructionism that has so much influenced childhood studies is positioned here by Martin and Barresi (2006: 271). It is seen as another extension of post-structuralism, which emphases the non-essential social self, constructed through language, culture and diverse lifestyles. In fission theory, analytic philosophers have questioned how, over time, the person is physically and psychologically the same, or divides into different persons, and how these seemingly different persons relate or do not relate to one another. And so the history closes in general contradictory disagreements among theorists about the meaning of the self, and therefore about the meaning and possibility of flourishing.

The early self

Before I discuss the history and its conclusions, I will add a few more contrasting examples of research about the early self. The above history mainly covered broadly *preliminary* research, in that thinkers proposed theories about the self that could potentially be rephrased as research hypotheses. Occasionally there were *deductive* research examples, when theories were tested, though generally in closed, partly self-fulfilling ways. Watson (1919), the behaviourist mentioned earlier, found that after a 6-month-old child had a small dog tossed into her pram, she was terrified of a mouse one year later. The above thinkers tended to omit MELD 1M, attempts to apprehend the real, complex ontology that exists before and after they encounter it. Although it is impossible to suspend all our prejudices, 1M is about the attempt to do so, and *inductive* research can begin by exploring and trying to be open to new insights before relating them to previous knowledge.

When Als (1999) looked past beliefs that premature babies cannot know or think, and discovered how to 'read' their 'language', this led her to record their 'strengths and sensitivities' (not deficits) and to treat the babies as major agents in their healthcare. In a neonatal unit led by her work, we observed John, born 14 weeks early (Alderson *et al.* 2004: 72–3). Six weeks later his care plan listed his 'competencies', which included: 'Initiating breathing movements much of the time; Smooth well organised movements to protect and calm himself; Making efforts to open his eyes in response to his mother's voice . . .'. The 'goals' section recorded: 'It appears that John's next steps are: Consistent efforts to breathe on his own; More time in restful sleep; Keeping firm muscle power with curled up posture; Being increasingly successful in calming himself . . .'. 'Recommended help to achieve his goals' advised the adults on responding to John's signals of discomfort, altering his bedding and moving his bed to somewhere 'less light and busy'. These kinds of observations and practices address the beginnings of flourishing and relief of suffering.

Charles Darwin observed that his son, when aged 6 months, 'instantly assumed a melancholy expression' when his nurse pretended to cry (Bloom 2012). Darwin's inductive views on human morality, like his theory of evolution, were drawn gradually from countless observations of many species. Darwin believed that the human conscience emerges from babies' love for their carers, and from humans' constant remembering of their past actions, often with regret. He thought that morality arises from our lasting affections and relationships, and that vulnerable early dependence seems to be essential towards forming these (Midgley 2010: 55–65).

Over a century of rich observations of children was extended in the late 1970s when psychologists began to observe, by the micro-second, video films of babies' eye movements. Young babies open their eyes wider in surprise, or show surprise, or preferences, or concern, by gazing longer at some objects than at others. Photographs record babies' growing awareness that other people express similar feelings of pleasure or anxiety, which the baby affects through smiles and cries (Murray and Andrews 2000). Emotional communications are likely to be prime motives for the gradual realisation that certain noises are sounds with specific meaning, and for wanting to make sense of words and learn to use them (Stern 1977; Murray and Andrews 2000). It used to be assumed that children's morality begins to develop with their language from around 18 months (Damon 1990; Kagan and Lamb 1986). However, careful experiments demonstrate younger babies' moral awareness: 5- to 10-month-old babies prefer helpful to obstructive or neutral puppets or cartoon shapes when they watch a short drama. When 8-month-olds watched an unhelpful puppet being rewarded or punished, although they usually preferred good to bad actions, they preferred a seemingly bad act (the puppet being punished) to a good one, if it seemed to be justly deserved. By 15 months, babies have a mental model of the world as understood by someone else. The babies smiled and clapped or frowned and shook their heads, and were intensely involved during the puppet plays (Bloom 2012). Bloom commented that even if their interest was instinctive, like hunger, 'cognitively empty but emotionally intense', adults' moral feelings are also often similarly instinctive.

Meanwhile, neuro-scans peer into children's brains for evidence of the self in the 100 billion brain cells or neurons we are born with and the massive growth of the connecting synapses (Oates *et al.* 2012). Geneticists search, so far unsuccessfully, for genes specifically identified with personality traits. And psychologists test developing and autistic children for their 'theory of mind' (the understanding that others have thoughts and feelings comparable to one's own, the ability to empathise and to share their viewpoint).

Early moral foundations and capacities are continually enriched through interaction and imitation, friendship and pretend play (Dunn 1988, 2004). Watching a 22-month-old child saying 'my turn', 'your turn', I saw her passionately feeling and seeing the fair shares. She had to give others their time on the trampoline if she was to get what she wanted, her own turn. Children solve problems without using language (Bruner 1996), while being deeply concerned with intention and meaning (Rogoff 2003). Colwyn Trevarthen (2006: 13) believes infants' learning satisfies their deep human need to be part of community, and to grow in experience and skill. He is impressed with children's powerful curiosity, their

> inborn clever awareness [and] powers of communication with the human world, and with their ability and need to make other persons communicate with them. [They want to] share the knowing and doing with people they love, and whose interests and purposes they respect.

'Purposes' echoes Antonovsky's views about basic needs for meaning and purpose in life, cited earlier. Trevarthen (2006: 13) contends that babies are

> born with the receptive awareness and expressive body needed to commu-
> nicate fully with others. They can feel and express curiosity, intention,
> doubt and anxiety, joy ... love and pride in admired accomplishment,
> shame or jealousy at being misinterpreted.

Without expressive, joy-seeking interactions, children are led towards despair or anger that deter new achievement. Again this relates to flourishing and misery in embodied, emotional and social terms.

Paul Connolly and colleagues (2009) reported awareness beginning in the early years, though without full understanding, of conflict between Catholics and Protestants in Northern Ireland, and of cultural dispositions and prejudices. At around 4 years children ask scientific and philosophical questions: 'Why do ships float?' (Tizard and Hughes 1984). From around 8 years, children show intricate, profound understanding of philosophical concepts and dilemmas (Matthews 1984). Contrasting the ethic of justice and the ethic of care, Carol Gilligan's prime example involved two 11-year-olds. Jake favoured justice and Amy care, and Gilligan asso-ciated their careful arguments with their differing sense of self. Jake described himself in terms of separation, hierarchy and abstract ideals, whereas Amy spoke of connection, contexts and reciprocal relationships (Gilligan 1982: 24–39, 50–1).

Central to personal morality is trust in others, and also to feel trusted and respected oneself. Yet unfortunately, children and young people often report feeling excluded, threatened and mistrusted in public spaces (*Guardian* and LSE 2011; Hillman *et al.* 1990; Jones 2012; Scraton 2006), and even in schools. My survey, of nearly 2,250 school students aged 7 to 17, found that only a quarter thought their teachers believed what they said, and about a half thought this varied. About a third of the students thought they could trust teachers to keep a secret, and to listen fairly (Alderson 1999a). Since then, schools have become ever more mistrustful of students and of teachers in terms of prescribing what must be learned and worn, how and when. There is also the need to secure expensive equipment, use of CCTVs, finger-printing, clocking in and out, and other close technological surveillance.

My final set of examples are more contested and draw on psychoanalysis of adults' recounted earliest memories and observations of young children, to trace and partly imagine babies' inner lives. The work is deductive in that it applies Sigmund Freud's theories, but inductive in exploring the little-known youngest age groups. Whether it accurately reports a reality or not, it continues to influence some public and professional thinking about babies and it addresses an enormous absence of knowledge about the origins of the self, flourishing and morality instead of negatively denying these possibilities.

When they observed withdrawn and violent young children in London nurs-eries during World War II, Anna Freud and colleagues perceived morality as being beyond language, teaching and texts (epistemology), and as a moment-by-moment, learning-through-doing-and-being experience (ontology), in babies' feeling, relating, initiating, interacting and reacting. The researchers believed that early consciousness and identity develop through babies' differentiation of the ego (the sense of the I or self) from the id (instincts and drives) and the super-ego (fear of parents' reprimands). They considered that babies internalise the super-ego; they develop the ego to mediate between the conflicting id and super-ego; and babies are informed and motivated by love for their mother to love other people and objects (Freud and Sandler 1985).

Melanie Klein similarly attributed babies' distress to overwhelming anxieties about hunger, discomfort and abandonment, with longing for the remembered comfort and bliss of human contact. Klein's object relations theory proposed that infants' earliest perceptions, for example of the mother and the breast, are split between wholly good experiences with 'good' objects and wholly bad experiences with 'bad' objects (Appignanesi 2006). Klein believed that besides projection of feelings about good and bad onto the objects, there is also introjection, when babies split and fragment their own ego into good and bad. Klein considered that the first four months after birth are dominated by the struggle to integrate the two primary drives, love and hate, and to realise that the mother, and the baby's own self, can be both good and bad, through constructive, complex, social interactions. Children, and adults, who continue to polarise good/bad are stuck, Klein contended, in the initial 'paranoid-schizoid position' of separate violent-sadistic versus positive-libidinal impulses.

A vital process during babyhood is gradually to break down the polarity between things that are loved, good and gratifying from things that are bad and frustrating. Then, instead of seeing things, and the split parts of things (of the mother, the breast) and of the self, as wholly good or bad, the infant gradually realises that people and objects and the self can be both good *and* bad, at the same time and at different times. Klein considered that progress into the subsequent 'depressive position' is the gradual, painful, lifelong journey towards accepting the complicated reality of oneself and other people and objects. If children and adults remain stuck in the initial schizoid position, their capacity for empathy and love and to feel and promote the good are thought to be severely impaired (Appignanesi 2006).

Steven Connor (1998) summarised Klein's theory:

> The bad object becomes the source of persecutory anxiety and threatens the destruction of the ego. In this stage, the ego can tolerate anxiety only by replicating the violent division between good and bad objects in its own self-constitution, taking in the good and disgustedly, anxiously, disavowing or expelling the bad . . . After about four months, the depressive position may be attained. In this, the mother may begin to be grasped as a whole person, in whom the good and the bad are combined. The anxiety here is not of imminent destruction by the aggressive bad object, but of the loss of the mother.

Connor reviewed how Wilfred Bion (1967) extended Klein's theories on baby–mother relationships, and the need of the baby's 'psyche to dispose of ego fragments produced by its destructiveness' and later to reintegrate good and bad parts of the self. Bion thought that mothers contain and interpret babies' feelings (Connor 1998):

> bad images are often not so much expelled, as loaned out to another, for possible reclaiming at some later time. This other is often the mother, provided she consents to act as the screen or detoxifying repository of the terrors and horrors expelled from the self in the interests of its self-preservation.

Though sceptical about over-attributions of adult psychic distress back to early life experiences, Bion associated certain adult problems with mothers and other close carers who had been unable to 'contain' the baby's over-powerful emotions of hatred, so that then hatred comes to be directed against all feelings, and the external reality that stimulates them, leading to hatred of life itself (Connor 1998).

This glimpse into an extensive literature illustrates the conviction of many psychoanalysts that babies' earliest feelings and experiences are complex, powerful and profound, far from blank, or empty, or solely learned from adult teachers, or reliant on language.[13] Winter's (2010) interviews with Crystal, Connor and other children (see p. 126) illustrate how young children have to grapple with the most profound feelings. Babies' earliest sensations and emotions could all the more overwhelm them for being novel, not yet contained or organised into clear memories, sequences, meanings or language, with no hope of explanations from anyone.

Interpreting the history of the self

This section returns to the above history of ideas about the self in relation to childhood, and then reviews the conclusions by the authors Martin and Barresi.

Over the centuries, most children and indeed adults endured hard lives, probably with little respect either given to them or expected, but children's low status differed little from that of most adults. There were powerful themes in religion and art of honouring children and women, although idealisations can work to oppress as much as to benefit the real people who fail to live up to them. The Enlightenment emphasis on the intellect and on rights related to reason became part of the distancing of adults from children, when men and later women became formally assumed to be competent, whereas children are assumed not to be (Alderson 1993). If the self is the incremental sum of memories or competencies, childhood can seem vacant. In wealthier societies, while the soul's relevance to worldly pragmatism faded, so too childhood became excluded from mainstream life in countless ways. The rise of culture over nature can also consign children to a pre-social limbo. Concepts of the sinful, or innocent, or learning child have been central to adults' efforts to understand themselves through the reflection or reverse mirror image of the child, and through projections, negations, idealisations, dislocations and redemptions of adult desires (Steedman 1994).

Children in wealthier societies greatly benefit today from being cared for, often more lavishly than ever before, but on average they live many more years of economic dependence in times when people are valued for their earning power. Ideas of the fragmenting self and identity appear to accompany fragmenting relationships and insecure uncertainties that can be especially hard for dependent groups such as children. They also complicate and undermine shared meanings and experiences of flourishing and misery.

Martin and Barresi (2006: 304–5) comment on their history by distinguishing between *scientifically* useful, explanatory theories, versus ideas of the self 'as a *practically* useful notion'. Scientific theories are scrutinised and critiqued while they advance and explain academic debates, and are replaced if they become sufficiently discredited. When the self came to be understood in more material and less in spiritual-metaphysical terms, the soul was no longer a scientifically useful concept. Today, the notion of a unified self of action and reflection does not fit fragmented, poststructural and developmental theories. (I would add that the subsplitting of topics such as the self serves the interests of academics, disciplines and departments when they each compete for status, funding and claims to unique knowledge.) With more and more knowledge about narrower components of the complex self-person, the coordinating and unifying of the knowledge and ways of knowing seem ever less likely.

Martin and Barresi ask whether this pluralism is healthy, or chaotic, or both, and whether the unified self was always an illusion. They contrast the fall of the *soul* in scientific theory with the religious belief in the soul still held by most people in the USA (although the authors see that as a confusing, retarding dogma). They set the fall of the *self* in scientific theory, against universal, daily practices, which essentially depend on the notion that everyone has some kind of unified self. The practices range from keeping promises to ownership, from responsibility to planning for the future. Martin and Barresi (pp. 304–5) see the self as 'a misleading, albeit socially indispensible and incredibly useful fiction'. They contend that we are not unified or constant in our self but we are in our body. They believe the soul was invented to elevate and exalt the 'I', a reigning 'demigod of sorts [with] essence, free will, consciousness', and immortality. As the soul dwindled, 'the unified self was called in to fill the void' and to continue the fictional and dangerous 'ego-trip' of human freedom and control above the natural world (see Volume 2, Chapter 9).

Although they might seem to be logical and inevitable, these conclusions leave us in an impossible hiatus, split between: an illusory fiction of the self and the practical reality; different and hardly reconcilable ways of knowing the self; scientific denial of the soul but much religious faith in it; fictional superhuman control but impotent mortality; and a constant, unified body but a transient, fragmented self or selves. This final split seems to be the most controversial, since bodies greatly change, and whatever the 'I' is, it cannot wholly be reduced to flesh. However much authors claim the non-existence or death of the self, in order to do so they have to rely on the continuing existence of their own self to do the denying (Bhaskar 2002a: 74). It seems unfortunate that Martin and Barresi have to conclude that their great history and all related academic thought inevitably ends in Cartesian, postmodern and pointless confusion. This returns us to the contradictions between positivists and interpretivists reviewed in Chapter 2.

Chapter 7 will review the major themes of this book, and show how DCR works to resolve some of these contradictions, when human flourishing is seen to involve living creatively in the dialectic between the fractured, contradictory fragmented self and the person's longing for unity, between free independent fulfilment, needy dependence and interdependent caring for others (Bhaskar [1993] 2008b: 286).

7

CONCLUSIONS TO VOLUME 1

The relevance of DCR to childhood studies

> It was so powerful for the young people because really it made them aware
> of what it is to have rights . . . and be able to exert your freedom of speech
> . . . The kids were driving the media coverage . . . They would go along to
> demonstrations and marches and speak in front of thousands of people.
> Twelve year old children perceived as being quite demure Muslim girls
> were primarily the driving force behind the campaign . . . [They came to
> know] how people can become involved in the democratic process and not
> see themselves as powerless but able to manipulate and control things.
>
> *(Rosie Mason, London schoolteacher, quoted in Pinson et al. 2010: 200)*

In their study of the politics of solidarity and compassion, Halleli Pinson, Madeleine
Arnot and Mano Candappa (2010) show the political awakening in English schools
of students aged from 6 years upwards. The catalyst was their shock when their
school friends, who were asylum-seekers, were suddenly threatened with being
deported or being detained in secure accommodation. The young students knew
something of the horrors that their friends had escaped from, and the memories they
had to live with. They were amazed that, in this democratic country, the justice
system could seem to be so harsh and unfair. They learned that together they could
challenge and sometimes stop the detentions and deportations. Pinson and colleagues
conclude that the students' growing political awareness and agency involves *questioning assumed values* – values of general childlike acceptance and compliance,
but also xenophobic values expressed in newspapers and by some of their parents
and neighbours. This questioning and awakening are central themes in this chapter.

Previous chapters have noted unresolved dissatisfactions and disagreements
among social scientists. And their proposed solutions tend to increase the
contradictions between simplistic empiricism and unrealistic interpretivism. This
chapter will refer to key themes in the debates that have lasted over 2,500 years

with DCR's proposed solutions, illustrated by the history of ideas about the self or person (see Chapter 6).

The topic of the person is also continued here, because it is so often ignored or assumed or fragmented among the sciences and social sciences. Yet, acknowledged or not, it is central to concepts of childhood, to children as persons who matter now, to beliefs about their well-being and needs, and to efforts to benefit them. A further reason for continuing the theme is that interdisciplinary childhood studies about the origins of the self could help to remedy present gaps and contradictions in research on the adult self.

After reviewing ideas about the self through key themes in DCR, I will look at Christian Smith's account of the person as a practical example of critical realist analysis. This Chapter ends by looking forward to Volume 2. To begin with, the next section starts by returning to the opening quotation, to consider when the questioning, resisting self or person begins.

Origins of the self

Zygmunt Bauman (2003) noted the great omission from sociology of concern about the Holocaust, a primary social event of the twentieth century. Also relatively neglected in sociology have been international human rights (UN 1948; European Council 1950), which emerged from the Nuremberg trials about the Holocaust, and which centre on each person as a rights-holder. The first stream on human rights was not held at a British Sociological Association annual meeting until the sixtieth meeting in 2011. Like the inner person, universal human rights can elude both empirical demands for direct evidence, and also interpretive attention to the cultural and contingent.

Bauman criticised Durkheim's and Parsons's view that we are born amoral or pre-moral, and are gradually educated and socialised away from animal passions and into becoming moral persons who conform to society's rules and norms. Bauman mistrusted modern civilisation, and he regarded the Holocaust as its product rather than its mistake or accident. With Hannah Arendt (1964) and Alvin Gouldner (1977), Bauman associated morality with the rare courage to resist and protest against unjust and cruel majority views, in compassion and solidarity with oppressed people. The example at the head of this chapter showed that even young children understand this. Piaget (1932) and Kohlberg (1981) researched children's interest in rules, but both saw morality in compliantly keeping rules, such as in boys' games. Piaget saw ignorant immaturity in imaginatively bending rules, such as when girls made allowances for younger children so that they could remain in the game and not be excluded for breaking a rule. The functionalist concept of necessary compliance regards each society as being the God-like keeper of its collective social conscience, each being understood on its own terms. That view prevents any independent evaluation or comparison of moralities. Functionalist research compounds the problems when it eschews explicit value judgements, and assesses all matters, including moralities, for their efficient, functioning utility in a smoothly run society, instead of for their moral worth. Compliance is the sole moral option if 'actions are evil because they are socially prohibited, rather than socially prohibited because they are evil' (Bauman 2003: 173).

Bauman and Arendt inverted this morality. For them, the perpetrators, bystanders and relatively few protestors in 1930s–40s Germany showed the extent of human good and evil. Ordinary good people can commit evil when they obey orders, transfer responsibility up the hierarchy, and fail to see victims as persons. Further, Bauman asked, where do concepts of morality come from if they are all somehow imagined and invented? Who invents them, how and why? The idea that morality must be imposed on primitive child savages implies that an alien morality works against human nature. Yet, as reviewed in Chapter 6, morality has meaning and urgency, and it protects the self and others, when it is rooted in vulnerable, needy human nature, which includes a long, dependent childhood, and when it promotes human flourishing. Morality can then be seen as an authentic part of human natural necessity, rather than being synthetic and arbitrary.

Bauman (2003: 177) suggested: '*For sociological theory, the very idea of pre-social grounds of moral behaviour augurs the necessity of a radical revision of traditional interpretation of the origins of the sources of moral norms and the obligatory power*' (emphasis added). He did not pursue this idea, but a vital contribution from interdisciplinary childhood studies to all the social sciences would be to explore these 'pre-social grounds' and the dialectic between the innate and the sociocultural, which I began to map in earlier chapters. Dominant sociological approaches seem to hold back such research when they side-step questions of power and justice, when value-free positivism can endorse moral indifference, interpretivism leads to moral relativism, and social constructionism implies that bodies and suffering do not really exist or matter. Gouldner considers that such positions remap or reorder the world towards other moralities of prudence or profit, utility, rule-keeping or performance. They replace older virtues of human attachment: 'kindness, courage, civility, loyalty, love, generosity and gratitude' with calculating self-interest and avarice, and they reduce personal worth into exchange value (Gouldner 1977: 75). These moves increase the risks of alienation, especially of the dependent youngest generations, whose own views, values and interests may be discounted by more powerful age groups. In contrast, this chapter will review and summarise DCR concepts introduced in previous chapters to show how they are useful if not essential in this task.

The epistemic fallacy, which reduces being into thinking, has driven traditional dismissal of young children as persons in the notion that thought and self-awareness can exist only through words, and not until at least the second year when children begin to talk. Like Connor in Chapter 6's opening example, children and adults frequently search for the right word or the forgotten word, illustrating how our complicated insights can be felt before they are both clarified and also reduced into words. Words are meaningless to us without some kind of related prior experiences. And if the prior experiences were meaningless without subsequent words, how would we know which words to search for without some former meaning to guide us? Partly subconscious, though highly aware, wordless thinking and meaning occur between experience and subsequent language, and babies' preverbal behaviours illustrate this interim state. Conversely, verbal warnings of joy or pain can partly socially construct expectations and, through them, later experiences.

This suggests that sensed experiences and emotions can be separate from language but not from thought (memory, patterns, order, comparisons, associations). Although these are all highly interdependent, words cannot wholly construct or convey experiences before, during or after they are sensed. There are problems with overly reducing living and doing (ontology) into language and verbal analysis (epistemology), but also problems with overly separating them. Chomsky (1984) commented:

> I don't think there is any scientific evidence about the question of whether we think only in language or not. But introspection indicates pretty clearly that we don't think in language necessarily. We also think in visual images, we think in terms of situations and events, and so on, and many times we can't even express in words what the content of our thinking is. And even if we are able to express it in words, it is a common experience to say something and then to recognize that it is not what we meant, that it is something else.

As mentioned earlier, the philosopher Mary Midgley (2010) draws on Darwin's theories of early human relationships, not in terms of unchanging, stone-age, human biology, but in seeing humans as social animals with much in common with complex pack, herd and flock species, with their 'pecking order'. This approach argues that we do not have language and reason because we are clever, but because we are intensely sociable. We are innately predisposed to relate, share and communicate like other animals, and additionally to reflect self-consciously and imaginatively, and to feel conscience-stricken guilt, regret and shame. Darwin contrasted such moral human feelings with swallows, who are not haunted by remorse if they leave their fledglings and follow their instinct to migrate in the autumn (Midgley 2010: 57).

DCR responses to problems in social science and philosophy

The history of ideas of the self (see Chapter 6) illustrated long-standing theoretical problems. Philosophy and research paint themselves into awkward corners when positivists and interpretivists cannot defend their own work against the others' criticisms, when academic disciplines cannot agree on a coherent view of the self, or when in theory they deny an enduring self or person on which they all have to rely in practice (Martin and Barresi 2006: 290–305). I will consider underlying problems and resolutions (listed in italics), partly summarised from previous chapters, which DCR has identified.

The *epistemic fallacy* (to collapse ontology, things and being, into episte-mology) leads researchers to try to validate their theorising within their own thoughts and signs. Instead, they also need to rely on the original, intransitive subject or referent of research, the third part of the *semiotic triangle* (Bhaskar [1993] 2008b: 223). Reality is lost when researchers rely on only two parts of the triangle, the *signified* (or their concepts of the original reality), and the *signifier* (the words as sounds or written marks), and they lose the original *referent*. Despite their seeming concern with reality, empiricists confuse it with their own sensed perceptions, and if something intangible, such as the self, cannot be proved through the senses, they deny its real existence and treat it as an invention or fiction.

This *primal squeeze on natural necessity* is the squeeze traced back to Plato and Aristotle, and later between Kantian idealism, metaphysics, speculation and reasoning versus Hume's empirical, sensed experience, and between today's positivists and interpretivists (Bhaskar [1994] 2010a). These swings and reactions between philosophical positions occur within their shared *TINA (there is no alternative)* assumptions about the epistemic fallacy and the primal squeeze. Research conclusions, policies and practices (in all areas of life such as health, education, welfare, economics, peace-keeping) tend to be based on actual and empirical evidence and then to fail or to become counterproductive if they override real deeper causes and alternatives.

Both deny the difference between *intransitive* reality and our *transitive* percep-tions of it. The denial of original reality that sets thought over being forces researchers to work far harder to try to construct the grounds and validation for their thinking within their thought, instead of in the original object of research. This leads into unrealistic and contested postmodern theories, in efforts to find validation. Yet the efforts move ever further away from the original reality that would validate the research.

Like the semiotic triangle, *flat actualism* also reduces three vital parts into two. It treats *actual* events and *empirical* records of them as if these two levels contain the whole of *reality*. It stays at the level of a world without depth. However, *natural necessity* recognises underlying, invisible, causal reality, which is only known in its effects. As when Newton and Darwin moved beyond observing objects and apparent patterns between them into seeing the patterns as the effects of the deeper causes of gravity or evolution, DCR recognises the three-layer natural necessity in both the natural and the social sciences. Paradoxically, unseen, unprovable realities, such as evolution, are respected more in the natural than in the social sciences, when causes such as class, gender and race may be dismissed as bias or speculation. DCR helps to strengthen and validate social research by showing, through the *possibility of naturalism* (Bhaskar 1998a), that the explana-tory theories in the social and natural sciences are more similar than is often assumed. Like gravity, the self can be seen as the unseen cause of an individual's thought and behaviour. A cause is real when it has practical effects. The reality of self helps to explain the natural necessity, the true nature, of being human, and to reveal the superficial weaknesses of behaviourist or poststructuralist research that ignores or denies underlying reasons and causes.

At their heart are misconceptions about the human self and also about *absence, change and difference*. Since Parmenides vetoed thinking about absence and 'what is not', about negativity, not-being, generating and perishing, western thinkers have concentrated on *ontological monovalence*. That is, the single value of the purely positive, actual-empirical presence, with denial of unseen non-being that drives change (Bhaskar [1993] 2008b, [1994] 2010a; Norrie 2010). That involves denial of real determinant absence, and therefore of change as complex transformation well beyond simple difference.

In Chapter 3, I gave the example of *difference* when Clare leaves a room and Tim enters it, versus *change* when Clare learned to read and absented her former total dependence on others to read to her. Change involves motive and agency, whereas noting a different child in a room does not explain Tim's motives or causes for being there. Difference involves two or more different entities – Clare and Tim can never be fused, whereas change involves alteration within one entity, tensed over time, with continuity as well as alteration. Change involves difference but cannot be reduced to it. Clare is the same and also different from her former non-reading self, in a being and becoming that continues throughout childhood and adulthood.

The history of the self showed how the self was either understood as an unchanging and therefore immortal soul or else, when religion and empirical science became incompatible, as a series of changing but therefore disconnected and invented selves. The example illustrates how change became divorced from continuity. This philosophy deeply affects daily thinking. While writing this section, I talked with a group of university student critical lawyers about children's human rights. They began by assuming that children cannot understand or exercise rights until they are 18 or 16 years old, although they were so near that age themselves. The view partly thrives on young adults' desire to distance themselves from non-emancipated childhood. They cited Piaget's stage theory, and relied on the implicit idea of the changing, volatile, not-yet-real child versus the *fixed, stable* adult who enjoys a lifelong career and marriage. Recent decades have overturned such adult stability, if it ever existed, but they have not ended folk tales about the *unreliable changeable* child who cannot make informed, long-term decisions.

Change and continuity are understood in DCR beyond monovalence by appreciating absence, what is not, as a great causal, determining, push-pull power like gravity. A world or a self with no inner absence or vacuums or deficiencies is fixed, because there is no room for change. At all ages, the self has to include presence and also absence in all the past, missed opportunities, in all the future, potential ones and in present flux.

The one and the other, and the one and the many

Denial of absence connects with the twin problems of *the one and the other* and *the one and the many*. There are two main kinds of explanation: one is taxonomic and assigns things to groups to explain their function; the other is causal and analyses processes of cause and effect. The first question, of the one and the other, asks how things can change but also endure as the same entity. What is the nature of change and how does it occur? If something changes does it become another different entity, or remain basically the same thing and, if so, how can that happen? Bhaskar ([1993] 2008b: 309 ff., 355) and Norrie (2010: 169 ff.) consider that this crucial, first question about ontology, being and becoming became 'dissolved', repressed and mystified into the second problem, the more static, conservative question about epistemology by Plato and his successors who questioned: *the one and the many*, or the universal and the particular. How can we *know* how to group different things into one category, or know the universal in each particular case? How is each separate entity the same as, or different from the many other things? How might they share, or not share, the same nature or substance? How can they be classified into groups? Attention to cause shifted to taxonomy, which allayed anxieties about how difference might be controlled and understood, order maintained and chaos prevented. Plato proposed the ideal Forms as fixed universals but still faced the problem of how to classify seemingly infinite actual diversity and flux into appropriate Forms.

The transfer, from concern with change to concern with difference (taxonomy), began when Parmenides vetoed thinking about absence, which is central to change, both personal and political. Platonic assumptions about the unchanging unity of the soul, and of God as the eternal, changeless observer are precursors to today's ideal of the detached, objective scientific observer. Interactive, reflexive research is still rejected by many scientists.[1] The epistemic fallacy invests great power in the observer to define and interpret the world unchallenged, politically as well as philosophically. Bhaskar ([1994] 2010a: 177) and others consider that the elite lawgivers Parmenides and Plato aimed to preserve the ruling order by denying non-being and change. Parmenides asserted that the world is a single whole to be understood only in positive terms of truth, never by negative, ignorant opinion concerning 'what is not', which cannot be recognised or mentioned. He saw being as an equilibrium, a complete, ungenerated, indestructible, eternal whole, like a well-rounded ball. Bhaskar analyses how Parmenides's untenable extreme bans not only change (absence, becoming, movement, transformation) but even difference (diversity, otherness).

In *The Sophist*, Plato (1997) subtly reduced, mystified and negated absenting transformative change into the more static and positive difference. He substituted Parmenides's One Universal Being into the ideal, epistemic Platonic Forms, and he continued to rely on knowledge as an alternative foundation for ontology, which became a matter of naming and classifying things. Plato thereby further developed the epistemic fallacy, and also the identity for philosophy of the knowing subject versus the passive object (Bhaskar [1994] 2010a:180 ff.; Norrie 2010: 166 ff.). The fixed, enduring, abstract, ideal Forms are assumed to underlie all matter, and they counter flux and perishing. To Plato, Forms establish the stable, epistemological basis for being (whereas in DCR natural necessity is the real causal basis). The Forms are as abstract, universal and independent of their visible expression, as numbers are abstract, universal and independent from the things they count.

Aristotle's response to the earlier questions of the one and the other and change were constrained, Bhaskar contends, by Plato's influence. Aristotle the biologist might appear to close Plato's thinking/being split, and to end his veto on change, when he intensely observed and recorded change as alteration, potential, movement and genesis. However, Bhaskar (p. 5) considers that Aristotle followed Plato in believing that he was guided by *nous*, the ultimate, divine, abstract power of knowing, and the power that constitutes everything as the designer and final cause. Aristotle split everything into its lasting form versus its transient matter or content. This set the method of western science: to identify and classify forms and laws. Modern science does investigate causes within the changing entities, and observes how change actually occurs, though it searches for natural laws and *closed systems*. Many social scientists feel doubtful and ambivalent about associating causes with open systems and with human agency and intentions. Like Aristotle, they avoid searching for internal, natural necessity that provides the *alethic* or inevitable truth about things and their emergent power and development towards perfection (whether in individual selves or in societies and economies). Instead, they tend to avoid discussion of cause or else attribute cause to the *external* forms, which for Aristotle was ultimately *nous*.

Norrie (2010: 173) quotes analysis by Collingwood (1945) and Lear (1988) of Aristotle's concept of changeable, raw matter, its indeterminate quality, and quantity, and unrealised potential unless form gives it meaning. Form is seen as the immanent essence of matter although, as abstract non-matter, form can only exist in the mind of the observer. The 'Platonic-Aristotelian fault-line or primal squeeze' (Bhaskar [1994] 2010: 183) leaves unresolved problems of the ideal universal beyond the world versus actual matter within the world, and knowing observers versus material objects. For centuries this may have consciously and unconsciously informed men who identified themselves with the abstract mind (form) and who identified children and women with bodies, feelings and flux (matter).

DCR proposes inner natural necessity as the grounds for universal change within each particular entity, within not beyond them. Aristotle's forms, and his view that the observer constitutes things and that the mind substitutes for the real ground of being, epitomise concepts of childhood as ephemeral, inferior matter waiting for the form of the rational adult mind to emerge (Stables 2008). Norrie (2010: 174) quotes Lear's (1988: 43) point that Aristotle advances a 'hypothetical' (not a natural) 'necessity of form', which 'flows backward from the achieved end to the process directed towards that end' and that the true cause or explanation is found in the end not the beginning. The phrase summarises attitudes towards children as the prelude to adulthood when 'life begins'. Norrie also quotes Cornford's comment that Aristotelian tradition privileges the adult observers' dismissal of young children's thoughts and experiences as formless because they lack language and therefore, it was believed, reason. This is despite the evidence that babies think and reason and form views long before they speak. They are emotionally motivated (both words involve movement) to struggle to learn language, not by pure reason, but primarily in order to relate to others through expressing their views and feelings.

Questions of the one and the many and the one and the other continue today to hover over the original 'fault-line' (Bhaskar [1993] 2008b: 355). Readers are referred to Bhaskar's and Norrie's histories of how philosophers have very differently addressed the problems of the primal squeeze, the universal ideal versus actual matter, the epistemic fallacy and the subject-object identity theory, without resolving or escaping from them. Real determinate absence with its link to change is lost in Descartes's reduction of everything into his ego. Cartesian doubt opened the way: to 'Lockean scepticism about essences, Berkeleian scepticism about matter and Humean scepticism about everything' (Bhaskar [1993] 2008b: 190); to Hume's induction that restricts a universal principle to its instances; to Kant's transcendental idealism with empirical realism and his split between the noumenal (unknown) and the phenomenal (known); through to Hegel's phenomenology; Wittgenstein's uncertainty about how we know the rules of the language games we play (p. 35); to Habermas, Strawson, Deleuze and postmodern relativism. The political and economic crises of the past hundred years have highlighted inadequacies in philosophy and sociology either to address or to advise on these problems, or to cross the gulf between a morality for (Kantian) rational beings and that for real human beings (Bhaskar [1994] 2010a: 205; Norrie 2010: 181).

DCR restores practical attention to the original ontological question of the one and the other, and how things, such as a child or a self, can change and yet still be the same, not replaced by another thing. This attends to the nature of being through validating determinate absence, causal natural necessity, and the *alethic* unavoidable truth through 'multi-tiered stratification of being, or ontological depth' (Bhaskar [1994] 2010a: 5). By centring determinate absence as well as presence in ontology, DCR aims to avoid the detotalising reifications, denials and splits that have riven western philosophy. The splits within and between many disciplines, as well as in many dichotomies, appear through the history by Martin and Barresi, and in their conclusion: 'we are not unified by the soul or the self. We are unified by the body' (2006: 305).

Emergence

One way to reconcile change with endurance is through *emergence*. Bhaskar (2002a: 74 ff.) sees human beings as agents bound in space and time, with a transcendentally real self, unlike modern concepts of a false self that is an isolated, atomistic ego linked to a vague abstract universal, neither of which exist. Bhaskar writes of 'those emergent totalities called persons [with their] geohistories, emergent rhythmic, multiple binds, reflectivity, openness and transformative agency'. The phrases raise questions about where or what persons might emerge from, and how fulfilled or empty or not-yet-unfolded their initial existence might be (Bhaskar [1993] 2008b:126).

DCR concepts of emergence work to overcome dichotomies, such as mind/body and material/abstract, which either reduce the mind into the brain and body, or else treat mind and body as separate dual entities. Neither approach can explain the relationship between mind and body-brain. DCR, however, treats the mind as emergent from the body-brain through the argument mentioned earlier. Water can quench thirst and extinguish fires, but it can only do so as H_2O and not as the separate components from which it emerged. Emergence has three meanings. First, it is a substance, entity, property or system that depends on another different substance, entity, property or system, as the mind depends on the body. Second, the emergent entity goes through fundamental change, for example, as the elements fuse in water, or the abstract mind emerges from the physical brain-body to combine neuro-physiological, psychological, social interactive and possibly spiritual attributes. Third, the emergent entity cannot be un-fused or reduced back into the original parts or the original substance, entity, property or system. This applies to all entities, from the chemistry of water to the history and emergent geo-politics of all societies (Morgan 2007a). The breaking down of divisions between natural and social sciences (the possibility of naturalism) shows how abstract social and cultural matters emerge and change out of natural and physical origins and can share their firm ontology.

Emergence and dialectic both work to overcome and resolve mind/body and agency/structure Cartesian dichotomies, when minds are seen to emerge from bodies, and agents emerge from social structures (language, schools, cultural traditions). Though they are all finally irreducible, they overlap and co-exist inter-dependently with their origins. Emergent societies are more than groups of people; they also have their own collective properties and powers. The concepts of the emergent can overcome divisions between philosophy, natural science and social science when an emergent account of consciousness 'avoids the mysticism of dualism and the basic intentionality contradiction of reductionism' (Morgan 2007a: 167). 'Mysticism' refers to inherent, unresolved contradictions in mind/body dualism, which separate solid bodies from mysterious minds. Reductionism tends to ignore or deny intentional, conscious agency, as seen in long-standing debates about whether lifting an arm, as an unconscious or unintentional reflex movement, differs from lifting an arm as an intended action. Through the concepts of emergence, DCR allows for both possibilities, depending on the agent's aware-ness, motivation and informed responses, and allows these contingencies to be examined, because diversions into mind-body dichotomies can be avoided (Bhaskar 1998a: 105).

Emergence can transcend large and small dichotomies: nature/society, indi-vidual/collective, body/mind, reasons/causes and facts/values. When a cause means something that produces an outcome, reasons can be seen to be causes that produce human actions and responses. This is not to say that everyone is entirely free and autonomous. There are many natural and social constraints; actions are frequently ineffective, they may be counterproductive, and often they have unintended consequences, but the original reasons still caused the outcomes. DCR re-vindicates the ontology of the physical and also of unseen entities such as the mind or self, and analyses their structure, their difference and change. Rather than seeing young children as vacant and pre-social, emergence can see people at every age as latent, emergent and unfolding, being and becoming, realising themselves and their relationships through their agency and contexts.

To combine continuity with change can suggest that flourishing (and alienation) mean much the same for children and young people as for adults, and they begin when children are respected (or rejected) as persons, even in small ways. Babies learn to talk, for example, not by being formally taught but, long before they understand, through living interactions, by being spoken to as if they already understand. The talking child is nurtured and imagined from birth as an emergent part of the pre-verbal child.

Emergence also illustrates the importance of merging childhood studies with the 'adult' world. This could increase our understanding of both children and adults, besides helping to counter dominant, oppressive myths about children's incapacities and irrelevance to the 'adult' world. From the earliest years, thought, language and morality and their gradual enrichment originate in and resonate with every aspect of being human in nature and culture. Sensed experiences and relationships give language and morality meaning, when their authentic, innate and intransitive aspects complement their learned, acquired and transitive aspects in the ontology of being human. Flourishing, suffering and morality matter as part of the whole sensitive person. *Eudaimonia* need not be confined to feeling states or the mind or intellect, but to all four interacting *planes of social being*. Long religious traditions of well-being and virtue respect capacities associated with childhood: friendship, delight, awe, attention to the moment. Childhood is then valued not only as a prelude, or an investment for future profit, but in its own right.

Changing the world

Many childhood researchers hope to improve policies and practices, but usually find their reports have little effect. DCR is concerned with practical transformation besides adding to knowledge. This section gives two examples of practical research, which have not intentionally used DCR concepts, but which will be analysed to illustrate how these DCR concepts underlie effective, emancipatory research. They are also described for their unusual range of approaches, a range likely to be necessary if researchers' aims to change the world are to be fulfilled.

I have referred several times to Heidelisa Als's (1999) intense, counterintuitive, psychological observations of premature babies and their capacities. The second example is the Children's Rights Alliance for England (CRAE).[2] Since ratifying the UN (1989) *Convention on the Rights of the Child* in 1991, the UK government undertook to report regularly to the UN Committee on the Rights of the Child on its progress in implementing the Convention. CRAE was formed to monitor progress, and children, young people and adults work together to collect immensely detailed evidence, which is reported every year (CRAE 2011). CRAE also coordinates the NGOs' (non-governmental organisations) alternative, critical report, which is submitted to the Committee with the government's complacent report. Young CRAE members presented their report to the UN Committee in Geneva (CRAE 2008) and, inspired by their work, the Committee advises other countries also to involve children and young people in composing their regular country NGO reports.[3] In 2008, the NGOs made 152 recommendations for change, at least 100 of which required urgent action. Annually after each UN review, CRAE monitors action on the UN Committee's recommendations.

Work in both projects fits DCR *four planes of social being*. Als began with studying individual babies' embodied needs and self-expression, then their inter-personal relationships and interactions with parents and neonatal staff, and third, social structures of neonatal care, the economics and politics, staff training and support, the design and routines in the units, and society's obligations to promote the well-being of sick babies and young families. Fourth, the study took premature babies seriously as persons, capable of suffering and of enjoying sensi-tive care, in early versions of flourishing. The Newborn Individualized Developmental Care and Assessment Program (NIDCAP) is now an international federation of advocacy for premature babies, training for neonatal staff, and transformation of neonatal care around the world, towards 'baby-led' units and policies.[4]

CRAE honours the rights of every child in England, and begins from their perspectives of need and hope and agency. All rights relate to the first two planes of social being, of bodies and interpersonal relationships, in how practical rights are honoured or violated, children's basic physical needs are met, they are protected from harm, abuse or neglect and they are able to express themselves freely. CRAE works at the third plane through local, regional, national and international structures to effect change, ranging from inequalities, exclusions and discriminations, to unjust laws, courts and police procedures, from failures in education, welfare and health services, to mistreatment of disadvantaged groups. Like NIDCAP, CRAE interacts with practitioners, policy-makers and other adults through meetings and publications, working with them, as well as with children and young people, for change. On the fourth plane, at the centre of CRAE's work is concern to promote each child's well-being or flourishing.

As considered earlier, *MELD 1M, first moment* concerns non-identity, alterity, sheer, irreducible other-being in an attempt to suspend epistemologies, such as deficit theories of the child, and to imagine the subjects studied as independent of the observer, and existing in their own right. Their 'non-identity' sets them beyond being reduced into classified groups and stereotypes. This process involves know-ingly separating the *intransitive* (though changeable) being of the subjects researched from the *transitive* perceptions and interpretations of the researcher, to avoid collapsing the former into the latter. While this is never wholly possible, there are many examples of efforts to suspend and search beyond prior assumptions and these include Als's attention to minute details of babies' being. There is also CRAE's involvement with (often disadvantaged, excluded) children and young people, which aims to suspend judgement and prejudice about them and to appreciate their capacities. Children are more than malleable, floating ideas. If 'there are only beliefs, knowledge, language, descriptions, you cannot refer to anything outside beliefs'. Further, you cannot think about 'a discourse which will allow you to critically evaluate our current claims to knowledge . . . its ideological function' (Bhaskar [1991] 2010b: 81–2). The essential separation of ontology from epistemology begins at *1M*.

First moment also involves looking beyond the empirical and actual to deeper reality. CRAE and NIDCAP are both concerned with children's inner being and their natural necessity, and also with underlying political and economic structural causes that shape children's lives and which have to be addressed if change is to occur. However, instead of seeing 1M difference as irreducible ontology, too often the intransitive real child is trebly confused, by adult observers, with their transitive (sometimes idealised) memories of their own childhoods, with misperceptions of children's actual behaviours and values, and with ambitions about each child's present and future achievements.

MELD 2E, *second edge*, negativity, begins with carefully identifying problems: in NIDCAP, the baby's fear, distress and pain, and the absence of sensitive care, besides the ignorance of neonatal staff and managers and their inattention to the babies' real needs. CRAE similarly begins with the real determinate absence of children's unmet and disrespected needs and rights, and the serious problems caused. The realisation of freedom 'consists in the self-transformation or replacement of unneeded, unwanted and oppressive sources of determination, or structures, by needed, wanted and empowering ones' (Bhaskar [1991] 2010b: 145). Removing unneeded oppressions partly involves beginning from the definitions and values of the children concerned, and working not simply for them but also with them as agents of change, as John's NIDCAP care plan (Chapter 6) demonstrated. 'When self-alienation is the root cause of the social ills, we cannot remove ills in the four planes of social being unless we are free as the *concrete singulars* that start from "the most ordinary desire" as the self' (Bhaskar 2002b: 23). The working together involves removing the inner 'self-alienation' as well as the outer oppressions, vital in NIDCAP's relieving of babies' distress and in CRAE's collective campaigning with young people. As 'concrete singulars' each is respected as unique, but also as sharing much in common with many of their peers and working on behalf of them too. Alienation involves separation from things that are essential to our well-being, and that includes realising the ability to realise this loss, or being mystified and deceived by the 'wicked spell cast over the world' that prevents people from realising their real utopian longings (Adorno [1964] 1989: 4, quoted in Hartwig 2007: 36).

At *MELD 3L*, *third level*, totality, relations and interactions between totalities are drawn together. Contrary to the splitting apart of the self within and between disciplines (see Chapter 6), NIDCAP and CRAE involve a wide range of disciplines, practitioners, policy-makers and the children and adults concerned, to promote shared understanding, agency and respect for the 'whole child' or young self. CRAE's agenda based on the UNCRC unites every aspect of childhood and youth. In 3L totality and dialectic of space-time-cause of human being, the past shapes the present and the future, far more than in any other species, through recorded, transferred culture and language over generations. This occurs among whole generations but also on the smallest level of individual conscience.

Enduring contradictions within a totality tend to split, disconnect or detotalise the totality. An example is when children are assumed to lack 'adult' maturity, although many children have these capacities of wisdom and altruism. Conversely adults may split off their spontaneous, care-free joy and call it 'the child within', instead of accepting that this can be as much a part of being an adult as being a child. Diffracted dialectic can understand, first, these detotalising tendencies that deny wholeness, second, that difference and change co-exist with connection and wholeness and, third, that connection itself can include splits and contradictions. 3L connects the natural and cultural, transitive and intransitive, internal relations between parts, and external relations between totalities. Dialectic draws together the dichotomies, thinking/being, past/present, mind/body, child/adult, process/ product, identity/change, universal/individual.

DCR's diffracting dialectic can see all the views as 'totalities within totalities . . . shot through with spaces . . . connected by all manner of negative, external and contingent as well as positive, internal and necessary determinations and relation-ships' (Bhaskar [1993] 2008b: 126). And multidisciplinary childhood studies can examine each account critically, while relating each to all the others and allowing that, in future, new disciplines may arise to enrich current understandings in social science and biology, biochemistry, genetics, neurology, psychology, psychoanal-ysis, religion and philosophy.

MELD 4D, fourth dimension, self-transformative agency, is achieved through the dialectic that is 'the pulse of freedom' (Bhaskar [1993] 2008b). NIDCAP and CRAE are led by babies', children's and young people's views, expressed through 'any media of the child's choice' (UN 1989: Articles 12 and 13) including body language. That is why the initial, attentive 1M is vital. '*Master–slave*' and *power₂*

relations epitomise negative, alienating adult–child relationships, at 4D and at plane four of our social being. This is the plane of personal freedom of conscience and agency, and working towards the flourishing good life for all in the good society, which aligns with the realisation of human rights. Childhood researchers tend to work in the Hegelian epistemological dialectic: thesis, antithesis, synthesis; collecting, analysing and reporting data within limited time and budgets. NIDCAP and CRAE show how transformative change involves the four-part MELD dialectic starting in 1M real ontology, then through negativity and totality towards emancipation, working over years for practical and political change with the people concerned, as well as writing reports.

Critical realism and the person

Christian Smith demonstrated the usefulness of critical realism's emphasis on ontology in his long analysis *What is a Person?* He identified 30 human capacities (Smith 2011: 42–54). These capacities respond to doubts about whether humanity can be united through such an entity as universal personhood, and beliefs that, instead, humanity is divided into countless, culturally contingent versions. The 30 capacities are validated when it seems unlikely that social researchers would deny having any of these capacities themselves. Logically and morally, therefore, it would then be hard for them to deny that other people also have them. If certain groups are assumed not to have these capacities apart, for example, from extremely disabled people, that would drain meaning away from the concept 'human' and, inevitably, from 'social' and 'society' and 'social research'. The problems and distress caused by conditions such as severe dementia illustrate how 'normal' human life is based on these 30 capacities.

The capacities, which partly but qualitatively differ from those of other species, are: consciousness; a partly unconscious being/mind with deep feelings; under-standing of the real properties of quantity, quality, time and space; making mental images about things; volition or will; practical consciousness with many tacit, 'auto-pilot' behaviours; understanding and assigning cause and effect; forming interests, values and priorities; feeling deep emotions; episodic and long-term remembering; intersubjective understanding; creativity; causal agency; using technologies; conducting long-term projects; self-transcendence and attending to others subjectively and intensely; making and communicating meanings; using symbols; using language; creating narrative; making valuations; anticipating the future; forming a personal identity; self-reflexivity; abstract reasoning; truth-seeking; morality; forming virtuous habits; appreciating aesthetics; interpersonal communion and love.

The very range and complexity of all these capacities allow immense cultural variations, and yet the core facilities exist in every person. The list is so extensive yet so basic that it counters spatial relativism, in notions that people in other cultures do not or cannot possess such capacities. The questions that temporal relativism poses for childhood studies and for future research include how these capacities endure over each lifetime in continuity from youth to age, and whether only adults and possibly young people are persons, while young children and certainly babies cannot be. So far, much detailed research has shown that most of these capacities exist, at least in latent, rudimentary, unfolding forms, in the early months after birth.

Volume 2

DCR does not propose an alternative social science. Instead, as a philosophy, it aims to clarify and explain underlying theories, beliefs and connections, omissions and contradictions, problems and also insights and achievements that already exist in social research, in order to assist more researchers to make informed decisions and analyses. By freeing social research from negative legacies, and showing its integral values, the hope is to promote emancipatory research, which challenges misunderstandings and also injustices.

My intention in this book was to merge the inevitably interacting personal and political, small- and large-scale matters. As there has not been space to do so much in one fairly short volume, the second volume deals more with the larger scale, while building on the DCR and childhood theories and examples set out in Volume 1. Chapter 9 will link to Chapter 3 on bodies in nature to see how the ecology, climate change, loss of biodiversity and dwindling resources especially affect the youngest generations.

Chapter 10, like Chapter 4, will examine interpersonal relations. Economics are central to human relationships, and Chapter 10 will consider the distribution of resources between the generations, and how current spending, debts and investments are likely to affect their lives in the next few decades. Interpersonal relations also involve whether young people are respected as active, equal citizens. Citizenship assumes a city context, and recently more people have begun to live in cities than to live outside them. While adults choose, more or less, to move into cities and to remain there, though many feel they have little choice, children and young people have even fewer options. How does urban or rural life particularly impact on them, their lifestyles, identities, health, opportunities and relationships?

Social structures that endure over time, the topics of Chapters 5 and 11, connect with ideas about change, progress and evolution. Do human capacities and prospects improve over time, or regress, or is there no definite pattern or purpose to human history? Given the growing ecological and economic challenges that face the burgeoning human societies, how can social structures be shaped to help or to harm them in the near future?

Chapter 12 will return to the topics of Chapter 6 on human identity, alienation or flourishing, to draw together themes from both volumes and all four planes of social being, and to consider how childhood studies can expand to work more closely with researchers of 'adult' societies.

Appendix

BACKGROUND SUMMARIES OF SELECTED RESEARCH STUDIES

General comments

Writing this book led me to realise that my extended family, with its overlapping generations and present living age-span of over 90 years, has been a kind of life-long case study that has framed my research on childhood.

The formal projects were approved by local research ethics committees.

All names have been changed; children often chose their own research name, parents usually chose their baby's second name.

I was the sole, or principal, or main co-researcher in each project, and always collected data. Many of the projects were interdisciplinary; co-researchers and advisers included experts in advocacy, anthropology, biology, education, epidemiology, genetics, history, information technologies, law, medicine, NGOs (non-governmental organisations), nursing, philosophy, psychology, social policy, social work and sociology, as well as users of services.

My approaches included an uncertain mixture of ethnography and critical theory with degrees of positivism and social constructionism. Writing this book has helped me to clarify my then under-acknowledged ambiguities. If I could begin again, I would be more clear and confident about realities, validations and links to social policy. The 'observations' listed below were interactive and involved talking and sometimes playing with participants. 'Ethnography' was a form of 'living alongside' and communicating, and was especially valuable with younger children and disabled children with speech difficulties. I would sit in class at their tables with school students, and spend weeks watching and talking with people in hospital wards and clinics, in schools and in families' homes. Semi-structured interviews were taped and transcribed. (I was greatly helped by my mother and by Sarah Johnson of One to One.)

There are details of hundreds of my reports on www.ioe.ac.uk/ssru and some are listed in the end references of this book.

1.1 Parents' consent to paediatric cardiac surgery

Dates	1984–1989
Researchers	Priscilla Alderson, supervisors, Caroline Ramazanoglu, Victor Seidler, Elliot Shinebourne, David Silverman
Funders	Economic and Social Research Council, Wingate Scholarships

Research aims and questions To research for a PhD in sociology on how concepts of patient autonomy and consent in law and medical ethics can apply to emotional parents giving consent to heart surgery on behalf of their child.

Data collection and samples Observations for two years in children's heart centres at the Royal Brompton and Great Ormond Street Hospitals London, in the wards, intensive care units and clinics; semi-structured taped interviews with staff and with over 100 parents; questionnaire surveys with over 400 parents and over 70 nurses.

Among the findings Kantian and utilitarian models of rational, informed and voluntary consent exclude the moral emotions which, far from disqualifying anxious parents, can inform their decisions.

Reports PhD thesis, University of London, 1988; book, Alderson (1990)

1.2 Children's consent to surgery

Dates	1989–1991
Researchers	Priscilla Alderson, Jill Siddle
Funders	Leverhulme Trust, Royal Liverpool Children's Hospital, Calouste Gulbenkian Foundation

Research aims and questions To research at which age children are able to give valid, informed and voluntary consent to major surgery.

Data collection and samples Observations in four hospitals; interviews with 120 patients aged 8–15 years before and after major elective surgery; interviews with their parents and 70 hospital staff.

Among the findings Children's competence to make informed and wise decisions are influenced by their experiences and by adults' expectations far more than by their age.

Reports Book, Alderson (1993) and series of papers

1.3 Civil rights in schools

Dates   1997–1999
Researchers   Priscilla Alderson, Sean Arnold
Funder   Economic and Social Research Council Childhood 5–16
                   Research Programme

Research aims and questions To investigate school students' views about the 1989 UN *Convention on the Rights of the Child* and its practical relevance in their schools.

Data collection and samples Questionnaire survey of 2,272 school students aged 7–17 years in 49 schools; 34 focus group interviews.

Among the findings Without necessarily using rights language, most students were highly aware about their rights and wanted these to be more fully respected in schools.

Reports Series of papers

1.4 Promoting positive behaviour at school

Dates   1997
Researcher   Priscilla Alderson
Funder   Calouste Gulbenkian Foundation

Research aims and questions To be a writer in residence in an unusual school that involved everyone, in transforming behaviours, relationships and routines in the school over five years, and to write a book in the words of the students and staff.

Data collection and samples Two weeks during summer and autumn terms of observing and interviewing in the school with students aged 7–11 years and the staff.

Among the findings There were many remarkable achievements by the school council and other groups and individual students, encouraged by the staff.

Reports Book (Highfield School 1997)

1.5 Enabling education

Dates   1994–1999
Researchers   Priscilla Alderson, Christopher Goodey
Funders   Calouste Gulbenkian Foundation, Gatsby Charitable Foundation

Research aims and questions To compare special and segregated versus inclusive and mainstream education for students with physical, sensory, behavioural or learning difficulties.

Data collection and samples Two education authorities, one highly inclusive, the other highly segregated; observations in 16 schools; taped interviews with 37 students aged 4–16 years and with 81 adults – parents, school and local authority staff.

Among the findings Inclusive education can benefit everyone, provided it is well planned and resourced; most of the special schools observed seriously failed their students.

Reports Book, Alderson and Goodey (1998) and other papers

1.6 An inclusive school

Dates	1998–1999
Researcher	Priscilla Alderson
Funder	Gatsby Charitable Foundation

Research aims and questions To be a writer in residence and to write a report of an inclusive mainstream primary school in the words of the students and staff.

Data collection and samples Observations and interviews with students aged 3–11 years, teachers and parents.

Among the findings Inclusion works when everyone is involved in equality and respect on grounds of ability, age, gender, 'race', ethnicity, religion, language and dress.

Reports Book, Alderson (1999b)

1.7 Other work on children's rights

Evaluation of the Office of Children's Rights Commissioner for London 2000–2002; book on young children's rights

Dates	1999–2002, 2007
Researchers	Priscilla Alderson, Lorna Clarke-Jones, Heike Schaumberg
Funders	Joseph Rowntree Foundation, Calouste Gulbenkian Foundation, Sainsbury Trusts, Save the Children

Research aims and questions To research and publicise the practical knowledge of children and young people in implementing the UN 1989 *Convention on the Rights of the Child* in their homes, schools and communities.

Data collection and samples Observing the work of the London office that was set up and run by and for London's children and young people; learning about their rights in their daily lives in schools, traveller sites and as young care-leavers; literature reviews.

Among the findings When encouraged and respected, children and young people, including ones who have been rejected by their schools and families, show considerable practical understanding of their shared human rights and ways to implement them.

Reports Alderson *et al.* (2002), Alderson (2008)

1.8 Foretelling futures

Dates	2002–2004
Researchers/colleagues	Priscilla Alderson, Kathryn Ehrich, Joanna Hawthorne, Margaret Killen, Inga Warren, John Wyatt
Funder	Wellcome Trust

Research aims and questions To research four neonatal intensive care units from the perspectives of the babies, parents and staff.

Data collection and samples Observations and interviews with parents and staff in four neonatal units.

Among the findings Policies ranged from world-leading 'baby-led' care to less family-friendly routines. We explored how and why the policies worked and varied.

Reports Series of papers including Alderson *et al.* (2005a, 2005b)

1.9 Evaluation of a London children's centre with children aged 0–2 years

Dates	2006–2007
Researchers	Priscilla Alderson, Elizabeth Brooker
Funder	The East London Nursery

Research aims and questions To assess, as far as possible from the children's perspectives, the quality of daily care in the nursery, and the links between play, care and learning, and to make recommendations.

Data collection and samples Observations, interviews with eight staff and 14 mothers, play sessions with 26 children aged 0–2 years.

Among the findings Our report on successes and problems in the nursery led to considerable changes.

Reports Alderson and Brooker (2007)

1.10 Living with diabetes

Dates	2005–2006
Researchers	Priscilla Alderson, Katy Sutcliffe, Katherine Curtis
Funder	Social Science Research Unit

Research aims and questions To investigate children's understanding and practical share in their daily management of their type 1 diabetes.

Data collection and samples Interviews in their homes and in three hospital clinics with 24 children aged 3–12 years and their parents.

Among the findings The children reported high levels of understanding, knowledge and skill gained from the experience of living with diabetes. They all wanted to be 'normal' and 'just get on with their lives'.

Reports Alderson *et al.* (2006a, 2006b)

1.11 Other projects on consent, rights and research ethics related to health, healthcare and genetics

Dates	1988 onwards
Researchers/colleagues included	Priscilla Alderson, Ann Oakley, Berry Mayall, Mary Madden, Ruth Wilkins, Valerie Hey, Helen Roberts, Naomi Pfeffer and Consumers for Ethics in Research, Elena Heminki, Clare Williams, Bobbie Farsides, Helen Penn, Jonathan Montgomery, Epigeum team
Funders included	King Edward's Hospital Fund for London, Economic and Social Research Council, Cancer Research Campaign, Gatsby Charitable Trust, Barnardo's, North East Thames Regional Health Authority, Institute for Public Policy Research, Institute of Education, BBC Children in Need, Sainsbury Trusts, Health Education Authority, European Commission, Wellcome Trust, Epigeum

Research aims and questions To design and conduct a series of projects on consent relating to healthcare treatment and research and prenatal screening; to convene a series of ESRC seminars on consent; to write books, guidelines and online courses about ethics standards in research with children and for healthcare and social research ethics committees.

NOTES

1 Introduction

1 International human rights concern the duties of states/governments to respect all their citizens' rights, enshrined in international treaties, which states ratify and undertake to implement. The most universally agreed treaty, except for the Geneva Conventions, is the UNCRC (1989), ratified by all states except for the USA and Somalia. Article 7 concerns the child's right to be registered immediately after birth and to have a name and a nationality. While there is concern that registration can risk oppressive and even dangerous intrusion from the state, which the UNCRC guards against, without registration many children's rights cannot be honoured. Of an estimated 134 million births per annum, 51 million go unregistered every year (see www.unicef.org/protection/Birth_ Registration_Working_Paper(2).pdf). The 2011 *Lancet* series recorded an estimated 2.6 million third trimester stillbirths per annum (see www.stillbirthalliance.org/). Over 40 per cent of deaths of children under 5 years occur in the first month after birth, and 75 per cent of these occur in the first week (see www.bmj.com/content/342/bmj.d346.full).

2 The complexity of the shift towards public medicine, with its precarious funding, politics and philanthropy, is recorded in George Eliot's 1874 historical novel *Middlemarch*.

3 During summer 2012, there were moves to expel Save the Children from Pakistan, although they said they had no connection at all with the fake programme.

4 CRIN (2012), see www.crin.org/Discrimination/Challenging/Media/index.asp, accessed 11 October 2012.

5 'Women half the population of the world' had 165,000,000,000 results on Google on 17 November 2011.

6 Anne Solberg's chapter has the most detailed examples in the book of children's lives, of 12-year-olds' share in domestic work, and of their practical autonomy and competence, although it does not quote their views directly; Jenny Kitzinger quotes abused girls in detail.

7 Jiri Kovarik lists timetables of his daughters aged 7 and 17, p. 119, and Judith Ennew asks an 8-year-old 'what is time?', p. 128.

8 The websites of UNICEF, Save the Children, Child to Child, and of street children's movements list many such activities, and see Appendix 1.7.

9 See http://ohchr.un, www.crae.org.uk and www.crin.org (accessed 10 October 2012) for details on countries' reports, the Committee's responses, and also the reports by children and young people. CRAE publishes an annual *State of England's Children*

report on the UK government's progress on implementing, or failure to respect, the UNCRC.

10 Such as *Children & Society, Childhood, Children's Geographies* and the *International Journal of Children's Rights.*

11 The problems are regularly discussed in *The Times Higher Education* journal, and among social researchers.

12 Mainstream sociologists in their research, journals and conferences continue largely to ignore children as if they are pre-social beings. At the sixtieth annual British Sociological Association conference in London in 2011, women were central to the hundreds of presentations, but children were rarely mentioned, and then mainly in the few sessions specifically about them.

2 Trends in research about children, childhood and youth

1 The popularity of 'lab based' psychology is shown by the covert observation mirror windows in rooms still used at the Institute of Education. New ones were installed of 2011, and elaborate lab tests were set for children in the BBC television series *Child of Our Time*, presented by Robert Winston and following 25 children from birth in an annual series.

2 Writing on research about the disastrous HMR (housing market renewal) programmes, Minton (2009) and Allen (2011) criticise university PR departments, which issue glossy press releases of 'banal', misleading research. This is funded by the HMR companies who pay researchers and journalists to promote their policies in the 'corporate capture', not only of formerly public urban space, but also of the cash driven universities, and once independent critical researchers.

3 Department for Work and Pensions *Households Below Average Income 2010/2011* (see www.dwp.gov.uk). Figures are after housing costs; 58 per cent of poor children live in households where at least one adult is employed (Save the Children 2012) www.savethechildren.org.uk/node/2764 (accessed 10 October).

4 I thank Martin Woodhead for rewriting my initial précis of this part of his chapter.

5 Children can openly be denigrated in terms that it is illegal to apply to women, ethnic minority or gay people, but are endorsed by almost half the British public. This is according to rather negative research by Barnardo's (2011), which listed the terms in the questionnaires, see www.barnardos.org.uk (accessed 2 January 2012). Racists can get round the law when they castigate black youths.

3 Real bodies: material relations with nature

1 There were strong public protests when the research was publicised, with complaints that it was extremely cruel and unethical. The researchers replied that they were certain that analgesia should routinely be administered, but they could not persuade their colleagues to agree, so they conducted the trial as a last resort. The publicity and protests possibly helped, along with the research, to change received medical opinion.

2 www.parliament.uk/about/living-heritage/. . ./overview/coalmines/*Cached* – *Similar* (accessed 11 October 2012).

3 Proceedings of the Old Bailey, 1674–1913, www.oldbaileyonline.org (accessed 11 October 2012).

4 Non-accidental child death rates have, however, fallen in the UK from three per week in 1974 to about one per week in 2008 (Sidebotham *et al.* 2011).

5 In May 2011, leading NGOs relaunched their campaign against Nestlé's promotion of formula milk, this time in Laos. Save the Children claims that formula-fed babies in majority world countries are four to six times more likely to die than breast-fed babies. See www.irinnews.org/report.aspx?ReportID=93040 (accessed 31 December 2011).

6 See www.dailymail.co.uk/news/article–2093223/Labour-MP-David-Lammy-Smacking-ban-led-riots.html#ixzz1lVrkkQT8 (accessed 29 January 2012).

7 'Logy' in both epistemology and ontology denotes how they overlap, and how our conscious analysis and knowing in time and space are inescapable and necessary in any conscious attempts to escape from them.

8 I have used hyphens to denote interaction and dialectic, and strokes to denote dichotomy and conflict.

4 Space: interpersonal relations

1 In Bronfenbrenner's child development system theory of concentric rings, each larger sphere of social life is more remote from the child though still influential. However, DCR traces constant interactions and constellations between all the planes (or spheres).

2 www.unicef.org/rosa/media_7046.htm (accessed 21 February 2012).

3 www.headliners.org/storylibrary/stories/2006/positivepress. A survey that found 71 per cent of the news about young people in the review to be negative. Report by Samantha and Samir on why and what can be done about it, *Headliners Positive Press* (accessed 17 July 2012).

4 See the Department for Education website and, for example, the arguments about the centrally directed early years curriculum, www.education.gov.uk/schools/teachingandlearning/curriculum/a0068102/early-years-foundation-stage-eyfs (accessed 14 September 2012).

5 BBC World Service, *'Orphanages' in Bali*, 11 December 2011.

6 For example, see *International Journal of Children's Rights* 1992–present.

5 Time: social relations and structures

1 A news item on the day this page was being written was Pierce, Y. (2011) Why persecute the poor for being poor?, *Guardian*, 19 August.

2 www.coping-project.eu reports the severe effects on children in Europe whose parents are in prison.

3 www.capt.org.uk; http://safetyblog.co.uk/uk-adult-children-road-death-injury-statistics-2010/ (accessed 12 December 2011).

4 Watkins, K. (2012) *The Missing Link: Road Traffic Injuries and the Millennium Development Goals*, www.fia.org (accessed 12 January 2012).

5 Toynbee, P. (2012) On charity George Osborne must stand up to the self-interested super-rich, *Guardian*, 16 April.

6 While the government was 'saving' millions of pounds on benefits for disadvantaged households, Save the Children claimed that 'one in eight of the UK's poorest children go without at least one hot meal per day' and launched an appeal for £500,000 to support them. Butler, P. (2012) Save the Children launches campaign to help UK families in poverty, *Guardian*, 5 September.

7 Among countless uncertainties, one example is the age at which children or their parents should be blamed for children's misdeeds. The legal age of criminal responsibility ranges from 8 years in Scotland to 16 in Spain.

8 Wilson, D. (2012) Murder isn't a question of whodunnit but why-did-they-do-it, *Guardian*, 19 July.

9 *Lancet* (1996) 348: 1189–96.

10 Documented, for example, in the annual UNICEF reports on *The State of The World's Children*, www.unicef.org.

11 Predictions by Marxist and heterodox economists are reviewed in Volume 2, Chapter 10.

12 Through ties-ligation, the 'li' in alienation, untied, shares etymological and spiritual origins with religion.

13 National Numeracy warned that the proposed schools mathematics curriculum in English schools is too atomised, filled with rote learning and remote from practical contexts: www.nationalnumeracy.org.uk (accessed 13 August 2012).

14 British parents should not deny school education to their children unless they provide 'education otherwise' at home. An estimated 10 per cent of children in the US are taught at home, primarily for religious reasons.

15 Each generation might appear to be more culturally diverse than united, locally, nationally and internationally. However, perhaps adversity particularly marks out distinctive age groups: Mannheim could compare generations in Europe born before and after World War I, and its immense upheaval in every aspect of society. He was 21 when the war began in 1914, and believed that youth (he did not mention childhood) was the defining time for each generation when making fresh contacts and forming new experiences.

16 For example, children's rights self-advocacy groups have an upper age bar of the eighteenth birthday: Children's Rights Alliance for England www.crae.org.uk.

17 In many policy reports, children only appear under the rubric 'childcare'.

18 High spending elderly groups attract advertisers who subsidise the mass media and the social and lobbying networks these groups enjoy.

19 Although the title of Vleminckx and Smeeding's book is *Child Well-being, Child Poverty and Child Policy in Modern Nations*, well-being seems to be mentioned on only 5 of 570 pages.

20 See most papers in *Childhood* and *Children & Society*.

21 The UNICEF Committee and commentaries on UNCRC tend to be mistakenly confused with the precise legal wording of UNCRC, much of it based on older Conventions.

22 Generally a very useful series on social justice online: www.bernardvanleer.org (accessed 18 September 2012).

6 Inner being: alienation and flourishing

1 The 1989 Children Act requires agencies to take account of 'the wishes and feelings' of the child (Section 8).

2 'You's' – the local Northern Ireland dialect. With her agreement, Crystal was referred for bereavement counselling.

3 www.statistics.gov.uk/hub/people-places/communities/societal-well-being (accessed 19 September 2012).

4 See, for example, www.esrc.ac.uk and the Cochrane reviews, www.cochrane.org.

5 Childhood studies books tend to have welfare but not well-being in their index, health but not happiness.

6 Rustin, S. (2012) The interview: can happiness be measured? *Guardian*, 20 July.

7 Antonovsky's concept of SOC is now the basis of large international research projects in 32 countries.

8 This much admired paper, which advanced cooperation in place of lethal competition in ecosystems, was notoriously rejected by peer reviewers and publication was delayed for 10 years.

9 Although Pascal's and Rousseau's *amour-propere* was an anxious self-love that depended on the opinion of others.

10 In 1913, German philosophers protested that university philosophy chairs were being filled by experimental psychologists and demanded that the disciplines be separated (Martin and Barresi 2006: 229–30).

11 The Honey Bee Network (www.sristi.org/cms/en) records thousands of practical inventions, many by extremely poor people (accessed 18 March 2012).

12 The philosophy department at the Institute of Education, London, which Peters founded, has still not explicitly revoked this view, and his recent successor opposes children's rights (Brighouse 2002).

13 The public's great fascination with the individual's lonely journey towards recognition, love and success has been reflected in the novel, from Cervantes, Defoe, Fielding, the Brontës, Austen, Eliot and Dickens onwards.

7 Conclusions to Volume 1: the relevance of DCR to childhood studies

1 Detached objectivity has, of course, been questioned in all disciplines. Some quantum physicists believe that wave-particles react to the observer, and some biologists believe that to understand a specimen you have to identify with it (Keller 1985), while environmental researchers are increasingly concerned with human political and emotional interactions with ecology.
2 www.crae.org.uk (accessed 4 July 2012).
3 Reports from all the countries that submit them, with responses from the Committee are published at www2.ohchr.org/english/bodies/crc/index.htm.
4 www.nidcap.org (accessed 4 July 2012).

REFERENCES

Abebe, T. (2009) Multiple methods, complex dilemmas: negotiating socio-ethical spaces in participatory research with disadvantaged children, *Children's Geographies*, 7(4): 451–65.

Acharya, L. (2010) Child reporters as agents of change, in B. Percy-Smith and N. Thomas (eds) *A Handbook of Children and Young People's Participation*. London: Routledge, pp. 204–214.

Adiga, A. (2010) *Between the Assassinations*. London: Atlantic.

Adorno, T. ([1964] 1989) Something's missing: on the contradictions of Utopian longing, in E. Bloch (ed.) *The Utopian Function of Art and Literature*. Cambridge, MA: MT Press.

Alanen, L. (1994) Gender and generation: exploring the child question, in J. Qvortrup, M. Bardy, G. Sgritta and H. Winterberger (eds) *Childhood Matters: Social Theory, Practice and Politics*. Aldershot: Avebury Press, pp. 24–42.

Alanen, L. (2011) Explorations in generational analysis, in J. Qvortrup, W. Corsaro and M. Honig (eds) *The Palgrave Handbook of Childhood Studies*. Basingstoke: Palgrave Macmillan, pp. 159–74.

Alanen, L. and Mayall, B. (2001) (eds) *Conceptualizing Child–Adult Relations*. London: Routledge Falmer.

Alderson, P. (1990) *Choosing for Children: Parents' Consent to Surgery*. Oxford: Oxford University Press.

Alderson, P. (1993) *Children's Consent to Surgery*. Buckingham: Open University Press.

Alderson, P. (1999a) Human rights in school: do they mean more than picking up litter and not killing whales? *International Journal of Children's Rights*, 7: 185–205.

Alderson, P. (1999b) *Learning and Inclusion: The Cleves School Experience*. London: David Fulton.

Alderson, P. (2008a) *Young Children's Rights*. London: Jessica Kingsley.

Alderson, P. (2008b)'When does citizenship begin? Economics and early childhood', in A. Invernizzi and J. Williams (eds) *Children and Citizenship*. London: Sage, pp. 108–119.

Alderson, P. (2011) Younger children's individual participation in 'all matters affecting the child', in B. Percy-Smith and N. Thomas (eds) *Handbook of Children's Participation*. London: Routledge, pp. 89–97.

Alderson, P. and Brooker, E. (2007) *Report of Children's Centre Evaluation*. London: SSRU, Institute of Education.

Alderson, P. and Goodey, C. (1998) *Enabling Education: Experiences in Special and Ordinary Schools*. London: Tufnell Press.

Alderson, P. and Morrow, V. (2011) *The Ethics of Research with Children and Young People: A Practical Handbook*. London: Sage.

Alderson, P., Clarke-Jones, L. and Schaumberg, H. (2002) *An Evaluation of The Office of Children's Rights Commissioner for London*. London: Social Science Research Unit.

Alderson, P., Ehrich, K., Hawthorne, J., Killen, M. and Warren, I. (2004) *Foretelling Futures: Dilemmas in Neonatal Neurology. A Social Science Project about Neonatal Care* 2002–2004. End of project report for funders. London: SSRU, Institute of Education.

Alderson, P., Hawthorne, J. and Killen, M. (2005a) The participation rights of premature babies, *International Journal of Children's Rights*, 13: 31–50.

Alderson, P., Hawthorne, J. and Killen, M. (2005b) Are premature babies citizens with rights? Provision rights and the edges of citizenship, *Journal of Social Science*, 9: 80–90.

Alderson, P., Sutcliffe, K. and Curtis, K. (2006a) Children as partners with adults in their medical care, *Archives of Diseases in Childhood*, 91: 300–3.

Alderson, P., Sutcliffe, K and Curtis, K. (2006b) Children's consent to medical treatment, *Hastings Center Report*, 36: 25–34.

Allen, C. (2011) Review of ground control, *Sociology*, 45:(2): 340–2.

Allen, M. and Ainley, P. (2007) *When Education Make You Fick, Innit?* London: Tufnell Press.

Als, H. (1999) Reading the premature infant, in E. Goldson (ed.) *Developmental Interventions in the Neonatal Intensive Care Nursery*. New York: Oxford University Press, pp. 18–85.

Anand, K., Sippel, W. and Aynsley-Green, A. (1987) Randomised trial of fentanyl anaesthesia, *Lancet*, 243–8.

Anderson, H. (2000) Reflections on the appeals and challenges of postmodern psychologies, societal practice and political life, in L. Holtzman and J. Morss (eds) *Postmodern Psychologies, Societal Practice, and Political Life*. New York: Routledge, pp. 202–16.

Antonovsky, A. (1979) *Health, Stress and Coping*. San Francisco: Jossey-Bass.

Antonovsky, A. (1987) *Unravelling the Mystery of Health: How People Manage Stress and Stay Well*. San Francisco, CA: Jossey-Bass Kessen.

Appignanesi, R. (ed.) (2006) *Introducing Melanie Klein*. London: Icon.

Apple, M. (2012) *Can Education Change Society?* London: Routledge.

Archer, M. (1995) *Realist Social Theory*. Cambridge: Cambridge University Press.

Archer, M. (2003) *Structure, Agency and the Internal Conversation*. Cambridge: Cambridge University Press.

Arendt, H. (1964) *Eichmann in Jerusalem: A Report on the Banality of Evil*. New York: Viking.

Ariès, P. (1962) *Centuries of Childhood*, trans. R. Baldick. London: Jonathan Cape.

Aristotle (2004) *The Nicomachean Ethics*, trans. J. Thomson. London: Penguin.

Armstrong, D. (1983) The invention of infant mortality, *Sociology of Health & Illness*, 8: 211–32.

Armstrong, K. (1993) *A History of God*. New York: Ballantine Books.

Axline, V. ([1964] 1990) *Dibs in Search of Self*. Harmondsworth: Penguin.

Bailey, A. (2011) Transnational mobilities and childhoods, in J. Qvortrup, W. Corsaro and M. Honig (eds) *The Palgrave Handbook of Childhood Studies*. Basingstoke: Palgrave Macmillan, pp. 408–21.

Ball, S. (2007) *Education: plc*. London: Routledge.

Baron-Cohen, S. (2011) *Zero Degrees of Empathy*. London: Allen Lane.

Barry, M. (ed.) (2005) *Youth Policy and Social Inclusion*. London: Routledge.

Baughman, F. and Covey, C. (2006) *The ADHD Fraud: How Psychiatry Makes Patients out of Normal Children*. Bloomington, IN: Trafford

Bauman, Z. (2003) *Modernity and the Holocaust*. Cambridge: Polity.

Baumrind, D. (1971) Current patterns of parental authority, *Developmental Psychology*, 4(1): 1–103.

Beauchamp, T. and Childress, J. (2001) *Principles of Biomedical Ethics*. New York: Oxford University Press.

Beazley, H., Bessell, S., Ennew, E. and Waterson, R. (2009) The right to be properly researched: research with children in a real messy world, *Children's Geographies*, 7(4): 365–78.

Beck, U. (1992) *The Risk Society*. London: Sage.

Becker, S., Dearden, C. and Aldridge, A. (2001) Children's labour of love? Young carers and care work, in P. Mizen, C. Pole and A. Boulton (eds) *Hidden Hands: International Perspectives on Children's Work and Labour*. London: Routledge Falmer, pp. 70–88.

Beckett, F. (2010) *What Did the Baby Boomers Ever Do For Us? Why the Children of the Sixties Lived the Dream and Failed the Future*. London: Biteback.

Beder, S. (2009) *This Little Kiddy Went to Market: The Corporate Capture of Childhood*. London: Pluto.

Belsky, J., Barnes, J. and Melhuish, E. (eds) (2007) *The National Evaluation of Sure Start*. Bristol: Policy Press.

Benton, T. (1977) *Philosophical Foundations of The Three Sociologies*. London: Routledge Kegan Paul.

Berlin, I. (2002) *Liberty*. Oxford: Oxford University Press.

Berne, E. (1968) *Games People Play*. Harmondsworth: Penguin.

Bhaskar, R. (1986) *Scientific Realism and Human Emancipation*. London: Verso.

Bhaskar, R. (1998a) *The Possibility of Naturalism*, 3rd edn. London: Routledge.

Bhaskar, R. (1998b) The logic of scientific discovery, in M. Archer *et al.* (eds) *Critical Realism: Essential Readings*. London: Routledge, pp. 48–103.

Bhaskar, R. (2002a) *Reflections on Meta-Reality*. London: Routledge.

Bhaskar, R. (2002b) *From Science to Emancipation: Alienation and Enlightenment*. Abingdon: Routledge.

Bhaskar, R. ([1975] 2008a) *A Realist Theory of Science*, 3rd edn. Abingdon: Routledge.

Bhaskar, R. ([1993] 2008b) *Dialectic: The Pulse of Freedom*, 2nd edn. Abingdon: Routledge.

Bhaskar, R. ([1994] 2010a) *Plato Etc*, 2nd edn. Abingdon: Routledge.

Bhaskar, R. ([1991] 2010b) *Philosophy and the Idea of Freedom*. Abingdon: Routledge.

Biaya, T. (2005) Youth and street culture in urban Africa, in A. Honwana and F. De Boeck (eds) (2005) *Makers and Breakers: Children and Youth in Postcolonial Africa*. Oxford: James Curry, pp. 215–28.

Bion, W. (1967) *A Theory of Thinking, Second Thoughts: Selected Papers on Psycho-analysis*. London: Karnac, pp. 111–19.

Bjørkvold, J.-R. (1992) *The Muse Within: Creativity and Communication, Song and Play from Childhood through Maturity*. New York: HarperCollins.

Black, R., Allen, L., Bhutta, Z., Caulfield, L., de Onis, M., Ezzati, M., Mathers, C. and Rivera, J. (2008) Maternal and child under-nutrition: global and regional exposures and health consequences, *Lancet*, 371: 243–60.

Blanden, J. (2006) *Bucking the Trend: What Enables Those Who are Disadvantaged in Childhood to Succeed Later in Life?* London: Department of Work and Pensions.

Blatchford, P., Russell, A. and Webster, R. (2012) *Reassessing the Impact of Teaching Assistants: How Research Challenges Practice and Policy.* Abingdon: Routledge.

Bloom, P. (2012) The moral life of babies, *New York Times,* 6 May.

Bluebond-Langner, M. (1978) *The Private Worlds of Dying Children.* Princeton, NJ: Princeton University Press.

Borba, R. and Nunes, T. (2000) Are young primary school pupils able to manipulate representations of negative numbers? *Proceedings of the Ninth International Congress on Mathematical Education,* Tokyo, p. 171.

Bourdieu, P. (1977) *Outline of a Theory of Practice.* Cambridge: Cambridge University Press.

Bowlby, J. (1964) *Childcare and the Growth of Love.* Harmondsworth: Penguin.

Boyden, J. (1997) Childhood and the policy makers, in A. James and A. Prout (eds) *Constructing and Reconstructing Childhood: Contemporary Issues in the Sociological Study of Childhood.* Abingdon: Routledge Falmer, pp. 190–229.

Boyden, J. and Bourdillon, M. (eds) (2012) *Childhood Poverty: Multidisciplinary Approaches.* Basingstoke: Palgrave Macmillan.

Bradley, B. (1989) *Visions of Infancy.* Cambridge: Polity Press

Brett, R. and Specht, I. (2004) *Young Soldiers: Why they Choose to Fight.* London: Lynne Rienner.

Brighouse, H. (2002) What rights (if any) do children have? in D. Archard and C. Macleod (eds) *The Moral and Political Status of Children.* Oxford: Oxford University Press.

Brooker, L. and Woodhead, M. (eds) (2008) *Developing Positive Identities: Diversity and Young Children.* The Hague: Bernard van Leer Foundation.

Brothers, C. (2012) The long walk to Europe, *Guardian Weekly,* 17 February.

Bruner, J. (1996) *The Culture of Education.* Cambridge, MA: Harvard University Press.

Buckingham, D. (2000) *After the Death of Childhood.* Cambridge: Polity.

Buckingham, D. (2011) *The Material Child: Growing Up in Consumer Culture.* Cambridge: Polity.

Burkitt, I. (2008) *Social Selves: Theories of Self and Society,* 2nd edn. London: Sage.

Burman, E. (2007) *Deconstructing Developmental Psychology,* 2nd edn. London: Routledge.

Butler, M. (1998) Negotiating place: the importance of children's realities, in S. Steinberg and J. Kincheloe (eds) *Students as Researchers: Creating Classrooms that Matter.* London: Falmer, pp. 94–112.

Callinicos, A. (2010) *Bonfire of Illusions.* Cambridge: Polity.

Carson, R. (1962) *Silent Spring.* Boston, MA: Houghton Mifflin.

Census.Gov. (2010) www.census.gov/cgi-bin/broker.

Chang, H-J. (2011) *23 Things They Don't Tell You About Capitalism.* London: Penguin.

Cho, H-J. (1995) Children in the examination war in South Korea, in S. Stephens (ed.) *Children and the Politics of Culture.* Princeton, NJ: Princeton University Press, pp. 141–68.

Chomsky, N. (1984) Interview with Wiktor Osiatynski, in *Contrasts: Soviet and American Thinkers Discuss the Future.* New York: Macmillan, pp. 95–101.

Chomsky, N. (1986) *Knowledge of Language: Its Nature, Origins and Use.* New York: Praeger.

Christensen, P. and James A. (eds) (2008) *Research with Children: Perspectives and Practices.* London: Falmer.

Collingwood R. (1945) *The Idea of Nature*. Oxford: Oxford University Press.

Connolly, P., Kelly, B. and Smith, A. (2009) Ethnic habitus and young children: a case study of Northern Ireland, *European Early Childhood Research Journal*, 17(2): 217–32.

Connor, S. (1998) 'Becket and Bion', lecture to *Beckett and London* conference, London: Goldsmiths College.

Coppock, V. (2002) Medicalising children's behaviour, in B. Franklin (ed.) *The New Handbook of Children's Rights*. London: Routledge, pp. 139–54.

Corsaro, W. (2011) Peer culture, in J. Qvortrup, W. Corsaro and M. Honig (eds) *The Palgrave Handbook of Childhood Studies*. Basingstoke: Palgrave Macmillan, pp. 301–15.

CRAE (Children's Rights Alliance for England) (2008) *Get Ready For Geneva Project. Report by Children and Young People to the UN Committee*. London: CRAE.

CRAE (Children's Rights Alliance for England) (2011) *State of England's Children*. London: CRAE.

Crouch, C. (2011) *The Strange Non-Death of Neoliberalism*. Cambridge: Polity.

Damon, W. (1990) *The Moral Child*. New York: New York Press.

Davies, H. and Joshi, H. (2001) Who has borne the cost of Britain's children in the 1990s? in K. Vleminckx and T. Smeeding (eds) *Child Well-being, Child Poverty and Child Policy in Modern Nations*. Bristol: Policy, pp. 299–320.

Davies, N. (2008) *Flat Earth News*. London: Vintage.

Davis, M. (2006) *Planet of Slums*. London: Verso.

Dawkins, R. (1976) *The Selfish Gene*. Oxford: Oxford University Press.

de Block, L. and Buckingham, D. (2007) *Global Children, Global Media: Migration, Media and Childhood*. Basingstoke: Palgrave.

De Boeck, F. (2005) The divine seed: children, gift, and witchcraft in the Democratic Republic of Congo, in A. Honwana and F. De Boeck (eds) (2005) *Makers and Breakers: Children and Youth in Postcolonial Africa*. Oxford: James Curry, pp. 188–214.

De Costa, C. (2002) The contagiousness of childbed fever: a short history of puerperal sepsis and its treatment, *eMJA, The Medical Journal of Australia*, 177(11/12): 668–71.

de Schweinitz, R. (2005) The 'shame of America': African-American civil rights and the politics of childhood, in J. Goddard, S. MacNamee, A. James and A. James (eds) *The Politics of Childhood: International Perspectives, Contemporary Developments*. Basingstoke: Palgrave Macmillan, pp. 50–70.

Dean, K. (2007) Needs, in M. Hartwig (ed.) *Dictionary of Critical Realism*, Abingdon: Routledge, pp. 323–4.

Dean, M. (2012) *Democracy Under Attack: How the Media Distort Policy and Politics*. Bristol: Policy.

Demos (2004) *The New Old*. London: Demos.

Denzin, N. (1977) *Childhood Socialization*. San Francisco: Jossey-Bass.

Denzin, N. (1988) Qualitative analysis for social scientists, *Contemporary Sociology*, 17(3): 430–2.

Denzin, N. and Lincoln, Y. (2000) *Handbook of Qualitative Research*. Thousand Oaks, CA: Sage.

Dex, S. and Joshi, H. (2005) *Children of the 21st Century: From Birth to Nine Months*. Bristol: Policy.

DfE (Department for Education) (2007) *The Children's Plan*. London: DfE.

Diamond, D. and Glynn, C. (2008) *Garden and Cosmos: The Royal Paintings of Jodhpur*. London: Thames & Hudson.

Donaldson, M. (1978) *Children's Minds*. Edinburgh: Fontana.

Donzelot, J. (1977) *The Policing of Families*. Trans R. Hurley. Baltimore: Johns Hopkins University Press.

Dorling, D. (2011) *Injustice*. Bristol: Policy.

Douthwaite, R. (1999) The need to end economic growth, in M. Scott Cato and M. Kennett (eds) *Green Economics*. Aberystwyth: Green Audit Books, pp. 27–35.

Drumbl, M. (2012) *Reimagining Child Soldiers in International Law and Policy*. Oxford: Oxford University Press.

Dunn, J. (1988) *The Beginnings of Social Understanding*. Oxford: Blackwell.

Dunn, J. (2004) *Children's Friendships: The Beginnings of Intimacy*. Oxford: Blackwell.

Eichsteller, G. (2009) Janusz Korczak – his legacy and its relevance for children's rights today, *International Journal of Children's Rights*, 17(3): 377–91.

European Council (1950) *European Convention on Human Rights*. Brussels: European Council.

Evans, R. and Becker, S. (2009) *Children Caring for Parents with HIV and AIDS: Global Issues and Policy Responses*. Bristol: The Policy Press.

Fassa, A., Parker, D. and Scanlon, T. (eds) (2010) *Child Labour: A Public Health Perspective*. Oxford: Oxford University Press.

Faulkner, R. (1990) *The Ancient Egyptian Book of The Dead*. Austin, TX: University of Texas Press.

Feinstein, L. (2003a) How can we predict future education achievement?, *LSE CentrePiece*, Summer: 24–30.

Feinstein, L. (2003b) Inequality in the early cognitive development of children in the early 1970 Cohort, *Economica*, 70: 73–97.

Field, F. (2010) *The Foundation Years: Preventing Poor Children Becoming Poor Adults: The Report of the Independent Review on Poverty and Life Chances*. London: HM Government, available at: www.frankfield.co.uk, accessed 21 December 2010.

Field, N. (1995) The child as labourer and consumer: the disappearance of childhood in contemporary Japan, in S. Stephens (ed.) *Children and the Politics of Culture*. Princeton, NJ: Princeton University Press, pp. 51–78.

Field, T. (2007) *The Amazing Infant*. Oxford; Blackwell.

Fine, B. (2010) *Social Capitalism: Researchers Behaving Badly*. Abingdon: Routledge.

Fine, C. (2006) *A Mind of Its Own: How Your Brain Distorts and Deceives*. London: Icon Books.

Fine, C. (2010) *Delusions of Gender: How our Minds, Society and Neurosexism Create Difference*. London: Icon Books.

Fischer, K. and Rose, S. (1994) Dynamic development of coordination of components in brain and behaviour: a framework for theory and research, in G. Dawson, and K. Fischer (eds) *Human Behaviour and the Developing Brain*. New York: Guilford Press, pp. 3–66.

Fitz, J. and Hood-Williams, J. (1982) The generation game, in D. Robbins (ed.) *Rethinking Social Inequality*. Aldershot: Gower, pp. 65–95.

Foucault, M. (1967) *Madness and Civilisation*. London: Tavistock.

Foucault, M. (1977) *Discipline and Punish*. London: Allen Lane.

Foucault, M. (1993) *The Birth of The Clinic*. London: Vintage.

Franklin, B. (2002) Children's rights and media wrongs, in B. Franklin (ed.) *The New Handbook of Children's Rights*. London: Routledge, pp. 15–42.

Freeman, M. (2007) Why it remains important to take children's rights seriously, *International Journal of Children's Rights*, 15(1): 5–23.

Freeman, M. (2011) Children's rights as human rights: reading the UNCRC, in J. Qvortrup, W. Corsaro and M. Honig (eds) *The Palgrave Handbook of Childhood Studies*. Basingstoke: Palgrave Macmillan, pp. 377–95.

Freeman, M. (ed.) (2012) *Law and Childhood Studies*. Oxford: Oxford University Press.

Freud, A. and Sandler, J. (1985) *The Analysis of Defense*. New York: International Universities Press.

Gardner, H. (1993) *The Unschooled Mind: How Children Think and How Schools Should Teach*. London: Fontana.

Garfinkel, H. (1967) *Studies in Ethnomethodology*. Englewood Cliffs, NJ: Prentice-Hall.

Garnett, M. (2007) *From Anger to Apathy*. London: Cape.

Gerhardt, S. (2004) *Why Love Matters: How Affection Shapes a Baby's Brain*. London: Routledge.

Giddens, A. (1984) *The Constitution of Society*. Cambridge: Polity.

Gilligan, C. (1982) *In a Different Voice: Psychological Theory and Women's Development*. Cambridge, MA: Harvard University Press.

Glaser, B. and Strauss, A. (1967) *The Discovery of Grounded Theory*. Chicago, IL: Aldine.

Glauser, B. (1997) Street children, in A. James and A. Prout (eds) *Constructing and Reconstructing Childhood: Contemporary Issues in the Sociological Study of Childhood*. Abingdon: Routledge Falmer, pp. 145–64.

Goddard, J., MacNamee, S., James, A. and James, A. (eds) (2005) *The Politics of Childhood: International Perspectives, Contemporary Developments*. Basingstoke: Palgrave Macmillan.

Goffman, E. (1969) *The Presentation of the Self in Everyday Life*. Harmondsworth: Pelican.

Goldson, B. and Muncie, J. (2009) *Youth, Crime and Juvenile Justice*, in 3 vols. London: Sage.

Goldstein, D. (2003) Nothing bad intended: child discipline, punishment and survival in a shantytown in Rio de Janeiro, in H. Montgomery, R. Burr and M. Woodhead (eds) *Changing Childhoods: Local and Global*. Chichester: John Wiley, pp. 89–91.

Goodey, C. (2011) *A History of Intelligence and 'Intellectual Disability': The Shaping of Psychology in Early Modern Europe*. Farnham: Ashgate.

Gordon, D., Nandy, S., Pantazis, C. and Townsend, P. (2002) *Child Rights and Child Poverty in Developing Countries*, report to UNICEF. Bristol: Townsend Centre for International Poverty Research.

Gordon-Smith, P. (2009) The morality of young children in their early years setting, *Childhoods Today*, June.

Gould, S. J. (2007) *The Richness of Life: The Essential Jay Gould*. London: Vintage.

Gouldner, A. (1977) *The Coming Crisis of Western Sociology*. London: Heinemann.

Graebner, D. (2011) *Debt: The First Five Thousand Years*. Brooklyn, NY: Melville House.

Green, H., McGinnity, A., Meltzer, H., Ford, T. and Goodman, R. (2005) *Mental Health of Children and Young People in Great Britain, 2004*. Basingstoke: Palgrave Macmillan.

Green, J. (1997) *Risk and Misfortune: A Social Construction of Accidents*. Abingdon: Routledge.

Greenfield, S. (2003) *Tomorrow's People: How 21st Century Technology is Changing the Way We Think and Feel*. London: Allen Lane.

Guardian and LSE (2011) *Reading the Riots: Investigating England's Summer of Disorder*. London: *Guardian* and LSE.

Guggenheim, M. (2005) *What's Wrong with Children's Rights?* Cambridge, MA: Harvard University Press.

Habermas, J. (1984) *The Theory of Communicative Action*, Vol 1, trans. Thomas McCarthy. Cambridge: Polity.

Habermas, J. (2006) *The Theory of Communicative Action*, Vol. 2, trans. Thomas McCarthy. Cambridge: Polity.

Hacking, I. (1999) *The Social Construction of What?* Cambridge, MA: Harvard University Press.

Haddad, M. (2012) *The Perfect Storm*. London: Oxfam GB.

Hall, G.S. (1904) *Adolescence: Its Psychology and Its Relations to Physiology, Anthropology, Sociology, Sex, Crime, Religion and Education*. New York: Appleton & Co.

Hammersley, M. (1995) *The Politics of Social Research*. London: Sage.

Hammersley, M. (2009) Why critical realism fails to justify critical social research, *Methodological Innovations Online*, 4(2): 1–11, available at: www.pbs.plym.ac.uk/mi/pdf/12-8-09/1.%20Hammersley_final%20August%209%2009.pdf.

Han, Xiaoli (2006) The everyday lives of rural-urban migrant workers' children in a Chinese city: how migrant children rebuild their daily lives after moving from rural areas to a city, unpublished MA dissertation. London: Institute of Education.

Hansen, K., Joshi, H. and Dex, S. (eds) (2010) *Children of the 21st Century*. Bristol: Policy.

Hardyment, C. (1984) *Dream Babies: Child Care from Locke to Spock*. Oxford: Oxford University Press.

Harris, M. (2008) *Exploring Developmental Psychology*. London: Sage.

Harris, M. and Butterworth, G. (2002) *Developmental Psychology*. Hove: Psychology Press.

Hart, R. (1997) *Children's Participation: The Theory and Practice of Involving Young Children in Community Development and Environmental Care*. London: Earthscan/UNESCO.

Hartas, D. (2008) *The Right to Childhoods*. London: Continuum.

Hartwig, M. (ed.) (2007) *Dictionary of Critical Realism*. Abingdon: Routledge.

Harvey, D. (2005) *A Brief History of Neoliberalism*. Oxford: Oxford University Press.

Harvey, D. (2011) *The Enigma of Capital and the Crises of Capitalism*. London: Profile.

Hatch, D. (1987) Analgesia in the Neonate, *British Medical Journal*, 294: 920.

Heesterman, W. (2005) Child labour and children's rights, in J. Goddard *et al.* (eds) *The Politics of Childhood: International Perspectives, Contemporary Developments*. Basingstoke: Palgrave Macmillan, pp. 73–89.

Hendrick, H. (1994) *Child Welfare: England 1872–1989*. London: Routledge.

Hendrick, H. (1997) Constructions and reconstructions of British childhood: an interpretive survey, 1800 to the present, in A. James and A. Prout (eds) *Constructing and Reconstructing Childhood: Contemporary Issues in the Sociological Study of Childhood*, Abingdon: Routledge Falmer, pp. 34–62.

Henry, J. (2012) *The Price of Off-Shore Revisited*. London: Tax Justice Network.

Highfield School (1997) *Changing Our School: Promoting Positive Behaviour*, ed. P. Alderson. London: Institute of Education.

Hill, M. and Tisdall, K. (1997) *Children & Society*. London; Longman.

Hillman, H., Adams, J. and Whitelegg, J. (1990) *One False Move . . . A Study of Children's Independent Mobility*. London: Policy Studies Institute.

HM Treasury *et al.* (2003) *Every Child Matters*. London: Stationery Office.

Hodgson-Burnett, F. ([1905] 2008) *A Little Princess*. London: Puffin.

Holmwood, J. (ed.) (2011) *A Manifesto for the Public University*. London: Bloomsbury.

Holt, J. (1964) *How Children Fail*. Harmondsworth: Penguin.

Holt, J. (1975) *Escape from Childhood*. Harmondsworth: Penguin.

Honwana, A. (2006) *Child Soldiers in Africa*. Pennsylvania, PA: University of Pennsylvania Press.

Honwana, A. and De Boeck, F. (eds) (2005) *Makers and Breakers: Children and Youth in Postcolonial Africa*. Oxford: James Curry.

Hörschelmann, K. and Colls, R. (eds) (2010) *Contested Bodies of Childhood and Youth*. Basingstoke: Palgrave Macmillan.

Horton, J. and Kraftl, P. (2006) What else? Some more ways of thinking and doing children's geographies, *Children's Geographies*, 4(1): 69–98.

Howker, E. and Malik, S. (2010) *Jilted Generation: How Britain has Bankrupted its Youth*. London: Icon.

Hrdy, S. (2009) *Mothers and Others: The Evolutionary Origins of Mutual Understanding*. Cambridge, MA: Harvard University Press.

Invernizzi, A. (2008) Everyday lives of working children and notions of citizenship in Portugal and Peru, in A. Invernizzi and J. Williams (eds) *Children and Citizenship*, pp. 131–41.

Invernizzi, A. and Williams, J. (eds) (2008) *Children and Citizenship*. London: Sage.

James, A. (2011) Agency, in J. Qvortrup, W. Corsaro and M. Honig (eds) *The Palgrave Handbook of Childhood Studies*. Basingstoke: Palgrave Macmillan, pp. 34–45.

James, A. and James, A. (2004) *Constructing Childhood*. Basingstoke: Palgrave Macmillan.

James, A. and Prout, A. (eds) ([1990] 1997) *Constructing and Reconstructing Childhood: Contemporary Issues in the Sociological Study of Childhood*. Abingdon: Routledge Falmer.

James, A., Curtis, P. and Birch, J. (2008) Care and control in the construction of children's citizenship, in A. Invernizzi and J. Williams (eds) *Children and Citizenship*. London: Sage, pp. 85–96.

James, W. ([1890] 1981) *The Principles of Psychology*. Cambridge, MA: Harvard University Press.

Jenks, C. (1982) *The Sociology of Childhood*. London: Batsford.

Jenks, C. (2005) *Childhood*. London: Routledge.

John, M. (2003) *Children's Rights and Power*. London: Jessica Kingsley.

Jones, O. (2008) 'Your geography quickly forgotten, giving away to an adult-imagined universe': approaching the otherness of childhood, *Children's Geographies*, 6(2): 195–212.

Jones, O. (2012) *Chavs: The Demonization of the Working Class*. London: Verso.

Jones, S. (2008) *Coral: A Pessimist in Paradise*. London: Abacus.

Kagan, J. and Lamb, S. (1986) *The Emergence of Morality in Young Children*. Chicago, IL: University of Chicago Press.

Kant, I. ([1781] 1965) *Critique of Pure Reason*, trans. N. Smith. New York: St Martin's Press.

Kant, I. (1972) *The Moral Law*, ed. H. Paton. London: Hutchinson.

Katz, C. (2004) *Growing up Global: Economic Restructuring and Children's Everyday Lives*. Minnesota, MN: University of Minnesota.

Katz, C. (2005) The terrors of hyper-vigilance, in J. Qvortrup (ed.) *Studies in Modern Childhood*. Basingstoke: Palgrave.

Keller, E. (1985) *Reflections on Gender and Science*. New Haven, CY: Yale University Press.

Kemp, P. (2005) Young people and unemployment, in M. Barry (ed.) *Youth Policy and Social Inclusion*. London: Routledge, pp. 139–60.

Kennedy, E. and Mendus, S. (eds) (1987) *Women in Western Political Philosophy*. Brighton: Wheatsheaf.

Kessen, W. (ed) (1965) *The Child*. London: Wiley.

Klein, M. (1964) *Love, Hate, and Reparation*. New York: W.W. Norton.

Klein, N. (2000) *No Space, No Choice, No Jobs, No Logo*. London: Flamingo.

Klein, N. (2007) *The Shock Doctrine*. London: Penguin.

Kohlberg, L. (1981) *Essays on Moral Development*. San Francisco, CA: Harper & Row.

Latour, B. and Woolgar, S. (1979) *Laboratory Life: The Social Construction of Scientific Facts*. Princeton, NJ: Princeton University Press.

Layard, R. (2006) *Happiness: Lessons from a New Science*. London: Penguin.

Layard, R. and Dunn, J. (2009) *A Good Childhood: Searching for Values in a Competitive Age*. London: Penguin.

Lear, J. (1988) *Aristotle*. Oxford: Oxford University Press.

Lee, N. (2001) *Childhood and Society: Growing up in an Age of Uncertainty*. Buckingham: Open University Press.

Lee, N. (2005) *Childhood and Human Value: Development, Separation and Separability*. Maidenhead: Open University Press.

Leveson, B. (2012) *The Leveson Inquiry: Culture, Practice and Ethics of the Press*, available at: http://www.levesoninquiry.org.uk, accessed 7 August 2012.

Liebel, M. (2004) *A Will of their Own: Cross-cultural Perspectives on Working Children*. London: Zed Books.

Liedloff, J. ([1975] 2004) *The Continuum Concept*. London: Penguin.

Lindstrom, B. and Erikson, M. (2010) A Salutogenic approach to attacking health inequalities, in A. Morgan, E. Ziglio, M. Davies and R. Barker (eds) *International Health Development: Investing in Assets of Individuals, Communities and Organisations*. London: Springer, pp. 17–40.

Locke, J. ([1690] 1997) *An Essay Concerning Human Understanding*, ed. R. Woolhouse. London: Penguin.

Lovelock, J. (2009) *The Vanishing Face of Gaia*. London: Basic Books.

LSE (The Centre for Economic Performance's Mental Health Policy Group) (2012) *How Mental Illness Loses out in the NHS*. London: LSE, available at: http://cep.lse.ac.uk/pubs/download/special/cepsp26.pdf, accessed 15 August 2012.

Lukes, S. (2005) *Power: A Radical View*, 2nd edn. Basingstoke: Palgrave.

Lukes, S. (2008) *Moral Relativism*. London: Profile.

Lundy, L. (2010) Review of 'The Palgrave Handbook of Childhood Studies', *International Journal of Children's Rights*, 18: 655–658.

Lynas, M. (2008) *Six Degrees: Our Future on a Hotter Planet*. London: Harper.

MacIntyre, A. (2002) *A Short History of Ethics*. London: Routledge.

Mannheim, K. ([1928] 1952) *The Problem of Generations*. London: Routledge & Kegan Paul.

Marmot, M. (2010) *Fair Society, Healthy Lives*. London: Improvement and Development Agency.

Martin, R. and Barresi, J. (2006) *The Rise and Fall of the Soul and Self: An Intellectual History of Personal Identity*. New York: Columbia University Press.

Marx, K. and Engels, F. ([1848] 1998) *Communist Manifesto*. London: Penguin.

Maslow, A. (1943) A theory of human motivation, *Psychological Review*, 50: 370–96.

Mason, P. (2009) *Meltdown: The End of The Age of Greed*. London: Verso.

Mason, P. (2012) *Why it's Kicking Off Everywhere: The New Global Revolutions*. London: Verso.

Matthews, G. (1984) *Dialogues with Children*. Cambridge, MA: Harvard University Press.

Matthews, H. (2005) Rising four: reflections on the state of growing up, *Children's Geographies*, 3(3): 271–3.

Mayall, B. (1993) Keeping children healthy, *Social Science & Medicine*, 3(1): 77–84.

Mayall, B. (1994) *Negotiating Health: Primary School Children at Home and School*. London: Continuum.

Mayall, B. (2002) *Towards a Sociology for Childhood: Thinking from Children's Lives*. Buckingham: Open University Press.

Mayall, B. (2011) Generational relations at family level, in J. Qvortrup, W. Corsaro, W. and M. Honig (eds) *The Palgrave Handbook of Childhood Studies*. Basingstoke: Palgrave Macmillan, pp. 175–87.

Mayall, B. (in press) *A History of the Sociology of Childhood*. London: Institute of Education.

Mayall, B. and Zeiher, H. (eds) (2003) *Childhood in Generational Perspective*. London: Institute of Education.

Mayhew, H. ([1861–1862] 2010) (ed.) R. Douglas-Fairhurst *London Labour and the London Poor*. Oxford: Oxford University Press.

Mead, G.H. (1934) *Mind, Self and Society*. Chicago, IL: Chicago University Press.

Médecins Sans Frontières (2011), available at: www.msf.org.uk/alleged_fake_cia_vaccination_campaign_undermines_medical_care_20110714, accessed 17 July 2011.

Meintjes, H., Hall, K., Marera, D. and Boulle, A. (2010) Orphans of the AIDS epidemic? The extent, nature and circumstances of child-headed households in South Africa, *AIDS Care*, 22(1): 40–9.

Midgley, M. (1979) *Beast and Man: The Roots of Human Nature*. Brighton: Harvester.

Midgley, M. (1996) *Utopias, Dolphins and Computers: Problems of Philosophical Plumbing*. London: Routledge.

Midgley, M. ([1985] 2002) *Evolution as Religion*. London: Routledge.

Midgley, M. (2010) *The Solitary Self: Darwin and the Selfish Gene*. Durham: Acumen.

Miller, A. (1983) *Thou Shalt not be Aware: Society's Betrayal of the Child*. London: Pluto.

Minton, A. (2009) *Ground Control: Fear and Happiness in the Twenty-First Century City*. London: Penguin.

Mizen, P., Pole, C. and Boulton, A. (eds) (2001) *Hidden Hands: International Perspectives on Children's Work and Labour*. London: Routledge Falmer.

Morgan, A., Ziglio, E., Davies, M. and Barker, R. (eds) (2010) *International Health Development: Investing in Assets of Individuals, Communities and Organisations*. London: Springer.

Morgan, J. (2007a) Emergence, in M. Hartwig (ed.) *Dictionary of Critical Realism*. Abingdon: Routledge, pp. 166–7.

Morgan, J. (2007b) Power, in M. Hartwig (ed.) *Dictionary of Critical Realism*. Abingdon: Routledge, pp. 372–3.

Morrow, V. (1998) If you were a teacher it would be harder to talk to you, *International Journal of Research Methodology*, 1(4): 297–313.

Morrow, V. and Mayall, B. (2010) Measuring children's well-being: some problems and possibilities, in A. Morgan, E. Ziglio, M. Davies and R. Barker, R. (eds) *International Health Development: Investing in Assets of Individuals, Communities and Organisations*. London: Springer, pp. 145–65.

Morrow, V. and Pells, K. (2012) Integrating children's human rights and child poverty debates: examples from Young Lives in Ethiopia and India, *Sociology*, 46(5): 906–20.

Morss, J. (1990) *The Biologising of Childhood: Developmental Psychology and the Darwinian Myth*. Hillsdale, NJ: Lawrence Erlbaum.

Morss, J. (1996) *Growing Critical*. Abingdon: Routledge.

Mount, F. (2012) *The New Few: Or A Very British Oligarchy*. London: Simon & Schuster.

Murray, L. and Andrews, H. (2000) *The Social Baby*. Richmond: The Children's Project.

Nadesan, M. (2005) *Constructing Autism: Unravelling the 'Truth' and Understanding the Social*. London: Routledge.

Nadesan, M. (2010) *Governing Childhood into the 21st Century: Biotechnologies of Childhood Management and Education*. New York: Palgrave Macmillan.

Nations, M. and Rebhun, L. (1988) Angels with wet wings won't fly: maternal sentiment in Brazil and the image of neglect, *Culture, Medicine and Psychiatry*, 12(2): 141–200.

Ndebele, N. (1995) Recovering childhood: children in South African national reconstruction, in S. Stephens (ed.) *Children and the Politics of Culture*. Princeton, NJ: Princeton University Press, pp. 321–34.

Nieuwenhuis, O. (2011) From child labour to working children's movements, in J. Qvortrup, W. Corsaro and M. Honig (eds) *The Palgrave Handbook of Childhood Studies*. Basingstoke: Palgrave Macmillan, pp. 289–300.

Nisbet, R. (1967) *The Sociological Tradition*. London: Heinemann.

Noddings, N. (2002) Education and happiness, in J. Dunne and J. Kelly (eds) *Childhood and its Discontents*. Dublin: Liffey Press, pp. 199–219.

Norrie, A. (2010) *Dialectic and Difference: Dialectical Critical Realism and the Grounds of Justice*. Abingdon: Routledge.

Nunes, T. and Bryant, P. (eds) (1996). *Children Doing Mathematics*. Oxford: Blackwell.

Nussbaum, M. and Sen, A. (eds) (1993) *The Quality of Life*. Oxford: Clarendon Press.

O'Neill, J. (1998) *The Market: Ethics, Knowledge and Politics*. London: Routledge.

O'Neill, O. (1988) Children's rights and children's lives, *Ethics*, 98(3): 445–63.

Oakley, A. (1981) Interviewing women: a contradiction in terms?, in H. Roberts (ed.) *Doing Feminist Research*. London: Routledge, pp. 30–61.

Oakley, A. (1994) Women and children first and last, in B. Mayall (ed.) *Children's Childhood and Observed and Experienced*. London: Falmer, pp. 13–32.

Oates, J., Karmiloff-Smith, A. and Johnson, M. (2012) *Developing Brains: Early Childhood in Focus*, 7. Milton Keynes: The Open University/The Hague: Bernard van Leer Foundation, download from www.bernardvanleer.org, accessed 1 October 2012.

Oldman, D. (1994) Adult-child relations as class relations, in J. Qvortrup, M. Bardy, G. Sgritta and H. Winterberger (eds) *Childhood Matters: Social Theory, Practice and Politics*. Aldershot: Avebury Press, pp. 43–58.

Osorio, AM. (2010) Pesticide exposure, in A. Fassa, D. Parker and T. Scanlon (eds) *Child Labour: A Public Health Perspective*. Oxford: Oxford University Press, pp. 137–50.

Palmer, S. (2007) *Toxic Childhood: How the Modern World is Damaging our Children and What We Can Do About It*. London: Orion.

Pantazis, C., Gordon, D. and Levitas, R.A. (eds) (2006) *Poverty and Social Exclusion in Britain: The Millennium Survey*. Bristol: Policy.

Parsons, T. (1951) *The Social System*. New York: Free Press.

Pembrey, M., Bygren, L., Kaati, G. *et al.* (2006) Sex-specific, male-line transgenerational responses in human, *European Journal of Human Genetics*, 14: 159–66.

Penn, H. (2005) *Unequal Childhoods*. Abingdon: Routledge Falmer.

Percy-Smith, B. and Thomas, N. (eds) (2010) *Handbook of Children's Participation*. London: Routledge.

Peters, R. (1966) *Ethics and Education*. London: George Allen & Unwin.

Peters, R. (1972) *Reason, Morality and Religion*. Swarthmore Lecture. London: Friends Home Service Committee.

Piaget, J. (1928) *The Child's Conception of The World*. London: Routledge & Kegan Paul.

Piaget, J. (1932) *The Moral Judgement of the Child*. London: Routledge & Kegan Paul.

Pilcher, J. and Wragg, S. (eds) (1996) *Thatcher's Children: Politics, Childhood and Society in the 1980s–1990s*. London: Falmer.

Pinson, H., Arnot, M. and Candappa, M. (2010) *Education, Asylum and The 'Non-Citizen' Child: The Politics of Compassion and Belonging*. Basingstoke: Palgrave Macmillan.

Place, B. (2000) Constructing the bodies of ill children in the intensive care unit, in A. Prout (ed.) *The Body, Childhood and Society*. Basingstoke: Macmillan, pp. 172–94.

Plato (1952) *Phaedrus*, ed. R. Hackforth. Cambridge: Cambridge University Press.

Plato (1964) *Protagoras and Meno*, trans. W. Guthrie. Harmondsworth: Penguin.

Plato (1997) *The Sophist*, in *Complete Works*, ed. J. Cooper. Indianapolis, IN: Hackett.

Plomin, R. and Spinath, F. (2004) Intelligence: genetics, genes, and genomics, *Journal of Personality and Social Psychology*, 86(1): 112–29.

Pollock, A. (2004) *NHS plc*. London: Verso.

Polman, L. (2010) *War Games: The Story of Aid and War in Modern Times*. London: Penguin.

Porpora, D. (2001) *Landscapes of The Soul*. New York: Oxford University Press.

Porpora, D. (2007) Social structure, in M. Hartwig (ed.) *Dictionary of Critical Realism*. Abingdon: Routledge, pp. 422–5.

Prout, A. (ed.) (2000) *The Body, Childhood and Society*. Basingstoke: Macmillan.

Prout, A. (2005) *The Future of Childhood*. Abingdon: Routledge Falmer.

Prout, A. (2011) Taking a step away from modernity: reconsidering the sociology of childhood, *Global Studies of Childhood*, 1(1).

Punch, S. (2005) The generationing of power, *Sociological Studies of Children and Youth*, 10: 169–88.

Qvortrup, J. (1985) Placing children in the division of labour, in P. Close and R. Collins (eds) *Family and Economy in Modern Society*. Basingstoke: Macmillan, pp. 129–45.

Qvortrup, J. (ed.) (1991) *Childhood as a Social Phenomenon.16 National Reports*. Vienna: European Centre.

Qvortrup, J. (2008) Diversity's temptation – and hazards, paper presented at *International Childhood Conference*, University of Sheffield.

Qvortrup, J., Bardy, M., Sgritta, G. and Winterberger, H. (eds) (1994) *Childhood Matters: Social Theory, Practice and Politics*. Aldershot: Avebury Press.

Qvortrup, J., Corsaro, W. and Honig, M. (eds) (2011) *The Palgrave Handbook of Childhood Studies*. Basingstoke: Palgrave Macmillan.

Reed, J. (2009) Why I let four-year-old rape victim give evidence in court, available at: www.cps.gov.uk/london/case_studies/why_i_let_rape_victim_age_, accessed 15 July 2009.

Reynolds, P. (1995) Youth and the politics of culture in South Africa, in S. Stephens (ed.) *Children and the Politics of Culture*. Princeton, NJ: Princeton University Press, pp. 218–42.

Ridge, T. (2002) *Childhood Poverty and Social Exclusion: From a Child's Perspective*. Bristol: Policy.

Robertson, J. and Robertson, J. (1989) *Separation and the Very Young*. London: Free Association Books.

Robinson, I. and Delahooke, A. (2001) Fabricating friendships, in I. Hutchby and J. Moran-Ellis, J. (eds) *Children, Technology and Culture*. London: Routledge Falmer.

Rogoff, B. (2003) *The Cultural Nature of Human Development*. Oxford: Oxford University Press.

Rolfe, A. (2005) There's helping and there's hindering; young mothers, support and control, M. Barry (ed.) *Youth Policy and Social Inclusion*. London: Routledge, pp. 233–50.

Rose, H. and Rose, S. (eds) (2001) *Alas Poor Darwin: Arguments against Evolutionary Psychology*. London: Verso.

Rose, N. (1999) *Governing the Soul*. London: Free Association Books.

Rose, S. and Rose, S. (2005) *The Future of the Brain: The Promise and Perils of Tomorrow's Neuroscience*. Oxford: Oxford University Press.

Rose, S., Lewontin, R. and Kamin, L. (1984) *Not in Our Genes*. Harmondsworth: Penguin.

Rosen, D. (2005) *Armies of the Young: Child Soldiers in War and Terrorism*. New Brunswick, NJ: Rutgers University Press.

Rotter, J. (1954) *Social Learning and Clinical Psychology*. New York: Prentice Hall.

Rusbridger, A. (2011) *Hacking Away at the Truth*. Orwell Lecture, London, 10 November.

Rutter, M. (1972) *Maternal Deprivation Reassessed*. Harmondsworth: Penguin.

Rutter, M. (2007) Sure Start local programmes, in J. Belsky, J. Barnes and E. Melhuish (eds) *The National Evaluation of Sure Start*. Bristol: Policy Press, pp. 197–210.

Rutter, M. (2011) Unsure about Sure Start, BBC Radio 4 *Analysis*, 17 July.

Saleem, S. (2011) Pakistani clerics attempt to dispel polio vaccination myths, *Guardian Weekly*, 11 November.

Saporiti, A. (1994) A methodology for making children count, in J. Qvortrup *et al.* (eds) *Childhood Matters: Social Theory, Practice and Politics*. Aldershot: Avebury Press, pp. 189–210.

Saussure, F. De ([1916] 1983) *Course in General Linguistics*. London: Duckworth.

Savage, M. and Burrows, R. (2007) The coming crisis of empirical sociology, *Sociology*, 41(5): 885–900.

Sayer, A. (2011) *Why Things Matter to People: Social Science, Values and Ethical Life*. Cambridge: Cambridge University Press.

Scambler, G. (2012) Health inequalities, *Sociology of Health & Illness*, 34(1): 130–46.

Scheper-Hughes, N. (1992) *Death Without Weeping: The Violence of Everyday Life in Brazil*. Berkeley, CA: University of California Press.

Scheper-Hughes, N. and Sargent, C. (1998) *Small Wars: The Cultural Politics of Childhood*. Berkeley, CA: University of California Press.

Scott, D. (2010) *Education, Epistemology and Critical Realism*. London: Routledge.

Scraton, P. (2006) The denial of children's rights and liberties in the UK and the North of Ireland, European Civil Liberties Network, Essay no. 14, available at: www.ecln.org/essays/essay-14.pdf, accessed 14 July 2012.

Seale, C. (1999) *The Quality of Qualitative Research*. London: Sage.

Seidler, V. (1986) *Kant, Respect and Injustice*. London: Routledge & Kegan Paul.

Sen, A. (1999) *Development as Freedom*. Oxford: Oxford University Press.

Sennett, R. (1998) *Corrosion of Character: The Personal Consequences of Work in The New Capitalism*. New York: W.W. Norton.

Sennett, R. (2008) *The Craftsman*. London: Penguin.

Serpell, R. (1993) *The Significance of Schooling: Life Journeys in an African Society*. Cambridge: Cambridge University Press.

Shaxson, N. (2011) *Treasure Islands and the Men Who Stole the World*. London: Bodley Head.

Shilling, C. (2012) *The Body and Social Theory*, 3rd edn. London: Sage.

Shiner, M., Scourfled, J., Fincham, B. and Langer, S. (2009) When things fall apart: gender and suicide across the life course, *Social Science & Medicine*, 69: 738–46.

Sidebotham, P., Bailey, S. and Belderson, P. and Brandon, M. (2011) Fatal child maltreatment in England, *Archives of Disease in Childhood*, 96: A93.

Siegal, M. (1997) *Knowing Children: Experiments in Conversion and Cognition*. Hove: Psychology Press.

Siegal, M. (2010) *Marvellous Minds: The Discovery of What Children Know*. Oxford: Oxford University Press.

Silverman, D. (2009) *Interpreting Qualitative Data*, 4th edn. London: Sage.

Smith, C. (2011) *What is a Person? Rethinking Humanity, Social Life, and the Moral Good from the Person Up*. Chicago, IL: University of Chicago Press.

Smith, E. (2012) *Luck: What it Means and Why it Matters*. London: Bloomsbury.

Socialnomics (2010) www.socialnomics.net/2010/04/13/over-50-of-the-worlds-population-is-under-30-social-media-on-the-rise, accessed 12 November 2011.

Solberg, A. (1996) The challenge in child research: from 'being' to 'doing', in J. Brannen and M. O'Brien (eds) *Children in Families: Research and Policy*. London: Falmer, pp. 53–65.

Stables, A. (2008) *Childhood and the Philosophy of Education: An Anti-Aristotelian Perspective*. London: Continuum.

Stainton-Rogers, W. and Stainton-Rogers, R. (1992) *Stories of Childhood*. London: Harvester Wheatsheaf.

Steedman, C. (1994) *Strange Dislocations: Childhood and the Idea of Human Interiority 1780–1930*. Cambridge, MA: Harvard University Press.

Stephens, S. (1995a) The 'cultural fallout' of Chernobyl radiation in Norwegian Sami regions, in S. Stephens (ed.) *Children and the Politics of Culture*. Princeton, NJ: Princeton University Press, pp. 292–318.

Stephens, S. (ed.) (1995b) *Children and the Politics of Culture*. Princeton, NJ: Princeton University Press.

Stern, D. (1977) *The First Relationship: Infant and Mother*. Glasgow: Fontana.

Tisdall, K., Davis, J., Hill, M. and Prout, A. (eds) (2006) *Children, Young People and Social Inclusion: Participation for What?* Bristol: Policy Press.

Tizard, B. and Hughes, M. (1984) *Young Children Learning*. London: Faber & Faber.

Townsend, P. (1979) *Poverty in the UK*. Harmondsworth: Penguin.

Townsend, P. and Gordon, D. (eds) (2002) *World Poverty: New Policies to Defeat an Old Enemy*. Bristol: Policy Press.

Toynbee, P. (2010) Frank Field must not let the unthinkable happen to Sure Start, *Guardian*, 3 December.

Trevarthan, C. (2006) 'Doing' education: to know what others know, *Early Education*, 46: 11–13.

Trevarthen, C. and Malloch, S. (2002) Musicality and music before three: human vitality and invention shared with pride, *Zero to Three*, 23(1): 10–18.

Trigg, R. (1985) *Understanding Social Science*. Oxford: Blackwell.

Tudor Hart, J. (1971) The inverse care law, *Lancet*, i: 405–12.

Turner, B. (2008) *The Body and Society*, 3rd edn. London: Sage.

UN (United Nations) (1948) UDHR – *Universal Declaration of Human Rights*. New York: UN.

UN (United Nations) (1966a) *International Covenant on Civil and Political Rights*. New York: UN.

UN (United Nations) (1966b) *International Covenant on Economic, Social and Cultural Rights*. New York: UN.

UN (United Nations) (1979) CEDAW – *Convention on the Elimination of all Forms of Discrimination against Women*. New York: UN.

UN (United Nations) (1989) UNCRC – *Convention on the Rights of the Child*. New York: UN.

UN (United Nations) (2006a) *Convention on the Rights of Persons with Disabilities*. New York: UN.

UN (United Nations) (2006b)*The United Nations Secretary General's Study on Violence Against Children*. New York: UN.

UN (United Nations) (2011) Security Council Report, 13 December, S2011/772 *The Situation in Afghanistan and its Implication for International Peace and Security*. New York: UN.

UNICEF (2010) *The Right to Childhood*. New York: UNICEF.

UNICEF (2007) *An Overview of Child Well-being in Rich Countries*. Geneva: UNICEF.

US (United States) (1776) *Declaration of Independence*, available at: www.ushistory.org/declaration/document, accessed 3 July 2012.

Van Blerk, L. (2010) Aids, mobility and commercial sex in Ethiopia: implications for policy, in K. Hörschelmann and R. Colls (eds) *Contested Bodies of Childhood and Youth*. Basingstoke: Palgrave Macmillan, pp. 232–246.

Van Valen, L. (1973) A new evolutionary law, *Evolutionary Theory*, 1: 1–30.

Vandenhole, W., Vranken, J. and De Boyser, K. (eds) (2010) *Poverty and Children's Rights*. Belgium: Intersentia.

Vleminckx, K. and Smeeding, T. (eds) (2001) *Child Well-being, Child Poverty and Child Policy in Modern Nations*. Bristol: Policy.

Vygotsky, L. ([1934] 1986) *Thought and Language*. Cambridge, MA: MIT Press.

Wacquant, L. (2008) *Urban Outcasts*. Cambridge: Polity.

Wacquant, L. (2009) *Punishing the Poor*. London: Duke University Press.

Wall, J. (2010) *Ethics in Light of Childhood*. Washington, DC: Georgetown University Press.

Ward, C. (1978) *The Child in the City*. London: Bedford Square Press.

Ward, C. (1988) *The Child in the Country*. London: Bedford Square Press.

Watson, J. (1919) *Psychology, From the Standpoint of a Behaviourist*. Philadelphia, PA: Lippincott.

Weber, M. ([1922] 1978) *Economy and Society*. Berkeley, CA: University of California Press.

Whitfield, G. and Williams, C. (2003) The evidence base for cognitive-behavioural therapy in depression: delivery in busy clinical settings, *Advances in Psychiatric Treatment*, 9: 21–30.

WHO (World Health Organisation) (2012) *Report on Polio Vaccination by WHO Board*, Chaired by L. Donaldson. Geneva: WHO.

Wilkinson, R. and Pickett, K. (2009) *The Spirit Level*. London: Penguin.

Wilkinson, R. and Pickett, K. (2012) The poison of inequality was behind last summer's riots, *Observer*, 5 August.

Winter, K. (2006) The participation of 'looked-after' children in their health care: a critical review of the research, *International Journal of Children's Rights*, 14(1): 77–97.

Winter, K. (2010) Ascertaining the perspectives of young children in care: case studies using reality boxes, *Children and Society*, online 14 September.

Winter, K. (2011) *Building Relationships and Communicating with Young Children: A Practical Guide for Social Workers*. Abingdon: Routledge.

Woodhead, M. (1997) Psychology and the cultural construction of children's needs, in A. James and A. Prout (eds) *Constructing and Reconstructing Childhood: Contemporary Issues in the Sociological Study of Childhood*. Abingdon: Routledge Falmer, pp. 63–84.

Woodhead, M. (2011) Child development and the development of childhood, in J. Qvortrup, W. Corsaro and M. Honig (eds) *The Palgrave Handbook of Childhood Studies*. Basingstoke: Palgrave Macmillan, pp. 46–61.

Wyness, M. (2006) *Childhood and Society*. Basingstoke: Palgrave Macmillan.

Yoshida, T. (2011) Corporal punishment of children: a critical realist account of experiences from two primary schools in urban Tanzania, PhD thesis. London: Institute of Education.

Zeiher, H. (2003) Intergenerational relations and social change in childhood, in B. Mayall and H. Zeiher (eds) *Childhood in Contemporary Perspective*. London: Institute of Education, pp. 157–78.

Zeiher, H. (2010) Childhood in German sociology and society, *Current Sociology*, 58(2): 292–308.

NAME INDEX

SUBJECT INDEX